"It's a great read, well researched, and very important for any student of the Israeli-Palestinian conflict to consider the information being presented. Even for people who are well read on the subject, there are many new details to learn and absorb."

—DOV HIKIND, former Democratic New York State Assemblyman (1983–2018) representing Brooklyn's Assembly district 48

"If you want to learn the whole unknown hidden truth of the Arab/Islamic war against Israel, read this book from cover to cover. Robert Spencer's book teaches you how to answer virtually every propaganda lie about Israel and Arabs one is confronted with by Israel-haters, Jew-haters, and those simply ignorant of the facts. This comprehensive treatise will eliminate the ability of newspapers and TV and radio and social media to convince you of their Mideast distortions and falsehoods. A critically necessary work in this Orwellian era."

—MORTON KLEIN, National President, Zionist Organization of America (ZOA)

"This is eye-opening history with enormous implications for foreign policy today. Taking us through the sad history of the Middle East peace process, Robert Spencer is the one analyst of the situation with the courage to identify why these peace negotiations have all failed, and will always fail. This book should be the occasion for a major reset of our policies toward Israel and the Palestinians, and a handy guide for everyone who is tired of the media spin on this all-important issue."

—STEVEN EMERSON, Investigative Project on Terrorism

"Spencer brings his formidable erudition and smooth keyboard to the knotty topic of the Palestinian assault on Israel. Deftly separating fact from fiction, he persuasively establishes the justice of Zionism and the barbarism of its opponents. Everyone should read this one-volume synthesis to understand the most complex conflict of our time."

—DANIEL PIPES, Middle East Forum

Also by Robert Spencer

Confessions of an Islamophobe

The History of Jihad

THE
PALESTINIAN
DELUSION

THE
PALESTINIAN
DELUSION

THE CATASTROPHIC HISTORY
OF THE MIDDLE EAST PEACE PROCESS

ROBERT SPENCER

BOMBARDIER
BOOKS

A BOMBARDIER BOOKS BOOK
An Imprint of Post Hill Press

The Palestinian Delusion:
The Catastrophic History of the Middle East Peace Process
© 2021 by Robert Spencer
All Rights Reserved
First Bombardier Books Hardcover Edition: December 2019

ISBN: 978-1-64293-623-0

Cover design by Cody Corcoran

Post Hill Press
New York • Nashville
posthillpress.com
Published in the United States of America

This book is dedicated to all those
who have given their lives to reestablish
and defend a homeland for the Jewish people.

Contents

CHAPTER ONE

How Israel Came to Be

Indigenous People?

"From the river to the sea, Palestine will be free."

This chant, long a favorite of Palestinian terror groups, has become increasingly mainstream in recent years, to the extent that in November 2018, CNN commentator and Temple University professor Marc Lamont Hill repeated the phrase while speaking at a United Nations event. CNN fired Hill, but Temple didn't, which is itself an indication of how widely accepted the phrase has become.[1]

"Freeing" Palestine from the river—the Jordan—to the sea—the Mediterranean—would mean the complete eradication of Israel, and likely a new genocide of the Jews, which is why the phrase is so controversial, but it also communicates a great deal more. The declaration that "Palestine will be free" assumes that it is being trodden underfoot by invaders and occupiers, and that the Palestinians are the indigenous people of the area.

This idea, too, is gaining increasing acceptance today. In early October 2018, Brown University's Office of Diversity and Multicultural Affairs sent out an announcement about "Indigenous Peoples' Day Weekend," the university's politically correct replacement for

Columbus Day weekend. The indigenous people being celebrated, the announcement stated, included "567 Federally Recognized tribes, 61 State Recognized tribes," as well as "Hawaiians and the people indigenous to its territories in the Caribbean and Pacific Oceans," all of whom have allegedly suffered "genocide and forced assimilation."[2] But gratuitously added to these oppressed indigenous people of North America were the Palestinians: "From Standing Rock to Palestine, Indigenous communities across the world continue to experience the pernicious effects of settler-colonialism on their sovereignty, their health, and their access to their traditional lands and practices."[3]

The backdrop of Brown's statement is an understanding of the situation of Israel and the Palestinians that is widely accepted today, and has been succinctly enunciated in the *Harvard International Review* by Hatem Bazian, a professor at the University of California, Berkeley of some of the keenest preoccupations of modern academia: Muslim American Studies; Colonialism and Post-Colonial Studies; Arab and Arab American Studies; Critical Race Theory; Palestine Studies; and Comparative Liberation Theologies: "Over a 50 year period, the indigenous Palestinians faced an emergent European nationalist movement that succeeded in dispossessing them and transforming their ancestral homeland into a modern nation state that locates its genesis in the biblical text."[4]

The Office of the United Nations High Commissioner for Refugees (UNHCR), popularly known as the UN Refugee Agency, agrees, stating: "Jewish nationalist ideology, Zionism, led to claims on Palestine for the Jewish people. Zionism began in Europe, in reaction to pogroms in the east and assimilation in the west. Early in the 20th century, Zionist leaders began planning for Jewish settlement in Palestine, and the removal of the indigenous population."[5]

Zionists believe that Jews should return to Zion, that is, the land of Israel, as their rightful home. Palestinian Authority president Mahmoud Abbas has directly contradicted the central Zionist claim, that the land of Israel is the ancestral home of the Jews, and has advanced a counterclaim: "Our narrative says that we were in this land since before Abraham. I am not saying it. The Bible says it. The Bible says, in these words, that the Palestinians existed before Abraham. So why don't you recognize my right?"[6] An Abbas spokesman has said in a similar vein: "The nation of Palestine upon the land of Canaan had a 7,000-year history B.C.E. This is the truth, which must be understood, and we have to note it, in order to say: 'Netanyahu, you are incidental in history. We are the people of history. We are the owners of history.'"[7]

Dimitri Diliani of the Fatah Revolutionary Council likewise declared that "the Palestinian people [are] descended from the Canaanite tribe of the Jebusites that inhabited the ancient site of Jerusalem as early as 3200 BCE."[8]

But is that really true? Are the Palestinians really the indigenous people of the area that the State of Israel now occupies, and were they really displaced by the Israelis?

There is no trace of support for such an idea in history. No archeological evidence, or evidence of any other kind, has ever been found to substantiate a link between the ancient Canaanites or Jebusites and the modern-day Palestinians.[9] The land that is now the State of Israel corresponds roughly to the lands known in ancient times as Judea, Samaria, Idumea, and Galilee, and was inhabited by Jews. In A.D. 134, the Romans expelled the Jews from the area in retaliation for a revolt against their rule led by the self-appointed messiah Simon Bar Kokhba; as an insult to the Jews and to efface any traces of their connection to the land, they renamed Jerusalem Aelia Capitolina and the region Palestine, a name they plucked from the Bible, as it was the name of the Israelites' ancient enemies, the Philistines.

Subsequently, Palestine was the name of a region but never of a people or of a political entity. The area that was Palestine was part of the Eastern Roman (Byzantine) Empire until it was conquered by the Arabs. Later it came under the control of the Turks, who ruled it until the Ottoman Empire collapsed at the end of World War I.

Jews in Palestine

Throughout all this time, even as invaders overwhelmed the land, a Jewish presence remained, particularly in Galilee. In the year 438, the Byzantine Empress Eudocia removed the prohibition on Jews' praying at the site of their ancient Temple in Jerusalem, a prohibition that had been in place for three hundred years. Jewish leaders in Galilee sent out a message to "the great and mighty people of the Jews" relaying the happy news and declaring: "Know then that the end of the exile of our people has come."[10]

It hadn't, but some Jews still persevered and continued to live in the region. In the tenth century, Jewish leaders in Palestine issued another call to the Jews to return to their homeland.[11] But the various invaders and occupiers of the land of Israel never made aliyah ("going up," or returning to the land of Israel) an easy or attractive option. On July 15, 1099, after some of their number had terrorized and murdered Jews all across Europe as they made their way to the Holy Land, the Crusaders finally entered Jerusalem, after a five-week siege. Once inside the city, they encountered a significant number of Jews, and were no kinder to them than they had been to their brethren in Europe. According to the twelfth-century Syrian Muslim chronicler al-Azimi, "they burned the Church of the Jews."[12]

A contemporary of al-Azimi and a fellow chronicler, Ibn al-Qalanisi, added: "The Franks stormed the town and gained possession of it. A number of the townsfolk fled to the sanctuary and a great host were killed. The Jews assembled in the synagogue, and the Franks burned it over their heads. The sanctuary was surrendered to them on guarantee of safety on 22 Sha'ban [14 July] of this year, and they destroyed the shrines and the tomb of Abraham."[13]

The Crusaders, expanding on the prohibition that the Romans had set centuries before, forbade Jews to enter Palestine, but some came anyway. In 1140, with the Crusaders still ruling Jerusalem, the Spanish philosopher and poet Yehudah Halevi wrote in his *Kuzari*, or *Book of Refutation and Proof in Support of the Despised Religion*, that Jews could be closest to the God of Israel within Israel itself. He himself then set out for the land, only to be killed in Jerusalem the following year, run down by an enraged Arab Muslim's horse as he sang his famous elegy, "Zion ha-lo Tish'ali."[14]

Yet still some Jews remained in the Holy Land, and Jews continued to emigrate to it, including another renowned philosopher, Maimonides, in the thirteenth century. But the Jews in the Holy Land always faced hardship. At the end of the fifteenth century, the Czech traveler Martin Kabátnik encountered Jews during a pilgrimage to Jerusalem, and reported that they still thought of the area as their land: "The heathens [that is, the Muslim rulers] oppress them at their pleasure. They know that the Jews think and say that this is the Holy Land that was promised to them. Those of them who live here are regarded as holy by the other Jews, for in spite of all the tribulations and the agonies that they suffer at the hands of the heathen, they refuse to leave the place."[15] Shortly thereafter, nearly thirty Jewish communities were counted in Palestine.[16]

These communities faced continual oppression. In 1576, the Ottoman Sultan Murad III ordered the deportation of one thousand Jews from the city of Safed to Cyprus, not as punishment for anything they had done but arbitrarily, because he wanted to bolster the Cypriot economy.[17] It is not known whether the order was carried out, but if it was, the deportees may have been better off, at least in material terms: two travelers who visited Safed in the early seventeenth century said that for the Jews of that city, "life here is the poorest and most miserable that one can imagine.... They pay for the very air they breathe."[18] But they were still there, and they remained.

The Turks taxed the Jews on the basis of the Qur'anic command that the "People of the Book" (primarily Jews and Christians) must be made to "pay the jizya [tax] with willing submission and feel themselves subdued" (9:29). In 1674, a Jesuit priest, Father Michael Naud, wrote that the Jews of Jerusalem were resigned to "paying heavily to the Turk for their right to stay here.... They prefer being prisoners in Jerusalem to enjoying the freedom they could acquire elsewhere…. The love of the Jews for the Holy Land, which they lost through their betrayal [of Christ], is unbelievable."[19] And Jews were coming from elsewhere to live there: "Many of them come from Europe to find a little comfort, though the yoke is heavy."[20]

It was indeed. Even aside from the political oppression, the land itself was increasingly inhospitable. By the end of the eighteenth century, only two hundred fifty thousand to three hundred thousand people, including ten thousand to fifteen thousand Jews, lived in what had become a backwater with a harsh and forbidding terrain and climate.[21] Yet still Jews came. In 1810, the disciples of the great Talmudic scholar known as the Vilna Gaon arrived in the land of Israel from the Russian Empire, and rejoiced even though they were well aware of the hardness of the land to which they had come:

> Truly, how marvelous it is to live in the good country. Truly, how wonderful it is to love our country…. Even in her ruin there is none to compare with her, even in her desolation she is unequaled, in her silence there is none like her. Good are her ashes and her stones.[22]

In 1847, the U.S. Navy commander William F. Lynch made an expedition to the Jordan River, the Dead Sea, and the surrounding areas, and encountered Jews all over the region. In Tiberias, wrote Lynch, "we had letters to the chief rabbi of the Jews, who came to meet us, and escorted us through a labyrinth of streets to the house of Heim Weisman, a brother Israelite."[23] He found that the Jews of the city "have two synagogues, the Sephardim and Askeniazim, but lived harmoniously together." He found evidence of continued Jewish immigration: "There are many Polish Jews, with light complexions, among them. They describe themselves as very poor, and maintained by the charitable contributions of Jews abroad, mostly in Europe."[24]

In Tiberias, the Jews outnumbered others: "There are about three hundred families, or one thousand Jews, in this town. The sanhedrim consists of seventy rabbis, of whom thirty are natives and forty Franks, mostly from Poland, with a few from Spain. The rabbis stated that controversial matters of discipline among Jews, all over the world, are referred to this sanhedrim. Besides the Jews, there are in Tiberias from three to four hundred Muslims and two or three Latins, from Nazareth."[25]

Lynch saw Ottoman oppression up close and held a dim view of the sultanate, of which he wrote presciently: "It needs but the destruction of that power which, for so many centuries, has rested like an incubus upon the eastern world, to ensure the restoration of the Jews to Palestine."[26]

Palestinians in Palestine?

So the Jews were always in the land they supposedly returned to only after two thousand years of absence as a result of the Zionist project. But the Palestinian Arabs were always there also, no?

No. Instead, travelers to the area over many centuries agree: the land was desolate and largely depopulated.

Writing some seventy years after the Romans expelled the Jews from their land in the year 134, the Roman historian Dio Cassius states: "The whole of Judea became desert, as indeed had been foretold in their sacred rites, fell of its own accord into fragments, and wolves and hyenas, many in number, roamed howling through their cities."[27]

An English visitor to Jerusalem wrote in 1590 (spelling as in the original): "Nothing there is to be scene but a little of the old walls, which is yet Remayning and all the rest is grasse, mosse and Weedes much like to a piece of Rank or moist Grounde."[28] In 1697, the English traveler Henry Maundrell found Nazareth to be "an inconsiderable village," while Acre was "a few poor cottages" and Jericho a "poor nasty village." All in all, there was "nothing here but a vast and spacious ruin."[29]

Some fifty years later, another English traveler, Thomas Shaw, noted that Palestine was "lacking in people to till its fertile soil."[30] The French count Constantine François Volney, an eighteenth-century historian, called Palestine "ruined" and "desolate," observing that "many parts" had "lost almost all their peasantry."[31] Volney complained that this desolation was unexpected, for the Ottoman imperial records listed larger populations, which led to tax collection efforts' being frustrated. Of one area, Volney wrote: "Upwards of three thousand two hundred villages were reckoned, but, at present, the collector can scarcely find four hundred. Such of our merchants as have resided there twenty years have themselves seen the greater part of the environs…become depopulated. The traveller meets with nothing but houses in ruins, cisterns rendered useless, and fields abandoned. Those who cultivated them have fled."[32]

Another English traveler, James Silk Buckingham, visited Jaffa in 1816 and wrote that it had "all the appearances of a poor village, and every part of it that we saw was of corresponding meanness."[33] In Ramle, said Buckingham, "as throughout the greater part of Palestine, the ruined portion seemed more extensive than that which was inhabited."[34] Twenty-two years later, the British nobleman Alexander William Crawford Lindsay, Lord Lindsay, declared that "all Judea, except the hills of Hebron and the vales immediately about Jerusalem, is desolate and barren."[35]

In 1840, another traveler to Palestine praised the Syrians as a "fine spirited race of men," but whose "population is on the decline." He noted that the land between Hebron and Bethlehem was "now abandoned and desolate," marked by "dilapidated towns."[36] Jerusalem was nothing more than "a large number of houses…in a dilapidated and ruinous state," with "the masses…without any regular employment."[37]

In 1847, the U.S. Navy's Lynch noted: "The population of Jaffa is now about 13,000, viz: Turks, 8000; Greeks, 2000; Armenians, 2000; Maronites, 700; and Jews, about 300."[38] Significantly, he counted no Arabs there at all.

Still another traveling English clergyman, Henry Burgess Whitaker Churton, saw the desolation of Judea as the fulfillment of Biblical prophecy. In 1852, he published *Thoughts on the Land of the Morning: A Record of Two Visits to Palestine*. "Soon after leaving the Mount of Olives," Churton recounted, "the country becomes an entire desolation for eighteen miles of mountain, until we reached the plain of the Jordan. It is foretold (Ezekiel, vi. 14), and is remarkably fulfilled, that Judea should be more desolate than the desert itself. That plain itself is now, in great measure, bare as a desert..."[39]

The following year, one of Churton's fellow clergymen, the Reverend Arthur G. H. Hollingsworth, published his own treatise, *Remarks Upon the Present Condition and Future Prospects of the Jews in Palestine.* Hollingsworth's observations are jarring to those who have uncritically accepted the idea that Palestine was always considered Arab land before the Jews arrived. According to Hollingsworth, the Arabs had no special affection for the land, and it was the Turks who claimed it:

> *The population of Palestine is composed of Arabs, who roam about the plains, or lurk in the mountain fastnesses as robbers and strangers, having no settled home, and without any fixed attachment to the land.*

Hollingsworth found the Christians of the area to be little better off:

> *In many of the ruined cities and villages there exists also, a limited number of Christian families, uncivilized, and not knowing from what race they derive their origin. Poor, and without influence, they tremblingly hold their miserable possessions from year to year, without security, and without wealth, in a land which they confess is not their own. The Turks monopolize for themselves the spoils and power of conquerors. They claim the land, they levy the uncertain and oppressive taxes.*[40]

Even the Ottoman government, however, was not at home there:

> *No Christian is secure against insult, robbery, and ruin. The Ottoman government is weak and violent, rapacious and uncertain in its justice, tyrannical and capricious; their soldiery and merchants amount to a few thousands, in a country where millions were formerly happy and prosperous. The influence of such a government never extends beyond the shadow of their standards. They are always in the attitude of a hostile army, encamped in a land which*

is only held by forcible possession; like a garrison under arms, they retain the country by the law of the sword and not by inheritance. It is a sullen conquest and not a peaceable settlement.[41]

Hollingsworth, like so many others, bore witness to the land's steady depopulation:

The Arab and Christian populations diminish every year. Poverty, distress, insecurity, robbery, and disease continue to weaken the inhabitants of this fine country.[42]

He did notice, however, one group that was increasing in number:

Amongst the scattered and feeble population of this once happy country, is found, however, an increasing number of poor Jews; some of their most learned men reside in the holy cities of Jerusalem, Hebron, and Tiberias. Their synagogues are still in existence. Jews frequently arrive in Palestine from every nation in Europe, and remain there for many years; and others die with the satisfaction of mingling their remains with their forefathers' dust, which fills every valley, and is found in every cave.[43]

The Jews weren't exactly thriving in Palestine. They eked out an existence there against enormous odds. Hollingsworth explains that the Turks made life extremely difficult for the Jews:

He creeps along that soil, where his forefathers proudly strode in the fulness of a wonderful prosperity, as an alien, an outcast, a creature less than a dog, and below the oppressed Christian beggar in his own ancestral plains and cities. No harvest ripens for his hand, for he cannot tell whether he will be permitted to gather it. Land occupied by a Jew is exposed to robbery and waste. A most peevish jealousy exists against the landed prosperity, or commercial wealth, or trading advancement of the Jew. Hindrances exist to the settlement of a British Christian in that country, but a thousand petty obstructions are created to prevent the establishment of a Jew on waste land, or to the purchase and rental of land by a Jew....

What security exists, that a Jewish emigrant settling in Palestine, could receive a fair remuneration for his capital and labour? None whatever. He might toil, but his harvests would be reaped by others; the Arab robber can rush in and carry off his flocks and herds. If he appeals for redress to the nearest Pasha, the taint of his Jewish blood fills the air, and darkens the brows of his oppressors; if he turns to his neighbour Christian, he encounters prejudice and spite; if he claims a Turkish guard, he is insolently repulsed and scorned. How can he bring his capital into such a country, when that fugitive possession flies from places where the sword is drawn to snatch it from the owner's hands and not protect it?[44]

By 1857, according to the British consul in Palestine, "the country is in a considerable degree empty of inhabitants and therefore its greatest need is that of a body of population."[45] Henry Baker Tristram, yet another in the seemingly endless stream of English travelers, reported in the 1860s that "the north and south [of the Sharon plain] land is going out of cultivation and whole villages are rapidly disappearing from the face of the earth. Since the year 1838, no less than 20 villages there have been thus erased from the map and the stationary population extirpated."[46]

The most celebrated chronicler of Palestine's pre-Zionist desolation was Mark Twain, who wrote about his travels in the Holy Land in *The Innocents Abroad* in 1869. It is Twain's literary genius that gives us the most indelible images of the wasteland that was Palestine:

Palestine sits in sackcloth and ashes. Over it broods the spell of a curse that has withered its fields and fettered its energies. Where Sodom and Gomorrah reared their domes and towers, that solemn sea now floods the plain, in whose bitter waters no living thing exists—over whose waveless surface the blistering air hangs motionless and dead—about whose borders nothing grows but weeds, and scattering tufts of cane, and that treacherous fruit that promises refreshment to parching lips, but turns to ashes at the touch. Nazareth is forlorn; about that ford of Jordan where the hosts of

Israel entered the Promised Land with songs of rejoicing, one finds only a squalid camp of fantastic Bedouins of the desert; Jericho the accursed, lies a moldering ruin, to-day, even as Joshua's miracle left it more than three thousand years ago; Bethlehem and Bethany, in their poverty and their humiliation, have nothing about them now to remind one that they once knew the high honor of the Saviour's presence; the hallowed spot where the shepherds watched their flocks by night, and where the angels sang Peace on earth, good will to men, is untenanted by any living creature, and unblessed by any feature that is pleasant to the eye. Renowned Jerusalem itself, the stateliest name in history, has lost all its ancient grandeur, and is become a pauper village; the riches of Solomon are no longer there to compel the admiration of visiting Oriental queens; the wonderful temple which was the pride and the glory of Israel, is gone, and the Ottoman crescent is lifted above the spot where, on that most memorable day in the annals of the world, they reared the Holy Cross. The noted Sea of Galilee, where Roman fleets once rode at anchor and the disciples of the Saviour sailed in their ships, was long ago deserted by the devotees of war and commerce, and its borders are a silent wilderness; Capernaum is a shapeless ruin; Magdala is the home of beggared Arabs; Bethsaida and Chorazin have vanished from the earth, and the "desert places" round about them where thousands of men once listened to the Saviour's voice and ate the miraculous bread, sleep in the hush of a solitude that is inhabited only by birds of prey and skulking foxes.

Palestine is desolate and unlovely. And why should it be otherwise? Can the curse of the Deity beautify a land?

Palestine is no more of this work-day world. It is sacred to poetry and tradition—it is dream-land.[47]

In Jezreel, Twain recounted the Bible's Song of Deborah and Barak, and then added: "Stirring scenes like these occur in this valley no more. There is not a solitary village throughout its whole extent—not for thirty miles in either direction. There are two or three small clusters of Bedouin tents, but not a single permanent habitation. One may ride ten miles, hereabouts, and not see ten human beings."[48] Twain found the Sea of Galilee and its surrounding areas no less desolate:

> It is solitude, for birds and squirrels on the shore and fishes in the water are all the creatures that are near to make it otherwise, but it is not the sort of solitude to make one dreary. Come to Galilee for that. If these unpeopled deserts, these rusty mounds of barrenness, that never, never, never do shake the glare from their harsh outlines, and fade and faint into vague perspective; that melancholy ruin of Capernaum; this stupid village of Tiberias, slumbering under its six funereal plumes of palms; yonder desolate declivity where the swine of the miracle ran down into the sea, and doubtless thought it was better to swallow a devil or two and get drowned into the bargain than have to live longer in such a place; this cloudless, blistering sky; this solemn, sailless, tintless lake, reposing within its rim of yellow hills and low, steep banks, and looking just as expressionless and unpoetical (when we leave its sublime history out of the question,) as any metropolitan reservoir in Christendom—if these things are not food for rock me to sleep, mother, none exist, I think.[49] [That is, the area was exceedingly tranquil.]

Sir John William Dawson stated the obvious in 1888 when he said: "No nation has been able to establish itself as a nation in Palestine up to this day. No national union and no national spirit has prevailed there. The motley impoverished tribes which have occupied it have held it as mere tenants at will, temporary landowners, evidently waiting for those entitled to the permanent possession of the soil."[50]

The wait would not be much longer. An English clergyman, Reverend Samuel Manning, described the Plain of Sharon as "a land without inhabitants" that "might support an immense population."[51] That immense population was beginning to come.

British Christian Zionists

The desolate land was catching the attention of Christian statesmen in nineteenth-century Britain. They began expressing the idea that it would be in the best interests of the Jews and the world if the Jews returned to Palestine and reclaimed it as their homeland.

In 1838, Lord Lindsay published the first edition of his *Letters on Egypt, Edom, and the Holy Land* after traveling through Palestine. He opined that "it is possible that, in the changes of the Turkish empire, Palestine may again become a civilised country, under Greek or Latin influences; that the Jewish race, so wonderfully preserved, may yet have another stage of national existence opened to them; that they may once more obtain possession of their native land, and invest it with an interest greater than it could have under any other circumstances."[52]

Lindsay characterized the absence of the land's actual indigenous people to be its chief drawback:

> *Many, I believe, entertain the idea that an actual curse rests on the soil of Palestine, and may be startled therefore at the testimony I have borne to its actual richness. No other curse, I conceive, rests upon it, than that induced by the removal of the ancient inhabitants, and the will of the Almighty that the modern occupants should never be so numerous as to invalidate the prophecy that the land should enjoy her Sabbaths so long as the rightful heirs remain in the land of their enemies.... [T]he land still enjoys her Sabbaths, and only waits the return of her banished children, and the application of industry commensurate with her agricultural capabilities, to burst once more into universal luxuriance, and be all that she ever was in the days of Solomon.[53]*

Anthony Ashley Cooper, seventh earl of Shaftesbury, a member of Parliament and a devout Christian, was of much the same mind. On July 24, 1838, he wrote that he was "anxious about the hopes and destinies of the Jewish people:"

Everything seems ripe for their return to Palestine; 'the way of the kings of the East is prepared.' Could the five Powers of the West be induced to guarantee the security of life and possessions to the Hebrew race, they would now flow back in rapidly augmenting numbers.... The inherent vitality of the Hebrew race reasserts itself with amazing persistence; its genius, to tell the truth, adapts itself more or less to all currents of civilization all over the world, nevertheless always emerging with distinctive features and a gallant recovery of vigour. There is an unbroken identity of Jewish race and Jewish mind down to our times: but the great revival can take place only in the Holy Land.[54]

Shaftesbury was determined not just to talk about this but to act upon it: "By the blessing of God I will prepare a document, fortify it by all the evidence I can accumulate, and, confiding to the wisdom and mercy of the Almighty, lay it before the Secretary of State for Foreign Affairs."[55]

Shaftesbury went to Lord Palmerston, who was the secretary of state for foreign affairs at the time, and laid the proposal before him. He recorded Palmerston's measured reaction in his diary:

August 1st, 1838.—Dined with Palmerston. After dinner left alone with him. Propounded my scheme, which seemed to strike his fancy; he asked some questions, and readily promised to consider it. How singular is the order of Providence! Singular, that is if estimated by man's ways! Palmerston had already been chosen by God to be an instrument of good to His ancient people, to do homage, as it were, to their inheritance, and to recognise their rights without believing their destiny. And it seems he will yet do more. But though the motive be kind, it is not sound. I am forced to argue politically, financially, commercially; these considerations strike him home; he weeps not like his Master over Jerusalem, nor prays that now, at last, she may put on her beautiful garments...[56]

Meanwhile, Shaftesbury continued to spread the idea that Jews should return to Palestine. He read Lindsay's work and was impressed.

In a January 1839 magazine article, he gave *Letters on Egypt, Edom, and the Holy Land* an enthusiastic review and proposed making Lindsay's hope a reality by resettling the Jews in Palestine under British rule or at least military protection. This would, he argued, be in the best interests of Britain itself:

> *The soil and climate of Palestine are singularly adapted to the growth of produce required for the exigencies of Great Britain; the finest cotton may be obtained in almost unlimited abundance; silk and madder are the staple of the country, and olive oil is now, as it ever was, the very fatness of the land. Capital and skill are alone required: the presence of a British officer, and the increased security of property which his presence will confer, may invite them from these islands to the cultivation of Palestine; and the Jews, who will betake themselves to agriculture in no other land, having found, in the English consul, a mediator between their people and the Pacha, will probably return in yet greater numbers, and become once more the husbandmen of Judaea and Galilee.*[57]

It was Lord Shaftesbury who coined the apposite phrase "A land without people, for a people without a land."[58]

In 1840, his meeting with the foreign secretary bore fruit: Palmerston offered the British government's protection to Jews in Palestine and even communicated to the Ottoman sultan his opinion that it would benefit the Ottoman Empire if "the Jews who are scattered throughout other countries in Europe and Africa should be induced to go and settle in Palestine."[59] The sultan did not respond favorably, and Zionism remained a concern primarily of the British.

Lieutenant-Colonel George Gawler, who had served as the British governor of Australia, issued this call in 1845: "Replenish the farms and fields of Palestine with the energetic people whose warmest affection are rooted in the soil."[60] In 1852, Gawler founded the Association for Promoting Jewish Settlement in Palestine.[61]

The Zionist idea was not forgotten in nineteenth-century Britain, and would continue to be considered at the highest levels of the

British government, along with, paradoxically, schemes that would challenge Zionism at its core.

The Ottomans attempted to stop the Zionist movement altogether by banning Jewish immigration to its domains. The British were concerned. On November 19, 1891, the interim British ambassador to the Ottoman Empire, Sir William Arthur White, wrote to British Prime Minister Robert Gascoyne-Cecil, third marquess of Salisbury, confirming that the prime minister had instructed him to ask the Sublime Porte for "further explanations with respect to the recent prohibition against Jewish immigrants entering the Ottoman Empire."[62]

Nonetheless those immigrants kept coming. After the outbreak of World War I, taking into account all the support for Zionism among highly placed Britons and reasoning that they would fare better if Palestine were under British rule rather than that of the Ottomans, many Jews in Palestine aided the British in numerous ways. The Ottomans responded with a campaign of mass deportations of Jews. In 1917, Ottoman officials rounded up the seven thousand Jews who were living in Jaffa and sent them north on a brutal forced march, out of Palestine.[63] This was not an isolated incident. By the end of the war, the Jewish population of Palestine had been reduced from its prewar total of ninety thousand to fewer than sixty thousand.[64]

Nevertheless, as they had throughout history, Jews continued to come to the land. The British Royal Commission stated accurately in 1937 that "always…since the fall of the Jewish state some Jews have been living in Palestine…. Fresh immigrants arrived from time and time…[and] settled mainly in Galilee, in numerous villages spreading northwards to the Lebanon and in the towns of Safad and Tiberias."[65]

The Muslim Arab Influx

Arabs began to come as well, although their presence in the land remained generally sparse. In 1830, Muhammad Ali of Egypt conquered Jaffa, Nablus, and Beisan and settled Egyptian and Sudanese Muslim

Arab soldiers there. Around the same time, the French conquest of Algeria led to an exodus of North African Muslims who refused to live under infidel rule. They came in large numbers to Palestine. Once there, they followed the pattern of the Turks and other Arab Muslims in making life as difficult as they possibly could for the Jews. "They constitute," noted another English clergyman, the Reverend W. M. Christie, who lived in Haifa in the early twentieth century, "the most fanatical section of the Palestine population."[66]

In a glimpse of what was to come, Christie added: "To a great extent without education, they are ready to accept any statement concerning things done to the detriment of Islam, and to act without sense of responsibility.... In 1889, we often heard it remarked that the 10,000 Moslems living in a state of barbarism in the Moghrabiyeh quarter were a real danger to the city. In the recent massacres [of Jews] in Safed, it was this party that carried through the nefarious work."[67]

These North African Muslims were not singular. Many, if not most, of the Arabs in Palestine were not the descendants of those who had conquered the land in the seventh century. Most of them had arrived from elsewhere. In 1930, Christie published a study entitled "Arabs and Jews in Palestine." He noted "the settlement of sections of Yemenite and Kaisite Arabs in Nazareth and Cana of Galilee," as well as "representatives of the Moslem rulers settled in the larger towns—Jerusalem, Hebron, Nablus, Jenin, Nazareth, and Acre. These are probably represented today by the Effendi class, who claim, without genealogical proof, however, to be the descendants of the conquerors."[68]

Muslims came from far-off lands. According to Christie, when the great twelfth-century jihad warrior Saladin "was hard pressed by the Crusaders, he begged help from Persia, and in response there came 150,000 Persian Moslems, who ultimately received for services rendered lands in Upper Galilee and in the Sidon district."[69]

Christie added: "Other Arabic-speaking settlers have come from various places outside of Palestine proper."[70] He explained that these included Christians, who were brought into the area in the latter half of the nineteenth century from Lebanon and many other places, "and the only soldering element is their common Arabic speech."[71] In Galilee, he said, "we meet with Maronites and Druses, both clearly immigrants," adding that the Shi'ite Muslims of that region had a "non-Galilean origin."[72] Christie concluded: "There remains the 'Arab' peasantry, or villagers. Every evidence points to their being Arabs only in the matter of language. They have much less Arabic blood than any of the sections of the people already named..."[73]

In 1938, the historian William B. Ziff wrote:

At the turn of the [twentieth] century there were 40,000 Jews in Palestine and about 140,000 others of all complexions. The inhabitants had no other feeling for this pauperized, disease-ridden country than a fervent desire to get away from it. Emigration proceeded steadily. Immigration was virtually non-existent. Not until the Zionists had arrived in numbers did the Arab population begin to augment itself. The introduction of European standards of wage and life acted like a magnet on the entire Near East. Abruptly Palestine became an Arab center of attraction. By 1922, after a quarter century of Jewish colonization, their numbers mushroomed to 488,000. Today they are over a million....

It is precisely in the vicinity of these Jewish villages that Arab development is most marked. Arab Haifa, profiting by the Zionist boom, grew from 1922 to 1936 by 130%, Jaffa by 80%, and Jerusalem by 55%. The Arab rural settlement in the Tel Aviv district increased by over 135%. The all-Arab city of Nablus, which held 33,000 before the war, has fallen to less than 12,000. Safed which had 20,000, dropped to less than 9,000.[74]

Winston Churchill observed drily in 1939, when Arab Muslims were ever more frequently presenting the British with claims of having been victimized by the Jews, that "far from being persecuted, the Arabs have crowded into the country."[75]

Eli E. Hertz, president of the organization Myths and Facts, which is devoted to setting forth the facts and dispelling myths about Israel, likewise notes that the Palestinian people are nonindigenous: "Family names of many Palestinians attest to their non-Palestinian origins. Just as Jews bear names like Berliner, Warsaw and Toledano, modern phone books in the Territories are filled with families named Elmisri (Egyptian), Chalabi (Syrian), Mugrabi (North Africa). Even George Habash—the arch-terrorist and head of Black September—bears a name with origins in Abyssinia or Ethiopia, *Habash* in both Arabic and Hebrew."[76]

Most of the indigenous people of Palestine, like Los Angelenos, seem to have come from somewhere else.

The Jews Benefit the Arabs

In 1896, the pioneering Zionist Theodor Herzl published his monumental manifesto *Der Judenstaat* (*The Jewish State*), calling upon Jews to return to their homeland. He wrote:

No one can deny the gravity of the situation of the Jews. Wherever they live in perceptible numbers, they are more or less persecuted. Their equality before the law, granted by statute, has become practically a dead letter. They are debarred from filling even moderately high positions, either in the army, or in any public or private capacity. And attempts are made to thrust them out of business also: "Don't buy from Jews!"

Attacks in Parliaments, in assemblies, in the press, in the pulpit, in the street, on journeys—for example, their exclusion from certain hotels—even in places of recreation, become daily more numerous. The forms of persecutions varying according to the countries and social circles in which they occur. In Russia, imposts are levied on Jewish villages; in Rumania, a few persons are put to death; in Germany, they get a good beating occasionally; in Austria, Anti-Semites exercise terrorism over all public life; in Algeria, there are travelling agitators; in Paris, the Jews are shut out of the so-called best social circles and excluded from clubs. Shades of anti-Jewish feeling are innumerable.[77]

His answer to this was a Jewish state in Palestine. He argued that this was not as far-fetched as it might seem:

> *The plan would, of course, seem absurd if a single individual attempted to do it; but if worked by a number of Jews in co-operation it would appear perfectly rational, and its accomplishment would present no difficulties worth mentioning. The idea depends only on the number of its supporters. Perhaps our ambitious young men, to whom every road of progress is now closed, seeing in this Jewish State a bright prospect of freedom, happiness and honors opening to them, will ensure the propagation of the idea.*[78]

Many did see exactly that, both before and after Herzl wrote these words. As European Jews began to immigrate in large numbers beginning in 1882, following a pogrom in Russia, in what came to be known as the First Aliyah, they did not foresee this fanatical hatred. In fact, they cherished the naïve hope that the Arabs of the land would welcome them. The Jews' presence meant Arab prosperity, they reasoned, so why wouldn't they? Herzl was confident about this:

> *The Jews are supported by none of the powers and have no military pretensions of their own. There need be no difficulty with the local population. Nobody is trying to remove non-Jews. The local population can only benefit from the prosperity that the Jews will bring.*
>
> *Do you believe that an Arab who has a house or land in Palestine whose value today is three or four thousand francs will regret seeing the price of his land rise five- or ten-fold? For that is necessarily what will happen as we Jews come. And that must be explained to the inhabitants of this country. They will become rich because of us. They will acquire excellent brothers just as the Sultan will acquire loyal and good subjects who will cause this region, their historic motherland, to flourish.*[79]

For a time, it seemed as if this hope wasn't as naïve as it appeared, and would actually turn out to be the case. Forty of the Jewish families that had just come to Palestine in 1882 settled in the village of Sarafand, which an early-twentieth-century Jewish writer termed "a forsaken ruin." There they built the settlement of Rishon l'Tsion, which was soon, in the characterization of the same writer, "thriving," so much so that these forty Jewish families were soon joined in the area by over four hundred Arab families.[80]

The desolate area began to show new life. In 1900, a British consulate report stated that "there can be no doubt that the establishment of the Jewish colonies in Palestine has brought about a great change in the aspect of that country."[81] Four years later, another British consular report declared that "the Jewish element is spreading all over Palestine and represents today the most enterprising part of the population."[82]

The Jewish presence in Palestine did make life better for everyone there, as Herzl had predicted. In 1936, following an Arab general strike in Palestine that lasted six months and the beginning of what came to be known as the Arab Revolt, with wholesale Arab murders of Jews and the grand mufti vowing the "revenge of God Almighty," the British government appointed a Royal Commission of Inquiry to investigate why there was so much unrest between Jews and Muslim Arabs in Palestine.[83] The Peel Commission, as it became known after its chief, Lord Peel, published its report the following year. The commission noted "the belief that Arab hostility" to the British approval for Jewish settlement in the land "would presently be overcome, owing to the economic advantages which Jewish immigration was expected to bring to Palestine as a whole."[84]

And even in the context of this study of Jewish-Arab conflict, the commission had to acknowledge that the Muslim Arabs had benefited from the Jewish presence, and that their numbers had accordingly increased:

The Arab population shows a remarkable increase since 1920, and it has had some share in the increased prosperity of Palestine. Many

Arab landowners have benefited from the sale of land and the prof-
itable investment of the purchase money. The fellaheen are better
off on the whole than they were in 1920. This Arab progress has
been partly due to the import of Jewish capital into Palestine and
other factors associated with the growth of the National Home. In
particular, the Arabs have benefited from social services which could
not have been provided on the existing scale without the revenue
obtained from the Jews.[85]

Stolen Land?

Another familiar theme of pro-Palestinian literature today is that the
State of Israel exists on "stolen land"—stolen, of course, from the
indigenous people of Palestine. In reality, the land is no more stolen
than the Palestinian Arabs are its indigenous inhabitants.

As the Ottoman Empire was in its death throes, the British
government began to look ahead. On November 2, 1917, British
foreign secretary Arthur Balfour issued a momentous statement in
a letter to Lord Lionel Walter Rothschild, the leader of the British
Jewish community:

His Majesty's government view with favour the establishment in
Palestine of a national home for the Jewish people, and will use their
best endeavours to facilitate the achievement of this object, it being
clearly understood that nothing shall be done which may prejudice
the civil and religious rights of existing non-Jewish communities in
Palestine, or the rights and political status enjoyed by Jews in any
other country.[86]

This was a significant boost for the Zionist project, as it was the
first time that a major power had expressed support for it, and Jewish
immigration into Palestine increased.

The British, however, were playing both sides. At the same time
that they committed themselves to the establishment of "a national
home for the Jewish people" in Palestine, they were also encouraging
the most vociferous opponents of the Zionist project, the Arabs.

Indeed, no less an authority than Colonel T. E. Lawrence, the celebrated "Lawrence of Arabia," admitted that the very concept of Arab nationalism was a British invention.

To be sure, the Arab Muslims of Palestine had always hated the Jews, but the Arabs in general had hated one another as well. According to Lawrence, however, "the phrase Arab Movement was invented in Cairo as a common denominator for all the vague discontents against Turkey which before 1916 existed in the Arab provinces. In a non-constitutional country, these naturally took on a revolutionary character and it was convenient to pretend to find a common ground for all of them."[87]

The British colonel Richard Meinertzhagen, who served as head of Britain's military intelligence in Cairo and later as His Majesty's chief political officer for Palestine and Syria, was blunter: "Arab national feeling is based on our gold and nothing else."[88]

Even worse, Colonel Lawrence, in the course of building the "Lawrence of Arabia" myth about himself, propagated, primarily in his massive 1926 book *Seven Pillars of Wisdom*, the idea that the Arabs, with a bit of help from Lawrence himself, had played a decisive role in the defeat of the Turks in World War I, driving them out of Arabia and ultimately even capturing Damascus, setting the stage for the fall of the empire itself.

Hollywood chimed in on this myth-making with the 1962 blockbuster film *Lawrence of Arabia*. This myth proved to be extraordinarily destructive, for after the Balfour Declaration, it became a staple of Arab Muslim propaganda that the Arabs had heroically and nobly come to the aid of the British against the Turks in World War I, and instead of being rewarded, were cruelly betrayed by the perfidious Albionites, who gave the land that had been promised to them to the Zionists instead.

Reality was far from this. Even Lawrence, after building his myth, admitted in a rare moment of candor that the help the Arabs offered to bring down the Ottoman Empire was not at all decisive, but "a sideshow of a sideshow."[89] Richard Aldington, whose 1955 book *Lawrence of Arabia: A Biographical Enquiry* does much to dispel the myths that Lawrence had woven, discounts the claim that the Arabs contributed much of anything at all to the British war effort, saying of its wartime activities: "To claim that these spasmodic and comparatively trifling efforts had any serious bearing on the war with Turkey, let alone on the greater war beyond is...absurd."[90]

Indeed, says Aldington, "much of the effort of the Arab forces... was diverted to hanging around on the outskirts of Medina and to attacks on that part of the Damascus-Medina railway which was of the least importance strategically."[91] Even worse, according to Aldington, was the Arab role in the British victory over the Turks in the Battle of Megiddo, which broke Ottoman power toward the end of the war. Aldington says that General Edmund "Allenby's great breakthrough in September 1918 provided [the Arabs] with sitting targets which nobody could miss, and the chance to race hysterically into towns which they claimed to have captured after the British had done the real fighting."[92]

The British encouraged the Arabs in this. The Muslim historian Muhammad Kurd Ali recounts that "whenever the British Army captured a town or reduced a fortress which was to be given to the Arabs it would halt until the Arabs would enter, and the capture would be credited to them."[93]

This was calculated to win Arab hearts and minds, but it did more than that. It gave impetus to the Arab claims after the war that the British owed them something, while owing the Jews nothing, and that they had been betrayed and were therefore justified in attacking Jews and resisting their settlement in Palestine.

The British did nothing to counter this impression; quite the contrary. They continued to play both ends against the middle.

One of the final acts of the dying Ottoman Empire in the early 1920s was to concede control of the lands that came to be known under British authority as Palestine and Transjordan to the League of Nations. On July 24, 1922, the league granted administrative control over these territories to Britain. The League of Nations Mandate for

Palestine paved the way for the Balfour Declaration's "national home for the Jewish people" to become a reality.

However, it did so with a significant caveat. The Mandate for Palestine stated that "the Administration of Palestine, while ensuring that the rights and position of other sections of the population are not prejudiced, shall facilitate Jewish immigration under suitable conditions and shall encourage, in co-operation with the Jewish agency referred to in Article 4, close settlement by Jews on the land, including State lands and waste lands not required for public purposes."[94]

However, the same document took away 77 percent of the land that had been originally intended for this purpose: all of the land east of the Jordan River. The British government added this significant clause into the "Mandate for Palestine" document:

> *In the territories lying between the Jordan and the eastern boundary of Palestine as ultimately determined, the Mandatory shall be entitled, with the consent of the Council of the League of Nations, to postpone or withhold application of such provision of this Mandate as he may consider inapplicable to the existing local conditions.*[95]

The "provision of this Mandate" that the British would "postpone or withhold application of" was Jewish settlement in the lands east of the Jordan. That the Jews were expecting these lands to be included in the mandate is clear from the great Zionist Ze'ev Jabotinsky's poem "Shtei Gadot L'Yarden—Zu Shelanu Zu Gam Ken": "There are two sides of the Jordan River—this is ours and that is also."[96] Jabotinsky didn't originate this idea; he got it from the original extent of the British Mandate, and its stated purpose.

So from whom was the land stolen? Not from the Ottomans, who had ceded it to the League of Nations. Not from the league, which had granted administrative powers over it to the British. Not from the British, who supported the creation of Israel, at least at this point. The only land that was actually stolen was from the Jews themselves, when the British arbitrarily reduced the size of the area that was to be opened for the Jewish national home.

But surely the Israeli immigrants displaced the native Arabs from their land, no?

No. The Jews who made aliyah in the nineteenth and early twentieth centuries didn't come as armed marauders, seizing land from its owners by force. They obtained the land in a far more conventional and prosaic way: they bought it. This is acknowledged even by *Al Jazeera* in an article claiming that Israel occupied stolen land: "The [Zionist] movement, citing the biblical belief that God promised Palestine to the Jews, began to buy land there and build settlements to strengthen their claim to the land. At the time, these settlements, built largely on the coastal plain and in the north of the country, were called 'Kibbutzim' and 'Moshavim.'"[97]

A 1930 British government report (which was, incidentally, generally favorable to restrictions on Jewish settlement in Palestine) noted that the Jews not infrequently overpaid: "The Jewish authorities have nothing with which to reproach themselves…. They paid high prices for the land, and in addition they paid to certain of the occupants of those lands a considerable amount of money which they were not legally bound to pay."[98]

Rewarding Terrorism

Some thirty-five thousand Jews came to Palestine in the First Aliyah, between 1882 and 1903, mostly from Eastern Europe.[99] Forty thousand more came, primarily from Russia after more pogroms there, in the Second Aliyah (1904 to 1914), and another forty thousand in the Third Aliyah (1919 to 1923).[100] In the Fourth Aliyah (in the 1920s), eighty-two thousand more immigrated, and in the Fifth Aliyah (1929 to 1939), nearly two hundred fifty thousand immigrated, as a result of the advent of Hitler and rising anti-Semitism in Germany and all over Europe.[101]

The Jewish population of Palestine increased from twenty-five thousand in 1881 to six hundred thirty thousand in 1947. A tacit testimony to how the Arabs benefited from the Jewish presence in the land was the fact that the Arab population was four hundred fifty thousand in 1881 and 1,300,000 in 1947.[102]

Yet despite the fact that the Muslim Arabs of Palestine benefited economically from the Jews' presence in the land, they lost no time in dispelling the naïve hopes that Herzl had expressed, that this would overcome any animosity the Arabs had toward the Jews. In 1919, scarcely two years after the Balfour Declaration, a Muslim leader, Amin al-Husseini, a member of a prominent Arab clan in Jerusalem, began a campaign of organized violence against the Jews. In 1919, al-Husseini orchestrated a series of attacks on Jews all over Palestine.

Al-Husseini had friends in high places. Despite the Balfour Declaration, the British authorities largely opposed Jewish settlement in Palestine. Colonel Meinertzhagen confided to his diary his belief that British authorities "incline towards the exclusion of Zionism in Palestine."[103] This, however, was no real secret; in fact, the British authorities encouraged the Arab Muslims to riot and attack Jews. Meinertzhagen recounted that Britain's financial adviser to the Military Administration in Palestine, Colonel Bertie Harry Waters-Taylor, told al-Husseini shortly before Easter in 1920 that "he had a great opportunity at Easter to show the world…that Zionism was unpopular not only with the Palestine Administration but in Whitehall; and if disturbances of sufficient violence occurred in Jerusalem at Easter, both General Bols [chief administrator in Palestine, 1919 to 1920] and General Allenby [commander of Egyptian force, 1917 to 1919, then high commissioner of Egypt] would advocate the abandonment of the Jewish Home."[104]

The British, in order to allow for this violence to take place more easily, withdrew their own troops as well as the Jewish police from Jerusalem.[105] Thus encouraged, al-Husseini instigated riots in Jerusalem during Passover in 1920; his men told crowds in Jerusalem that "the government is with us."[106] Amid mass looting and rapes, six Jews were murdered and over two hundred more injured. A court of inquiry found that "the Jews were the victims of a peculiarly brutal and cowardly attack, the majority of the casualties being old men, women and children."[107]

Then the British authorities, showing why their nation is sometimes called Perfidious Albion, arrested the man they had encouraged to mount these riots, al-Husseini, but he escaped. Undaunted, the British tried him in absentia and sentenced him to ten years in prison. This was, however, just for show. On April 11, 1921, the British high commissioner Herbert Samuel met with al-Husseini and rewarded him with the title grand mufti of Jerusalem, saying that he hoped that this would pacify him to the extent "that the influences of his family and himself would be devoted to tranquility."[108]

It didn't work. Al-Husseini continued to instigate riots. Just weeks after he became mufti, he orchestrated riots in Petach Tikvah and Jaffa in which forty-three Jews were murdered. A British government report admitted that "the Arab majority, who were generally the aggressors, inflicted most of the casualties."[109]

This violence became a recurring aspect of life for the Jews in Palestine. In August 1929 in Jerusalem, rioting Arabs murdered 133 Jews and injured over two hundred more, many in their homes. In Hebron, they murdered another sixty-seven Jews, and in Safed, twenty more. The British government-appointed Shaw Commission found that the riots "took the form, in the most part, of a vicious attack by Arabs on Jews accompanied by wanton destruction of Jewish property. A general massacre of the Jewish community at Hebron was narrowly averted. In a few instances, Jews attacked Arabs and destroyed Arab property. These attacks, though inexcusable, were in most cases in retaliation for wrongs already committed by Arabs in the neighbourhood in which the Jewish attacks occurred."[110]

The Shaw Commission found that the riots were entirely the fault of the Muslim Arabs, and blamed the Jews. It determined that "the outbreak in Jerusalem on 23 August was from the beginning an attack by Arabs on Jews for which no excuse in the form of earlier murders by Jews has been established," and that "there can, in our view, be no doubt that racial animosity on the part of the Arabs" led to the attacks.[111] However, it attributed this animosity to "the disappointment of their national political aspirations and fear for their economic future."[112] The road to rewarding the Muslim Arabs for this violence was paved by giving them political and economic concessions, thereby encouraging more terrorism.

The irony of this was that the British government had established a British protectorate in April 1921 right next door to Palestine and on land originally part of the area designated for the site of the Jewish national home, the Emirate of Transjordan, a national home for the Arabs—Arabs who were no different culturally, religiously, or linguistically from the Arabs of Palestine. How, then, their national political aspirations had been frustrated was hard to see. Nonetheless, as far as the Shaw Commission was concerned, the real problem was not marauding, murderous Muslims but Zionism:

Jewish enterprise and Jewish immigration, when not in excess of the absorptive capacity of the country, have conferred material benefits upon Palestine in which the Arab people share. We consider, however, that the claims and demands which from the Zionist side have been advanced to the future of Jewish immigration into Palestine have been such as to arouse among the Arabs the apprehensions that they will in time be deprived of their livelihood and pass under the political domination of the Jews.[113]

The Shaw Commission exonerated the mufti, asserting that he was "influenced by the twofold desire to confront the Jews and to mobilise Moslem opinion on the issue of the Wailing Wall. He had no intention of utilising this religious campaign as the means of inciting to disorder."[114]

The Shaw Commission recommended that in order to prevent such massacres in the future, the British government should limit Jewish immigration to Palestine. It called for "a revision of the methods of regulating immigration to prevent a repetition of the excessive immigration of 1925 and 1926 and to provide for consultation with non-Jewish representatives with regard to it."[115]

This was rewarding terrorism, and the British government rewarded it again the following year in the Report on Immigration, Land Settlement and Development, more commonly known as the Hope Simpson Report, after John Hope Simpson, the chief of the commission. "The present position" of the Arabs, according to this report, was "undesirable, from the point of view both of justice and of the good government of the country." It added: "The Arab population already regards the transfer of lands to Zionist hands with dismay and alarm. These cannot be dismissed as baseless..."[116]

Orde Wingate

The Arabs continued to express their "dismay and alarm" at the Jewish presence in Palestine through attacks on Jews. In 1936, however, the British captain Orde Wingate arrived in the land. Deeply sympathetic to Zionism as a result of his devout Christian faith, Wingate offered his help to Zionist leaders. But they, having noticed how most of the British authorities were on the opposite side, at first regarded his offer with suspicion.

Wingate, however, was sincere. He had a plan to stop the Muslim Arab attacks on Jews: "There is only one way to deal with the situation, to persuade the gangs that, in their predatory raids, there is every chance of their running into a government gang which is determined to destroy them."[117] These "government gangs" would "produce in their minds the belief government forces will move at night and can and will surprise them either in villages or across country."[118]

Even though these would be British government forces, they would be partially made up of Jews as well. British authorities, however, were reluctant to side with the Jews and initially hesitated, but ultimately approved Wingate's plan to create his Special Night Squads (SNS). Wingate and his men began to fight back against al-Husseini's Arab Muslim mobs.

Wingate's British comrades were not pleased. They made fun of his eccentricities, which included wearing an alarm clock around his wrist and eating raw onions for their healthful properties. They disliked his arrogance, his rudeness, his slovenliness, and his (to them) exceedingly odd attachment to Jews and Zionism.[119] British authorities disliked his recommendation that Britain ally with the Jews rather than the Arabs, and his recommendation that one million more Jews be allowed to immigrate to Palestine.

Finally the British had had enough of Wingate's advocacy for the Jews; in May 1939, he was transferred out of Palestine. This was no ordinary transfer of a career military officer: British officials ordered that his passport be stamped with instructions that if he returned to Palestine, he would be forbidden to enter.[120] In a formal appeal against the treatment he had received, Wingate conceded nothing, saying: "I am not ashamed to say that I am a real and devoted admirer of the Jews.... Had more officers shared my views the rebellion would have come to a speedy conclusion some years ago."[121]

He was not heeded. Indeed quite the opposite happened. That same month, the British rewarded al-Husseini again, limiting Jewish settlement in the land to seventy-five thousand over the next five years, just as Hitler and his henchmen were readying their Final Solution to their problem of Jews in Europe.

While al-Husseini was largely responsible for the riots, he didn't have to work very hard to convince the Muslim Arabs in Palestine that killing Jews was in their best interests. The British authorities professed they found this puzzling. The 1937 Peel Commission expressed surprise that the tensions hadn't died down: "There were outbreaks of disorder in 1920 and 1921, but in 1925 it was thought that the prospects of ultimate harmony between the Arabs and the Jews seemed so favourable that the forces for maintaining order were substantially reduced."[122]

The commission ascribed this in large part to the lack of an independent Arab state in Palestine: "These hopes proved unfounded because, although Palestine as a whole became more prosperous, the causes of the outbreaks of 1920 and 1921, namely, the demand of the Arabs for national independence and their antagonism to the National Home, remained unmodified and were indeed accentuated by the 'external factors,' namely, the pressure of the Jews of Europe on Palestine and the development of Arab nationalism in neighbouring countries."[123]

There were other reasons, however, entirely unnoticed by British officialdom, for the ongoing Arab Muslim attacks on Jews and their unstinting opposition to a Jewish state.

CHAPTER TWO

The Roots of the Hatred of Israel

It's Your Country, but Leave It Alone

On March 1, 1899, a Muslim Arab leader in Jerusalem, Yusuf al-Khalidi, wrote a letter to the chief rabbi of France, who opposed the Zionist project:

> *In theory, the Zionist idea is completely natural, fine and just. Who can challenge the rights of the Jews in Palestine? Good Lord, historically it is really your country.*
>
> *But in practice you cannot take over Palestine without the use of force. You will need cannons and battleships. Christian fanatics will not overlook any opportunity to incite the hatred of the Muslims against the Jews.*
>
> *It is necessary, therefore, in order for peace to reign for the Jews in Turkey [that is, throughout the Ottoman Empire, which included Palestine] that the Zionist movement stop. Good Lord, the world is vast enough and there are still uninhabited countries where one can settle millions of poor Jews who may perhaps be happy there and one*

day constitute a nation. That would perhaps be the best and most rational solution to the Jewish question. But, in the name of God, let Palestine alone. Let it remain in peace.[1]

Al-Khalidi's reference to Christian fanatics inciting the hatred of Muslims against the Jews was prescient in light of the British authorities' incitement of Arab riots against Jews in Palestine, but the Muslims had no trouble hating Jews on their own, without any help from outsiders.

Qur'anic Anti-Semitism

This is because of the hatred of Jews that is embedded in the Islamic holy texts. There is a strong native strain of anti-Semitism in Islam, rooted in the Qur'an. The Qur'an puts forward a clear, consistent image of the Jews: they are scheming, treacherous liars and the most dangerous enemies of the Muslims.

The Qur'an presents Muhammad as the last and greatest in the line of Biblical prophets, preaching a message identical to theirs. The identical character of their messages may seem odd to those who know very well that the Qur'an's contents are quite different in character from those of the Bible, but the Qur'an has an ingenious explanation for this: the original message of all the Biblical prophets was Islam, and they were all Muslims. Only later did their followers corrupt their messages to create Judaism and Christianity.

Consequently, in the Qur'an, Abraham is not a Jew or a Christian, but a Muslim (3:67); his message was identical to Muhammad's. The Islamic claim is that the authentic Torah actually commands Jews to follow Muhammad and recognize his prophecy. Those who refuse to accept Muhammad as a prophet are, in the Muslim view, rejecting both Moses and the prophecies of the Torah. It is no surprise, then, that in the Qur'an both David and Jesus curse the disbelieving Jews for their disobedience (5:78).

Yet of course, Torah-observant Jews did not and do not accept Muhammad as a prophet, and this, according to Islamic tradition, enraged the prophet of Islam during his lifetime. According to Islamic tradition, Muhammad initially appealed energetically to the Jews, hoping they would accept his prophetic status. He even had the Muslims imitate the Jews by facing Jerusalem for prayers, and he adopted for the Muslims the Jews' prohibition of pork. But he was infuriated when the Jews rejected him, and Allah shared his fury in Qur'anic revelation: "And when there came to them a messenger from Allah, confirming what was with them, a party of the people of the Book threw away the Book of Allah behind their backs, as if they did not know!" (2:101).

Another Jewish leader noted that "no covenant was ever made with us about Muhammad." Allah again responded through his Prophet: "Is it ever so that when they make a covenant a party of them set it aside? The truth is, most of them do not believe" (2:100). In fact, Allah gave food laws to the Jews because of their "wrong-doing," and "for their turning many from the way of Allah" (4:160), and by doing so, "repaid them for their injustice" (6:146). Some Jews are "avid listeners to falsehood" who "distort words beyond their usages." These are "the ones for whom Allah does not intend to purify their hearts," and they will be punished not just in hellfire but in this life as well: "For them in this world is disgrace, and for them in the Hereafter is a great punishment" (5:41).

Jews dare to deny divine revelation, claiming that "Allah did not reveal to a human being anything," to which Muhammad is told to respond, "Who revealed the Scripture that Moses brought as light and guidance to the people? You [Jews] make it into pages, disclosing some of it and concealing much" (6:91).

Muslims should not get close to such people: "O you who have believed, do not take the Jews and the Christians as friends. They are friends of one another. And whoever is a friend to them among you, indeed, he is of them. Indeed, Allah does not guide the wrong-doing people" (5:51). It would hardly be appropriate for Muslims to act peaceably toward the Jews when the Jews, according to the Qur'an, are prone to war—especially against Muslims. Whenever the Jews "kindle the fire of war," says the Qur'an, "Allah extinguishes it" (5:64).

Ultimately, Allah transforms disobedient Jews into apes and pigs (2:63–66, 5:59–60, 7:166). While the Qur'an says that Muslims are the "best of people" (3:110), the unbelievers are "like livestock" (7:179). "Indeed, the worst of living creatures in the sight of Allah are those who have disbelieved, and they will not believe" (8:55).

The Jews also "strive to do mischief on earth"—that is, *fasaad*, for which the punishment is specified in Qur'an 5:33: "they will be killed or crucified, or have their hands and feet on alternate sides cut off, or will be expelled out of the land."

The rebellion against Allah that has resulted in the Jews' degradation—the "terrible agony" that those who have rejected Islam are to feel "in this world" as well as in the next (3:56)—is a frequent preoccupation of the Qur'an. Departing from his earlier tendency to appeal to the Jews as the authorities on what Allah had revealed, Muhammad began to criticize them for concealing parts of that revelation. The Qur'an several times criticizes Jews for refusing to follow Muhammad, asking, "Why don't the Jews' rabbis stop their evil behavior?" (5:63)

Someone who believes in the Qur'an as the perfect and eternal word of Allah, and the authentic Hadith as the records of the statements and actions of the man whom the Qur'an designates as the "excellent example" (33:21) for Muslims to emulate will accordingly form a negative view of Jews.

How could such a believing Muslim ever accept being friends and neighbors with "the most intense of the people in animosity toward the believers"? How can he carry out good-faith negotiations for peace with people who fabricate things and falsely ascribe them to Allah (2:79, 3:75, 3:181)? How can he trust those who claim that Allah's power is limited (5:64) and who are "avid listeners to falsehood" and "distort words beyond their usages" (5:41)?

A pious and knowledgeable Muslim will discover in his Qur'an that the Jews are busy hiding the truth and misleading people (3:78).

They staged rebellion against the prophets and rejected their guidance (2:55), and even killed them (2:61). They prefer their own interests to the teachings of Muhammad (2:87). They wish evil for people and try to mislead them (2:109), and even feel pain when others are happy or fortunate (3:120). They're arrogant about their status as Allah's beloved people (5:18) while devouring people's wealth by subterfuge (4:161); slandering the true religion (4:46), and killing the prophets (2:61). They're merciless and heartless (2:74), unrestrained in committing sins (5:79), cowardly (59:13–14), and miserly (4:53). They are under Allah's curse (4:46, 9:30).

An informed and committed believer will look at the Jews, and in particular at Zionism and the State of Israel, and not see a struggle over land or boundaries that can be solved through negotiations if a sufficient amount of goodwill exists on both sides. Such a believer is much more likely to see the Israeli-Palestinian conflict as an eschatological struggle against the great spiritual enemies of the Muslims, as the Jews are designated in the Qur'an: "You will surely find the most intense of the people in animosity toward the believers to be the Jews..." (5:82)

There can be no negotiated settlement, and no peace, with these treacherous, untrustworthy, mendacious enemies. And the Qur'an's condemnations of the Jews are repeatedly sweeping: the Muslim holy book refers again and again to "the Jews," not simply to one party among them. The Qur'an does include the Jews (along with "Christians and Sabeans") among those who "will have their reward with their Lord, and no fear will there be concerning them, nor will they grieve" (2:62), but mainstream Muslim commentators are not inclined to see this as an indication of divine pluralism. The Qur'an translators Abdullah Yusuf Ali, Mohammed Marmaduke Pickthall, and Muhammad Asad all add parenthetical glosses that make the passage mean that the Jews referred to in this passage will be saved only if they become Muslims. Qur'an.com adds "before Prophet Muhammad" in brackets after "Jews or Christians or Sabeans," making it clear that those three could be saved as such only before the advent of Islam, and that now they must convert to Islam to be saved.

What's more, the Qur'an also says that "they who disbelieved among the People of the Book and the polytheists will be in the fire of hell, abiding eternally in it. Those are the most vile of created beings." (98:6) Those who "disbelieved among the People of the Book" are the Jews and Christians who did not convert to Islam.

These rebellious people can never legitimately govern a state. Syed Abul Ala Maududi (1903–1979), founder of the Pakistani political party Jamaat-e-Islami, declared that non-Muslims have "absolutely no right to seize the reins of power in any part of God's earth nor to direct the collective affairs of human beings according to their own misconceived doctrines."[2] If they did, "the believers would be under an obligation to do their utmost to dislodge them from political power and to make them live in subservience to the Islamic way of life."[3]

Indeed. Islamic law never grants the People of the Book the same rights as those enjoyed by Muslims. Being designated People of the Book accords to Jews, Christians, and a few others only the ambiguous privilege of being allowed to practice their religions under the "protection" of Islamic law, which mandates severe restrictions to make them "feel themselves subdued" (Qur'an 9:29). The "protected peoples" (dhimmis) do not enjoy equal rights with Muslims, but they are allowed to maintain their religious identity as long as they accept the hegemony of Muslims in an Islamic state, and various humiliating and discriminatory regulations.

Thus the Qur'an demonizes Jews in all manner of ways, and envisions their living in subservience and submission to the Muslims, not governing their own state. In light of these teachings, the Jewish State of Israel constitutes a perpetual affront to Muslims and Islam, on Qur'anic grounds.

And Islamic tradition is no kinder to the Jews.

Jews in the Hadith

The Hadith, reports of Muhammad's words and deeds that, if deemed authentic by Islamic scholars, are normative for Islamic law, contain a great deal of anti-Semitic material. In one, as if apes and pigs weren't bad enough, Muhammad says that a group of Jews "assumed the shape of rats."[4] In another, he exclaims: "May Allah's curse be on the Jews for they built the places of worship at the graves of their Prophets."[5]

Islam's most frequently repeated prayer is a passage from the Qur'an in which the believers ask of Allah: "Guide us to the straight path, the path of those upon whom you have bestowed favor, not of those who have evoked anger or of those who are astray." (1:6–7) Muhammad explains: "The Jews are those who Allah is angry with, and the Christians have strayed."[6]

The most notorious anti-Semitic passage in all of the Hadith is the one in which Muhammad is made to prophesy that Muslims will bring about the End Times by killing Jews wholesale: "The last hour would not come unless the Muslims will fight against the Jews and the Muslims would kill them until the Jews would hide themselves behind a stone or a tree and a stone or a tree would say: Muslim, or the servant of Allah, there is a Jew behind me; come and kill him; but the tree Gharqad would not say, for it is the tree of the Jews."[7]

This passage gives all the anti-Semitism in Islam an edge of menace. Muslims are taught in their holiest books not just to despise and mistrust Jews, but that Muslims are doing a good and virtuous deed if they kill them, a deed that will bring about the consummation of all things and the dawning of eternal justice for mankind.

"Drive Them out From Where They Drove You Out"

But even that genocidal Hadith is not the primary obstacle rendering all peace negotiations between Israel and the Palestinians fruitless. The principal stumbling block on the path to peace is the phrase "drive them out from where they drove you out" (Qur'an 2:191).

Palestinians routinely claim (falsely, as we shall see) that they were driven from their land by the Jews when Israel declared independence on May 14, 1948, and the Arab League—primarily Egypt, Syria, Iraq, Transjordan, Lebanon, and Saudi Arabia—declared war on the nascent Jewish state, determined to destroy it in its cradle. Accordingly, a Palestinian Muslim is likely to believe that driving out the Israelis from where the Muslims themselves were driven out is a divine command that must be obeyed without question.

Destroying Israel is, in light of this, a religious imperative, even an act of worship. In 2012, Hamas published a music video that included a lyric apparently inspired by the "drive them out from where they drove you out" command and the Hadith calling on Muslims to kill Jews in order to hasten the Last Day: "Killing Jews is worship that draws us close to Allah."[8]

A Muslim who believes that Allah has commanded him to drive out the Jews from where he was driven out, and that this command is no more negotiable or susceptible to being questioned than the Ten Commandments is by a Jew or Christian, is not likely to believe that negotiations will bring about a lasting agreement allowing Israelis and Palestinians live side by side in peace.

"Jihad," Arabic for "struggle," in Islamic theology primarily means warfare against unbelievers in order to establish the supremacy of the Muslims over them, and the hegemony of Islamic law. This is a religious imperative, based on the Qur'an's command to fight against the People of the Book and ensure that they "feel themselves subdued" (9:29). It makes it impossible for Muslims to accept a Jewish state in which Muslims live, for then the People of the Book are not living in submission to the Muslims as they should, but upending the natural order of things and daring even to rule over the Muslims.

Rule of Muslims by infidels, especially those whose enmity toward the Muslims is the strongest (Qur'an 5:82) is unacceptable under any circumstances and can never be tolerated.

The Israeli-Palestinian conflict is, in short, what no policymaker, no negotiator, no one who has ever been involved with the Middle East "peace process" has ever admitted it to be: a religious war.

An Islamic Jihad

These policymakers and diplomats could have known better, however, if they had simply listened to the people who were prolonging that war. They have never made their intentions secret. The moderator at a 2012 event commemorating the forty-seventh anniversary of the founding of Fatah, the dominant group within the Palestine Liberation Organization, declared: "Our war with the descendants of the apes and pigs [that is, Jews] is a war of religion and faith."[9]

To be sure, other Palestinian leaders on numerous occasions have been actively deceptive about how they see the conflict. One brazen example of this deception came from Mahmoud al-Habbash, a close adviser to Palestinian Authority president Mahmoud Abbas and the Palestinian Authority's supreme sharia judge, when he stated flatly on September 24, 2018, on official Palestinian Authority television: "Our people's conflict with the occupation is a political conflict and not religious, as Israel is trying to market it to the world."[10]

Yet the same al-Habbash emphasized on October 23, 2015, also on official Palestinian Authority television, that "this is a conflict between two entities, good and evil, between two projects: Allah's project versus Satan's project, a project connected to Allah, which is his will—true and good—and a project connected to oppression and Satanism, to Satanism and animosity, occupation and barbarism."[11]

Yet on May 4, 2018, al-Habbash insisted on *Quranic Horizons*, a program on official Palestinian Authority television, that the conflict was all about occupation, not about anti-Semitism: "We were never supporters of hatred, and were not enemies of peace. We did not exploit anyone, did not attack anyone, and did not deny anyone's right…and here—what we have said and are saying and will continue to say—we do not resist the occupation, we do not resist the occupiers because they are Jewish. No, we resist occupiers whatever their religion may be.

You know, if the occupation was Muslim Arab we would resist. What more do you want? We are not against the Jewish religion."[12]

However, while Judea and Samaria (the West Bank) were occupied by Jordan and the Gaza Strip by Egypt from 1948 to 1967, there was no protest among the Palestinian Arabs against the "occupation," and there were no calls for a Palestinian state including those areas. Palestinian spokesmen have again and again made it clear that the Qur'an and Islam in general, not quarrels over various patches of land or occupation or settlements, are what make the Israeli-Palestinian conflict intractable. And contrary to al-Habbash's insistence, they have made it abundantly clear that one of their chief objections to Israel is that it is governed by, and full of, Jews.

A Qatari sheikh, Muhammad Al-Muraikhi, stated this plainly on Qatar TV on January 9, 2009. "We do not treat the Jews as our enemies just because they occupied Palestine," he explained, "or because they occupied a precious part of our Arab and Islamic world. We will treat the Jews as our enemies even if they return Palestine to us, because they are infidels. They rejected Allah and His messengers."[13]

An Egyptian imam, Muhammad Hussein Ya'qoub, declared eight days later in a televised sermon that Muslim hatred of Jews had nothing to do with Israel and everything to do with the Qur'an:

> *If the Jews left Palestine to us, would we start loving them? Of course not. We will never love them. Absolutely not. The Jews are infidels— not because I say so, and not because they are killing Muslims, but because Allah said: "The Jews say that Uzair is the son of Allah, and the Christians say that Christ is the son of Allah. These are the words from their mouths. They imitate the sayings of the disbelievers before. May Allah fight them. How deluded they are." [Qur'an 9:30] It is Allah who said that they are infidels.*
>
> *Your belief regarding the Jews should be, first, that they are infidels, and second, that they are enemies. They are enemies not because they occupied Palestine. They would have been enemies even if they*

did not occupy a thing. Allah said: "You shall find the strongest men in enmity to the believers to be the Jews and the polytheists." [Qur'an 5:82] Third, you must believe that the Jews will never stop fighting and killing us. They [fight] not for the sake of land and security, as they claim, but for the sake of their religion: "And they will not cease fighting you until they turn you back [from] your religion, if they can." [Qur'an 2:217] This is it. We must believe that our fighting with the Jews is eternal, and it will not end until the final battle—and this is the fourth point. You must believe that we will fight, defeat, and annihilate them, until not a single Jew remains on the face of the Earth.14

Ya'qoub's peroration was just as chilling:

As for you Jews—the curse of Allah upon you. The curse of Allah upon you, whose ancestors were apes and pigs. You Jews have sown hatred in our hearts, and we have bequeathed it to our children and grandchildren. You will not survive as long as a single one of us remains.[15]

Also on Egyptian television on the same day, January 17, 2009, two other Muslim clerics, Sheik Said Al-Afani and Sheik Muhammad Abd Al-Salam, reiterated that the war against Israel was all about Islamic imperatives. The Jews, said Al-Afani, "are the accursed people, who incurred the wrath of Allah. They are the offspring of snakes and vipers, the slayers of our Prophet Muhammad, whose death was a consequence of his being poisoned by a Jewish woman."[16]

Contradicting the accepted wisdom in the West, he continued: "Our hatred of them is purely on religious grounds, and not because of the pure, sacred land, which was blessed by Allah, or because of Gaza...not only because of Al-Aqsa and so on. We hate them, first and foremost, because of their enmity towards Allah, and because they slayed our prophets."[17]

Then Muhammad Abd Al-Salam added: "Let me clarify that it is our duty to hate them, as part of our faith." To this Al-Afani readily agreed. Al-Salam explained: "People have become confused about this. Some think that it is a territorial or a national issue, or that it has to do with the blessed Al-Aqsa Mosque, but the issue is much broader—it is a matter of faith. We are obligated to hate them because they are a murderous people, and the enemies of all that is good and of Islam."

A Muslim cleric from Egypt, Sheikh Salam Abd Al-Qawi, emphasized on Egypt's Al-Nas TV on January 8, 2009, that hatred of the Jews is a religious obligation mandated by Islam: "Hating the enemies of Allah is very important. We must teach our children, our youngsters, our brothers, and all the Muslims to hate the accursed Zionist Jews. Why not? They teach their children to hate us. Our hatred of the Jews is based upon our faith. The Koran tells us to hate them, not to love them…. We must teach our children to obey Allah, to obey the Prophet Muhammad, and to hate the Jews, the Zionists, and what the Zionists are planning. We must raise them on the Koranic verses that call to fight and wage jihad for the sake of Allah. We want to raise our children to love jihad for the sake of Allah. We must teach our children that death for the sake of Allah is our most lofty goal."[18]

Abdallah Jarbu, Hamas' deputy minister of religious endowments, on Al-Aqsa TV on February 28, 2010, condemned on Islamic grounds anyone who wants to negotiate with the Israelis:

[The Jews] suffer from a mental disorder, because they are thieves and aggressors. A thief or an aggressor, who took property or land, develops a psychological disorder and pangs of conscience, because he took something that wasn't his.

They want to present themselves to the world as if they have rights, but, in fact, they are foreign bacteria—a microbe unparalleled in the world. It's not me who says this. The Koran itself says that they have no parallel: "You shall find the strongest men in enmity to the believers to be the Jews."

May He annihilate this filthy people who have neither religion nor conscience. I condemn whoever believes in normalizing relations with them, whoever supports sitting down with them, and whoever believes that they are human beings. They are not human beings. They are not people. They have no religion, no conscience, and no moral values.[19]

On October 5, 2018, on *Not a Neighbor*, a program on official Palestinian Authority television, Sharia judge Muhannad Abu Rumi likewise denounced the idea that the Israeli-Palestinian conflict is about territory and could thus be subject to negotiations:

People could be deluded or think…that we have no way out with the Jews…. The liberation of this land is a matter of faith, which will happen despite everyone. The Jews leaving this land is a divine decree…. The war is not only over this strip of land, as you all know the Jews want everything and not just a part. They want to subjugate us, and that we be slaves to their command…[20]

A week later, during a Friday sermon at the Islamic Center of South Florida, Imam Hasan Sabri offered a succinct encapsulation of the principle of "Drive them out from where they drove you out" (Qur'an 2:191): "If a land is occupied or plundered, it should be liberated from its occupiers and plunderers, even if this leads to the martyrdom of tens of millions of Muslims."[21]

Sabri ridiculed the very idea of negotiations: "Take the Palestinian cause, for example. It is not being plotted against with a deal they call 'the Deal of the Century.' Why do they call it a 'deal'? Because whoever is involved in this treason is not a man of principles. These are peddlers, not men with a cause. All they want are positions and jobs. That is why for them, the cause is nothing but a deal, a matter of give and take. For them, it is nothing but a deal."[22]

To this, Sabri contrasted the "position of a believing Muslim about the Palestinian cause," which he characterized in this way: "That Palestine in its entirety is Islamic land, and there is no difference between what was occupied in 1948 and 1967. There is no difference between this village or that village, this city or that city. All of it is Islamic *waqf* land that was occupied by force. The responsibility for it lies with the entire Islamic nation, and the [Palestinians] should benefit from this land. If a land is occupied or plundered, it should be liberated from the occupiers and plunderers, even if this leads to the martyrdom of tens of millions of Muslims. This is the ruling, and there is no room for discussion or concessions."[23]

There is no room for discussion or concessions because of the nature of the foe as these spokesmen describe that enemy to their people. In a Friday sermon on November 23, 2018, an imam in Gaza, Sheikh Musa Abu Jleidan, mined the Qur'an's vilification of the Jews to explain to Palestinians and to his Muslim audience worldwide (video of the sermon was uploaded to YouTube) how evil and implacable their enemy really was:

> *The Jews are treacherous and conniving cheaters. Allah said about them: "Is it not true that every time they enter into a pact, a group from among them casts it aside? In fact, most of them do not believe." They are the pinnacle of terrorism. [Allah said:] "Whenever they kindle the fire of war, Allah extinguishes it, but they strive to do mischief on earth. Allah loves not those who do mischief." They are the strongest among people in enmity to our religion. Even if snakes gave up their venom and scorpions their stinging, the Jews would not relinquish their enmity towards Muslims. [Allah said:] "You shall find the strongest among people in enmity towards believers to be the Jews and the polytheists." In addition, they are the slayers of the prophets.[24]*

Every one of his assertions, as we have seen, is straight from the Qur'an (2:100, 5:64, 5:82, 2:61, 2:91, 3:21, and many other verses).

An Egyptian Muslim cleric, Sheikh Masoud Anwar, on Al-Rahma TV on January 9, 2009, also stated that negotiations with the Israelis were worthless because Jews could not be trusted. He declared: "The worst enemies of the Muslims—after Satan—are the Jews. Who said this? Allah did." He enumerated some of what he claimed to be the negative characteristics of the Jews, including these:

Cowardice is a deep-rooted characteristic of every single Jew. Cowardice.... Clinging to life.... The third characteristic of the Jews is their treacherous nature. The Jews are violators of covenants. Whoever believes that the Jews can honor an agreement is deluding himself. Whoever claims that the Jews honor their commitments is gullible. Whoever makes fun of us, saying the Jews are divided into doves and hawks, is a liar. There are neither hawks nor doves among them. You cannot even dream of a peaceful solution with the Jews. Forget about your dreams. They are either vultures or wolves—not doves. There are no doves or hawks among them. They are all wolves. They are all wolves. The Jew holds an olive branch in one hand, and a dagger in the other.[25]

Another imam told a Muslim audience in November 2018 that while the struggle against Israel is an Islamic cause, this is best kept hidden for public relations purposes. At a "Workshop for Palestine" hosted by American Muslims for Palestine at the Islamic Center of Union County, New Jersey (ICUCNJ), on November 17, 2018, ICUCNJ Imam Sa'id Elkasaby explained: "Although our cause is Islamic, when we market and present it to people, I believe that it should be presented as a 'humanitarian cause.' If I talk to Jews and tell them that my cause is Islamic, they're out. It's over. They won't support me because they're Jews and I'm a Muslim. The same is true when I tell a Christian that my cause is Islamic. When I tell him that my cause is humanitarian, it means that every human being must acknowledge that truth. I know that I have the right to Palestine, but I want to be supported by everybody—by the Muslims, the Christians, the Chinese, the Sikhs, and the nonreligious. They will all support my cause because all humans will support my cause. I am a human being. I have rights. I own a land. So I present this cause to people.... If we keep telling the Americans that our cause is Islamic, only the Muslims will support us. The non-Muslims will not support us. So I want to generalize the cause so everybody will sympathize with us."[26]

Yet numerous Muslim clerics have for many years contradicted the general assumption that the Israeli-Palestinian conflict is over land and could be settled through negotiations. As Barack Obama pressed Israel to resume peace talks with Palestinian Authority president Mahmoud Abbas, in the summer of 2013 Sheikh Hammam Saeed, the leader of the Jordanian branch of the Muslim Brotherhood, thundered that eradicating all Jewish presence from the Holy Land was a matter of Islamic law. He termed the idea of a negotiated settlement "heresy, according to Islamic law, because Allah says that Palestine belongs to the Islamic nation, while they say that Palestine belongs to the Jews. Anyone who says that Palestine belongs to the Jews has no place in the religion of Allah, and no room in this creed. This is an issue of heresy and belief."

In another address Saeed added: "This is what we say to the Jews: We will not accept you on the land of Palestine.... I say to you, oh Jews: The time of your reckoning has come. By Allah, we will hold you accountable for every drop of blood you have spilled, for every inch of land you attacked, and for every mosque-goer whose entry into the Al-Aqsa Mosque you have prevented." But he was not fighting just to redress perceived grievances: "Woe betide you, oh Jews, do you realize that this is mentioned in the Qur'an and the hadith?" And the crowd began chanting that Palestine was "the graveyard of the Jews."[27]

That genocidal vision is not unique. In June 2013, the Jordanian newspaper *Assawsana* published an article by Muhammad Qasem Batayena chillingly and frankly entitled, "Let's Kill the Jews Everywhere." In it, Batayena insisted: "I'm not an extremist, nor racist.... I'm not bloodthirsty and not vengeful.... I'm not a terrorist and I've never been a killer." Nonetheless, he laments that "I am an Arab for sure," but "our blood is permitted, while the blood of the apes and pigs is forbidden...because the Arab tyrants sold us for a cheap price and served us on golden plates as sacrifice for the Zionists."

Batayena saw a brighter future ahead: "Yes, we will triumph, pray in Jerusalem and take revenge on the filthy murderers.... [W]e will

kill them wherever we find them, as the Holy Qur'an told us....
[W]e will make them taste the taste of death, in which they became
masters all over the Islamic and Arab lands.... Yes, we will kill them,
and I swear that if I get the chance, I won't miss it...since I believe
in Allah and his Messenger, and I know that this world is nothing
but the enjoyment of a delusion."28 The exhortation to "kill them
wherever you find them" appears three times in the Qur'an (2:191,
4:89, 9:5); and the statement "what is the life of this world except the
enjoyment of delusion" is also Qur'anic (3:185).

An Eschatological Struggle

Because the Jews are the enemies of Islam, to fight them is to defend
Islam. Mahmoud al-Habbash explained on official Palestinian
Authority television on June 30, 2018, that "Jerusalem is the arena of
conflict between us and the colonialist project"—that is, Israel. This
conflict is not just about driving out the alleged colonialist occupier. Al-Habbash said that it is, in fact, nothing less than "the Battle
of History between Islam and the enemies of Islam; between the
Muslims and the enemies of Muslims; between the Islamic culture in
all its splendor and human glory and the culture of Satan attempting
to establish oppression and aggression at the expense of the culture
of truth and goodness." The al-Aqsa Mosque on the Temple Mount,
said al-Habbash, "is decreed to be the arena of the battle between
good and evil."29

Al-Habbash added: "Jerusalem is the heading of this battle, this
conflict, and this round, which I and many others see as the key, as
the first step, as the spark of the battle of the 'final promise.'" Al-Habbash was referring to this passage from the Qur'an: "Then when the
final promise came, [We sent your enemies] to sadden your faces and
to enter the Temple in Jerusalem, as they entered it the first time,
and to destroy what they had taken over with destruction" [17:7],
until, of course, the Muslims fought back and drove them out. So
al-Habbash was envisioning conflict with the Israeli authorities over

the Temple Mount in the context of the Qur'an's prophecy of a battle between the Muslims and the Jews heralding the end of days.

Because of the treachery of the Jews, according to another Gaza imam, Ahmad Okasha, the only solution to the problems of the Palestinians was decreed by Muhammad himself in his own End Times prophecy of Muslims killing Jews. On Hamas' Al-Aqsa TV on November 5, 2018, Okasha said: "The most obvious Jihad on the face of the Earth is the Jihad in Palestine. There is no doubt or dispute about it. Muslims fighting Jews who occupied their land—there is no dispute here."[30]

Indeed, Okasha added, Jerusalem itself

shall only be liberated in the way decreed for us by Allah: "Judgment Day shall not come until you fight the Jews, and the trees and the rocks will say: 'Oh Muslim, oh servant of Allah, there is a Jew behind me, come and kill him.'"[31]

That genocidal Hadith is a favorite motif among contemporary jihadists. On March 30, 2007, a spokesman for Hamas, Dr. Ismail Radwan, said on Palestinian Authority television:

The Hour [Resurrection] will not take place until the Muslims fight the Jews and the Muslims kill them, and the rock and the tree will say: "Oh, Muslim, servant of Allah, there is a Jew behind me, kill him!"

We must remind our Arab and Muslim nation, its leaders and people, its scholars and students, remind them that Palestine and the Al Aqsa mosque will not be liberated through summits nor by international resolutions, but it will be liberated through the rifle. It will not be liberated through negotiations, but through the rifle, since this occupation knows no language but the language of force.... O Allah, strengthen Islam and Muslims, and bring victory to your Jihad-fighting worshipers, in Palestine and everywhere.... Allah take the oppressor Jews and Americans and their supporters.[32]

As for the tree that Muhammad referred to as "the tree of the Jews," the Saudi sheikh Muhammad al-Arefe explained in 2008 that "studies conducted in Tel Aviv and in the Palestinian lands occupied by the Jews showed that they plant trees around their homes, because the Prophet Muhammad said that when the Muslims fight the Jews, each and every stone and tree will say: 'Oh Muslim, oh servant of Allah, there is a Jew behind me, come and kill him.'" The Jews planted these trees, al-Arefe said, because they are "not man enough to stand and fight" the Muslims."[33]

On official Palestinian Authority television on January 9, 2012, Palestinian Authority mufti Muhammad Hussein invoked the genocidal Hadith as he commemorated the forty-seventh anniversary of the founding of Fatah: "Forty-seven years ago the [Fatah] revolution started. Which revolution? The modern revolution of the Palestinian people's history. In fact, Palestine in its entirety is a revolution, since [Caliph] Umar came [to conquer Jerusalem, A.D. 637], and continuing today, and until the End of Days. The reliable Hadith [tradition attributed to Muhammad], [found] in the two reliable collections, Bukhari and Muslim, says: 'The Hour [of Resurrection] will not come until you fight the Jews. The Jew will hide behind stones or trees. Then the stones or trees will call: "Oh Muslim, servant of Allah, there is a Jew behind me, come and kill him." Except the Gharqad tree [which will keep silent].' Therefore it is no wonder that you see Gharqad [trees] surrounding the [Israeli] settlements and colonies."[34]

On July 27 and 28, 2018, the Palestinian Al-Quds TV channel broadcast speeches from the second international conference of the Al-Aqsa Forum for Preachers, which was being held in Istanbul. One of the speakers, the Mauritanian Muslim cleric Muhammad Al-Hassan Ould Al-Dadou Al-Shanqiti, purported to find the future of Israel and Palestine in Islamic prophecy:

The Prophet Muhammad informed us of the two defeats that the Zionists would suffer in this blessed land. The first defeat would occur before the return of Jesus son of Mary: "You shall fight the Jews and kill them, while you are on the east bank of the Jordan River and they are on the west bank."

...After that, the second war will take place, when Jesus son of Mary fights the Antichrist. The Jews from all over the land will gather around the Antichrist, with 70,000 Jews from Esfahan in the right wing of his army, wearing scarves on their heads. The Muslims will kill them, and the trees and the rocks will say: "Of servant of Allah, of Muslim, there is a Jew behind me, come and kill him— except for the Gharqad, which is one of the trees of the Jews." That is when the ultimate defeat of the brothers of apes and pigs will take place, and after that, nothing will remain of them.[35]

Even imams in the West have referred to the genocidal Hadith. In December 2016, the Jordanian Muslim cleric Sheikh Muhammad bin Musa Al Nasr preached at Dar Al-Arqam Mosque in Montreal, and his sermon was posted on the mosque's YouTube channel. In the course of his sermon, Al-Nasr recited the genocidal Hadith, concluding: "O Muslim, O servant of Allah, there is a Jew behind me, come and kill him."[36] And an imam in Toulouse, France, Mohammed Tatai, said in a sermon in June 2018: "The Prophet Muhammad told us about the final and decisive battle: 'Judgment Day will not come until the Muslims fight the Jews. The Jews will hide behind the stones and the trees, and the stones and the trees will say: Oh Muslim, oh servant of Allah, there is a Jew hiding behind me, come and kill him—except for the Gharqad tree, which is one of the trees of the Jews.'"[37] When a controversy arose in France over his remarks, Tatai complained that video of his sermon "takes what I said out of context."[38] Of course.

On March 31, 2017, the imam Mundhir Abdallah of the Al-Faruq Mosque in Copenhagen, Denmark, preached that soon there would be a "caliphate, which will instate the shari'a of Allah and revive the Sunna of His Prophet, which will wage Jihad for the sake of Allah, which will unite the Islamic nation after it disintegrated, and which will liberate the Al-Aqsa Mosque from the filth of the Zionists, so that the words of the Prophet Muhammad will be fulfilled."[39]

Which words in particular? Abdallah continued: "Judgement Day will not come until the Muslims fight the Jews and kill them. The Jews will hide behind the rocks and the trees, but the rocks and the trees will say: 'Oh Muslim, oh servant of Allah, there is a Jew behind me, come and kill him.'"[40] He said that the Muslims would soon "liberate Jerusalem, and will uproot the Jewish entity, that colonialist and Crusader base."[41]

After being charged with hate speech, Abdallah claimed that he was just speaking critically of the latest round of the Israeli-Palestinian "peace process":

In that sinful summit, the [Arab] rulers of treachery and depravity called for the Palestinian issue to be resolved through negotiations. What negotiations? Negotiations that would have given the Jews— in keeping with the "Deal of the Century," which was brought about by that foolish, hateful, Crusader pig Trump, in order to break the will of the Muslims, to strengthen the Jewish entity, and to give the Palestinians 10% of historical Palestine. Palestine is not up for partitioning or bargaining. The only solution for Palestine is Jihad. There is no other solution."[42]

Abdallah shot back against the hate-speech charges by saying that instead of himself, "the first to be placed on trial should be the people who planted the Jews in our lands."[43]

To at least one Muslim cleric, that would be Allah himself. Imam Ahmad Al-Rawashdeh in December 2017 delivered a Friday sermon at the Old Tila Al-Ali Mosque in Amman, Jordan, in which he asserted that "as long as they are dispersed, it is impossible to annihilate the Jews," but that the Palestinians had divine help, as Allah himself had provided a remedy for this: he "informed us that he would gather the Jews in one place, so that they could be dealt a mortal blow." Allah would, said al-Rawashdeh, "gather them so that they can meet their end...because they constitute an epidemic," and would gather them, of course, in Palestine. He went on to cite Adolf Hitler, quoting him as saying: "One cannot find a single act of immorality or crime against society in which the Jews are not involved."[44]

So what was to be done? A Muslim cleric affiliated with Hamas, Wael Al-Zarad, offered the solution on Al-Aqsa TV on February 28, 2008:

> *In short, these are the Jews. As Muslims, our blood vengeance against them will only subside with their annihilation, Allah willing, because they tried to kill our Prophet several times....*
>
> *What should we do with these people? What is the best solution for them? Should it be by shamelessly bestowing kisses, regardless of our religion and our morals, on satellite TV and in clear view of the whole world? Should it be through futile meetings, which are usually conducted on carpets red with the blood of martyrs? Or should it be through an exchange of despicable smiles and ugly handshakes?...*
>
> *What is the best solution for these people, who have perpetrated every possible thing against us? They have destroyed our homes, killed our children, taken our land, and plundered our resources. They have turned our mosques into pubs and bars, where they drink alcohol and get women drunk. From the dome of the Al-Aqsa Mosque, they proclaim that Ezra the Scribe is the son of God.*
>
> *By Allah, people, the Jews do not deserve such a fuss. They do not deserve to be feared. The Jews are not a terrorizing bogeyman. The Jews are nothing but human scum, who came as scattered gangs to occupy our land. By Allah, if each and every Arab spat on them, they would drown in Arab spit. By Allah, if each and every Muslim spat on them, they would drown in saliva. By Allah, if the Arabs and Muslims turned into flies, the Jews would die from their buzzing. Therefore, my dear brothers, the Jews do not deserve to be feared so much. Therefore, I ask with pain and sorrow: Isn't there a single reasonable man in any of the Arab air forces? Isn't there a single reasonable man among them, who will break through these aerial borders, and bomb the Jews deep in their own land? Where are all the Arabs and Muslims?[45]*

No Israel for Jews

Others, however, have agreed that Allah gathered the Jews in Israel, even going so far as to claim that the Qur'an promises the land of Israel to the Jews, and that the Muslim claim to Israeli land is therefore illegitimate on Islamic grounds.

This is a comforting message that some of these spokesmen have taken to Jewish audiences, reinforcing in them the idea that the Islamic jihad imperative against Israel is simply the province of a tiny minority of extremists among Muslims, and that the voices of reason and moderation—and Qur'anic authenticity—will eventually prevail in the Islamic world.

Alas, these spokesmen are spreading a false message based on a partial and highly misleading reading of the Qur'an.

Those who make this argument usually base it primarily upon Qur'an 5:21, in which Moses declares, "O my people! Enter the holy land which Allah has assigned to you, and turn not back ignominiously, for then you will be overthrown, to your own ruin." The London-based imam Muhammad al-Husseini emphasizes the views of the ninth-century Islamic scholar al-Tabari, who explains that this statement is "a narrative from God...concerning the saying of Moses...to his community from among the children of Israel and his order to them according to the order of God to him, ordering them to enter the holy land."[46]

Al-Tabari is not unique in this. The revered Qur'an commentator Ibn Kathir says in his interpretation of 5:21 that the Jews "were the best among the people of their time"—a designation reminiscent of the Qur'an's calling the Muslims "the best of people" (3:110).[47] And the parallels Ibn Kathir imagines he sees between the Muslims and the Jews don't end there—he even has the Jews waging jihad:

Allah states next that Musa [Moses] encouraged the Children of Israel to perform Jihad and enter Jerusalem, which was under their control during the time of their father Ya`qub [Jacob]. Ya`qub and his children later moved with his children and household to Egypt *during the time of Prophet Yusuf [Joseph]. His offspring remained in Egypt until their exodus with Musa. They found a mighty, strong people in Jerusalem who had previously taken it over. Musa, Allah's Messenger, ordered the Children of Israel to enter Jerusalem and fight their enemy, and he promised them victory and triumph over the mighty people if they did so.*

That is not the end of the story, however. Predictably, the Jews disobeyed Allah. Consequently, says Ibn Kathir, they "were punished for forty years by being lost, wandering in the land uncertain of where they should go. This was their punishment for defying Allah's command." In contrast stand the Muslims: "The Muslim Ummah [community] is more respected and honored before Allah, and has a more perfect legislative code and system of life, it has the most honorable Prophet, the larger kingdom, more provisions, wealth and children, a larger domain and more lasting glory than the Children of Israel."[48]

And the idea that the "glory" of the Children of Israel was not "lasting" is the key to seeing the weakness of the argument that Allah promised the Land of Israel to the Jews. One might wonder why, if this exegesis is correct, the Islamic world from Morocco to Indonesia manifests such hostility to Israel. Why have so few Muslims ever noticed that Allah actually wants the Jews to possess the Land of Israel? One reason may be that they read Qur'anic passages such as 2:61, which says that some Jews who rebelled against Moses were "covered with humiliation and misery; they drew on themselves the wrath of Allah. This because they went on rejecting the Signs of Allah and slaying His Messengers without just cause. This because they rebelled and went on transgressing."

The Qur'an also says the Jews broke whatever covenant with Allah they had:

And because of their breaking their covenant, We have cursed them and made hard their hearts. They change words from their context and forget a part of that whereof they were admonished. You will not cease to discover treachery from all except a few of them. But bear with them and pardon them. Lo! Allah loves the kindly. (5:13)

Being thus accursed according to the Qur'an, the Jews are not the legitimate inheritors of the promise made in Qur'an 5:21. The ones who are the inheritors of that promise are those who have remained faithful to Allah—the Muslims—not those whom he has accursed—the Jews.

The Muslim Claim to Jerusalem

When discussing the Israeli-Palestinian conflict, pundits and politicians often tell us that Jerusalem is one of the holy cities of Islam—indeed, its third-holiest city, right after Mecca and Medina.

But in reality, the Islamic claim to Jerusalem is extremely tenuous, based only on a legendary journey of Muhammad—a journey that is at best a dream and at worst a fabrication. The Qur'an refers to this journey only obliquely and in only one place; Islamic tradition fills in the details and connects Jerusalem with the words of the Qur'an. But the Qur'an itself never mentions Jerusalem even once—an exceptionally inconvenient fact for Muslims who claim that the Palestinians must have a share of Jerusalem because the city is sacred to Islam.

Muhammad's famous Night Journey is the basis of the Islamic claim to Jerusalem. The Qur'an's only reference to this journey appears in the first verse of chapter seventeen, which says that Allah took Muhammad from "the Sacred Mosque" in Mecca "to the farthest [in Arabic, *al-aqsa*] Mosque." There was no mosque in Jerusalem at this time, so the "farthest" mosque probably wasn't really the one that now bears that name in Jerusalem, the al-Aqsa Mosque located on the Temple Mount, with its location chosen purposely to humiliate the Jews and declare the victory of Islam over Judaism. Nevertheless, Islamic tradition is firm that this mosque was in Jerusalem.

According to Islamic tradition as written by Muhammad's first biographer, Ibn Ishaq, Muhammad described the journey as beginning "while I was lying in Al-Hatim or Al-Hijr," that is, an area in Mecca opposite the Ka'bah, identified by Islamic tradition as the burial place of Hagar and Ishmael, when "Gabriel came and stirred me with his foot."[49] Soon after that "someone came to me and cut my body open from here to here"—and he gestured from his throat to his pubic area. The one who had come to him, Muhammad continued, "then took out my heart. Then a golden tray full of Belief was brought to me and my heart was washed and was filled (with Belief) and then returned to its original place."[50] At that point Muhammad was presented with the Buraq, an animal he described as "half mule, half donkey, with wings on its sides with which it propelled its feet."[51]

"When I came up to mount him," Muhammad reported, according to Ibn Ishaq, "he shied. Gabriel placed his hand on its mane and said, 'Are you not ashamed, O Buraq, to behave in this way? By God, none more honorable before God than Muhammad has ever ridden you before.' The animal was so ashamed that he broke out into a sweat and stood still so that I could mount him."[52]

They went to the Temple Mount, and from there to Paradise itself. According to a Hadith, Muhammad explained,

I was carried on it, and Gabriel set out with me till we reached the nearest heaven. When he asked for the gate to be opened, it was asked, "Who is it?" Gabriel answered, "Gabriel." It was asked, "Who is accompanying you?" Gabriel replied, "Muhammad." It was asked, "Has Muhammad been called?" Gabriel replied in the affirmative. Then it was said, "He is welcomed. What an excellent visit his is!"

Muhammad entered the first heaven, where he encountered Adam. Gabriel prodded Muhammad, "This is your father, Adam; pay him your greetings." The Prophet of Islam duly greeted the first man, who responded, "You are welcome, O pious son and pious Prophet." Gabriel then carried Muhammad to the second heaven, where the scene at the gate was reenacted, and once inside, John the

Baptist and Jesus greeted Muhammad: "You are welcome, O pious brother and pious Prophet." In the third heaven, Joseph greeted him in the same words, and Muhammad and Gabriel went on, greeted by other prophets at other levels of heaven.

In the sixth heaven was Moses, occasioning another dig at the Jews. "When I left him," Muhammad said, "he wept. Someone asked him, 'What makes you weep?' Moses said, 'I weep because after me there has been sent (Muhammad as a Prophet) a young man, whose followers will enter Paradise in greater numbers than my followers.'"

In the seventh heaven, Muhammad met Abraham, had more visions, and received the command that the Muslims must pray fifty times daily. But returning, Muhammad passed by Moses, who told him to go back and argue Allah down to a more manageable number. Muhammad complied, finally agreeing with Allah for five daily prayers.[53]

Muhammad's account of his journey to Paradise was met with considerable skepticism even in the earliest Islamic account of it. Muhammad lost followers over this claim, likely at least to some degree because of his wife Aisha's statement that "the apostle's body remained where it was but God removed his spirit by night."[54]

Despite the obvious apologetic and ahistorical character of this fable, it is the foundation of the Muslim claim to Jerusalem to this day, and one of the key reasons why Muslims do not accept Jewish historical and contemporary political claims to Jerusalem. The Palestinian claim to Jerusalem is based not on political or even historical claims, but on an Islamic fable. So here again the conflict is entirely religious. From beginning to end, the conflict with Israel is all about Islam. Hajj Amin al-Husseini, the grand mufti of Jerusalem who did everything in his power to prevent the establishment of the State of Israel, confirmed this in 1937 when he declared:

> *The battle between Jews and Islam began when Mohammed fled from Mecca to Medina.... Just as the Jews were able to betray Mohammed, so they will betray the Muslims today.... [T]he verses*

*of the Koran and the Hadith assert that the Jews were Islam's most
bitter enemy and moreover try to destroy it.*[55]

"Do You Want to Start a Holy Jihad?"

During World War II, rabbis Stephen S. Wise and Abba Hillel Silver
tried to convince U.S. president Franklin D. Roosevelt that Jewish
refugees from Europe should be moved Palestine. Roosevelt responded:
"Do you want to be responsible by your actions for the loss of hundreds
of thousands of lives? Do you want to start a holy jihad?"[56]

Roosevelt, unlike the leaders of the West today, knew that Muslim
intransigence, based on the command to "drive them out from where
they drove you out" and the Islamic demonization of the Jews, would
never accept a Jewish state in Palestine under any circumstances. Like
many Western leaders today, Roosevelt was disinclined to offend or
provoke the warriors of jihad, and so he wasn't willing to aid Jewish
settlement in Palestine.

Others were, however, and on May 14, 1948, the State of Israel
declared its independence. But Roosevelt was right: the new state
was born not in peace but amid rage, hostility, and a "holy jihad."

The Zionists had always expected that they would have to fight.
Naftali Hertz Imber, the nineteenth-century author of the lyrics of
what would become Israel's national anthem, *Hatikva*, wrote a poem
to that effect:

If you long to inherit the land of your birth,
Buckle on the sword and take up the bow,
And go in the footsteps of your fathers.
With weeping and tearful pleadings
Zion will not be won.
With sword and bow—hark ye!
Jerusalem will be rebuilt.[57]

And so it would be.

CHAPTER THREE

The Jihad of 1948

The Solution That Has Never Solved Anything

"The two-state solution has for decades been the primary focus of efforts to achieve peace in the Israeli-Palestinian conflict," the *New York Times* informed us in 2016, with support from Secretary of State John Kerry, who called it "the only way to achieve a just and lasting peace between Israelis and Palestinians."[1]

On November 28, 2018, the International Day of Solidarity with the Palestinian People, United Nations secretary-general António Guterres called on Israel and the Palestinians "to restore faith in the promise of Resolution 181, of two States living side-by-side in peace and security, fulfilling the legitimate national aspirations of both peoples, with borders based on the 1967 lines and Jerusalem as the capital of both states—East Jerusalem being the capital of the Palestinian state."[2] Guterres declared that this was "the only way to achieve the inalienable rights of the Palestinian people."

The UN General Assembly had passed Resolution 181, calling for the creation of an Arab state and a Jewish state in Palestine, on November 29, 1947, a day short of seventy-one years before

Guterres again called for its implementation. The Arabs had rejected it immediately. Neither Guterres nor Kerry, nor anyone else who still advances the "two-state solution" and Resolution 181 as the only path to peace for both Israelis and Palestinians, ever seems to ponder why so many years have gone by since Resolution 181 was originally passed without its ever being implemented even for a single day. They don't seem to regard the seven decades of its not being in force as any indication that maybe it isn't the path to peace after all. There has been no indictment of its status as the "only way to achieve a just and lasting peace."

In the United States, both Democratic and Republican presidents have endorsed it. Even U.S. president Donald Trump, whose maverick presidency has rejected so much of what has been taken for granted by the foreign policy establishment in so many areas, said in September 2018: "I like a two-state solution. That's what I think works best…. That's my feeling."[3]

Yet it never has worked best, or at all, since it was first adopted.

The Birth of the Original Two-State Solution

The two-state solution was born out of the British duplicity regarding the Arabs and Jews in Palestine. The Balfour Declaration had called for the establishment of a "Jewish national home" in Palestine, an ambiguous phrase that may or may not have meant a Jewish state. But then Colonel Bertie Harry Waters-Taylor encouraged the grand mufti al-Husseini to incite the Muslim Arabs to riot in 1920, and helped pave the way by withdrawing British troops and the Jewish police from Jerusalem.[4]

British officials continued to demonstrate a decided preference for the Muslim Arabs thereafter, while keeping up appearances regarding support for the Jews in Palestine. There were, or appeared to be, pressing geopolitical reasons for this stance: in 1935, Benito Mussolini sent Italian forces into Ethiopia; the following year, he merged Italian Somaliland, Eritrea, and Ethiopia into the colonial entity Italian East Africa. The Italians began sending Arabic-language broadcasts into the British and French holdings in the Middle East and North Africa, presenting Mussolini as the "friend and protector of Islam."[5]

With the theology of jihad underlying their hostility to any Jewish state or even presence in Palestine, this kind of language was bound to appeal to the Muslim Arabs of the region. Mussolini's allies in Nazi Germany were broadcasting into the Middle East as well. In 1937, just before the Peel Commission's report was released, German foreign minister Konstantin von Neurath told German legations in Middle Eastern countries:

> *The formation of a Jewish state or a Jewish-led political structure under a British Mandate is not in Germany's interest, since a Palestinian state would not absorb world Jewry, but would create an additional position of power under international law for international Jewry, somewhat like the Vatican state for political Catholicism or Moscow for the Comintern.... Germany therefore has an interest in strengthening the Arab world as a counterweight against such a possible increase in power for world Jewry.*[6]

The German overtures to the Arabs, like those of the Italians, were specifically Islamic. On Muhammad's birthday in May 1937, Arab protesters in Palestine carried German and Italian flags, as well as photographs of Hitler and Mussolini. Arab newspapers rejoiced over this "significant gesture of sympathy and respect...with the Nazis and Fascists in their trials at the hands of Jewish intrigues and international financial pressure."[7]

The British, appalled, were determined to out-Herod Herod and act as even more of a "friend and protector of Islam" than Mussolini or Hitler could ever hope to be. The British government continued to back away from its commitment to a Jewish national home. In January 1937, a member of the Peel Commission, Dr. Reginald Coupland, had already broached the idea of a partition of the land that had originally been meant for the Jewish national home with the great Zionist leader Chaim Weizmann. "If there were no other way out to peace," said Coupland delicately, "might it not be a final and peaceful settlement—to terminate the Mandate by agreement and split Palestine into two halves, the plain being an Independent Jewish State...and the rest of Palestine, plus Trans-Jordania, being an Independent Arab State."[8]

Weizmann was initially dismayed at the further British diminishment of the land allotted to the Jewish national home: "Of course, it is cutting the child in two."[9] However, his shock quickly gave way to enthusiasm: here at last was a way forward to a Jewish state. However small or truncated it would be, it would be a Jewish state.

The British plowed ahead with this idea. The Peel Commission recommended the partitioning of Palestine into an Arab area and a Jewish area: "The idea of Partition has doubtless been thought of before as a solution of the problem, but it has probably been discarded as being impracticable. The difficulties are certainly very great, but when they are closely examined they do not seem so insuperable as the difficulties inherent in the continuance of the Mandate or in any other alternative arrangement."[10]

Sounding much like António Guterres eighty years later, the Commission added: "Partition offers a chance of ultimate peace. No other plan does."[11]

The British strongly opposed the establishment of, as the Peel Commission put it, a single state in which one group would rule the other: "The problem cannot be solved by giving either the Arabs or the Jews all they want. The answer to the question which of them in the end will govern Palestine must be Neither. No fair-minded statesman can think it right either that 400,000 Jews, whose entry into Palestine has been facilitated by he [sic] British Government and approved by the League of Nations, should be handed over to Arab rule, or that, if the Jews should become a majority, a million Arabs should be handed over to their rule. But while neither race can fairly rule all Palestine, each race might justly rule part of it."[12]

And yet the British government was also aware of the difficulties confronting such a plan. A November 1938 report stated:

"His Majesty's Government, after careful study of the Partition Commission's report, have reached the conclusion that this further examination has shown that the political, administrative and financial difficulties involved in the proposal to create independent Arab and Jewish States inside Palestine are so great that this solution of the problem is impracticable."[13]

The London Round Table Conference

That impression was only reinforced when Arab Muslim and Jewish leaders met with the British at a conference in London in February and March 1939. The goal was to find a solution for Palestine, but the chances of success were dim from the start. The conference was held when it was fresh in memory that Muslims had kidnapped and killed a Jewish family in August 1938 and murdered nineteen Jews in Tiberias in October 1938, but the Irgun, the National Military Organization in the Land of Israel, had begun to fight back against Arab attacks, and so the Arab delegates in London adopted a posture of aggrieved victimhood, a pose that their successors would assume on innumerable occasions thereafter.

In London, they played the victim card to the hilt. The Arab delegation refused to sit in the same room as the Jewish delegation, or even to enter the St. James Palace, where the conference was being held, through the same entrance through which the Jews passed, an insistence that may have been inspired as much by the Qur'an's description of the "idolaters" as being "unclean" (9:28) as by the exaggerated sense of grievance that they wanted to display before the British.[14]

The British were as solicitous of this posturing as the Muslims were intransigent. Instead of insisting that the Arabs sit in the same room with the Jews, and walk through the same doorways, pointing out that this haughtiness was hardly conducive to achieving what was the very object of the conference itself, the British acceded to the Arab demands, and in effect conducted two separate conferences. There were even two opening ceremonies on February 7, 1939, both attended by Prime Minister Neville Chamberlain and other top British officials: one for the Arabs (which was held first, of course), and one for the Jews, after the Arabs had left (through the door that the British had ensured no Jews had passed through).[15]

Having been thus accorded proof yet again that the British were ready to reward their intransigence, the Arab delegates presented demands that showed no willingness whatsoever to grant the legitimacy of any Jewish presence in Palestine at all, ignoring the fact that Jews had been there since time immemorial, even when the land was universally characterized as waste and desolate. The Arabs demanded an independent Arab state and that the British repudiate the Mandate endeavor to establish a Jewish national home in Palestine. Jewish immigration to Palestine must, in line with this, be forbidden outright.[16]

For its part, the Jewish delegation, seeing that the Arabs were not disposed to give an inch, stood their ground as well. David Ben-Gurion, the leader of the delegation, presented what was essentially the opposite of the Arab demands: the continuation of Jewish immigration to Palestine; the continuation of the Mandate—that is, ongoing British rule rather than Arab rule; and ultimately, independence for the Jews as well as for the Arabs in Palestine.[17]

The conference, predictably, came to nothing.

Not a Jewish State, Not an Arab State

The British fumbled about for another way forward, opting in a new white paper, approved by the House of Commons on May 23, 1939, for a one-state solution, an idea that has experienced something of a revival in recent times.

One state, however, would have had to have someone in charge, and that posed more problems. The choices were a Jewish state or an Arab state, and both were fraught with peril. The British therefore came out against both. In line with the by-then well-established British policy of playing both sides of the street, the 1939 white paper, known as the MacDonald White Paper after Secretary of State for the Colonies Malcolm MacDonald, discussed the ambiguity of the phrase "Jewish national home" and stated: "His Majesty's Government therefore now declare unequivocally that it is not part of their policy that Palestine should become a Jewish State."[18]

Yet at the same time, the British did not throw their support to a Palestine entirely under Arab rule, either. The Zionists had already made it clear that such an idea was unacceptable to them, and that they knew what Islamic rule would mean for religious minorities. Weizmann didn't refer to Islam in his December 31, 1937, letter to the U.K. Colonial Office's permanent undersecretary of state, Sir John Shuckburgh, but his letter demonstrates that he knew very well Islam's legal strictures for Jews and the hardships that Jews had suffered in Islamic lands for centuries:

> *Jews are not going to Palestine to become in their ancient home "Arabs of the Mosaic Faith", or to exchange their German or Polish ghetti for an Arab one. Whoever knows what Arab government looks like, what "minority status" signifies nowadays, and what a Jewish Ghetto in an Arab State means—there are quite a number of precedents—will be able to form his own conclusions as to what would be in store for us if we accepted the position allotted to us in these "solutions."[19]*

The British, despite their post-Balfour animus toward Jewish settlement in Palestine, gave the appearance of having heeded Weizmann's warning. The 1939 white paper reiterated British support for an Arab state while trying gently to clear up Arab "misunderstandings" about where that state would or should be:

> *In the recent discussions the Arab delegations have repeated the contention that Palestine was included within the area in which Sir Henry McMahon, on behalf of the British Government, in October 1915, undertook to recognise and support Arab independence.... His Majesty's Government regret the misunderstandings which have arisen as regards some of the phrases used. For their part they can only*

adhere, for the reasons given by their representatives in the Report,
to the view that the whole of Palestine west of Jordan was excluded
from Sir Henry McMahon's pledge, and they therefore cannot agree
that the McMahon correspondence forms a just basis for the claim
that Palestine should be converted into an Arab State.[20]

This white paper, however, was not as even-handed as it endeavored to appear to be. It noted with satisfaction that since 1922, "more than three hundred thousand Jews have immigrated to Palestine, and that the population of the National Home has risen to some four hundred fifty thousand, or approaching a third of the entire population of the country."[21] However, it limited further Jewish immigration to Palestine to seventy-five thousand "over the next five years," that is, from April 1939 to April 1944, the years during which European Jews felt with the most tragic urgency the need for a place to which they could immigrate.[22]

While ensuring that the Jews could not become a majority in Palestine, the British also did their best to make sure the Jews would not be able to govern themselves, and that Weizmann's dark vision of Jews in Palestine living under Arab Muslim government would become a reality. "As soon as peace and order have been sufficiently restored in Palestine," the white paper directed blandly, "steps will be taken to carry out this policy of giving the people of Palestine an increasing part in the government of their country, the objective being to place Palestinians"—that is, both Arabs and Jews who lived in Palestine; the modern usage of "Palestinians" as referring only to Muslim Arabs had not yet begun—"in charge of all the Departments of Government, with the assistance of British advisers and subject to the control of the High Commissioner."[23] That assistance was to be exercised with scrupulous even-handedness: "Arab and Jewish representatives will be invited to serve as heads of Departments approximately in proportion to their respective populations."[24]

So the British recognized that the Jewish population was less than one-third of Palestine in 1939, and restricted it so that it could not grow much larger, while stipulating that government officials would be selected in accordance with the size of the populations of the respective groups. This essentially ensured that an independent Palestine would become an Arab state, making Weizmann's nightmare come true. In his letter to Shuckburgh, he declared:

> It is not for the purpose of subjecting the Jewish people, which still stands in the front rank of civilization, to the rule of a set of unscrupulous Levantine politicians that this supreme effort is being made in Palestine....
>
> Could there be a more appalling fraud of the hopes of a martyred people than to reduce it to ghetto status in the very land where it was promised national freedom?[25]

Yet here were the British, the appointed guarantors of a Jewish national home, laying the groundwork for exactly that appalling fraud.

Winston Churchill was vehemently opposed to this white paper, which he correctly labeled a "surrender to Arab violence."[26] However, it did not appease the very people it had been designed to placate. Hajj Amin al-Husseini demanded instead that Jewish immigration to Palestine be halted altogether, that the British withdraw from the territory, and that an independent Arab state be established.

Weary of this insoluble problem, the British might have been ready to accede to these demands. Malcolm MacDonald himself recommended that the British wash their hands of the whole problem and leave the Jews to the tender mercies of the Muslim Arabs: "As long as the Jews have the British government behind them, they will never meet the Arabs halfway."[27]

But before any such pressure could be brought on the Zionists, events in Europe intervened.

Abandoning the Jews of Europe

Even after the Nazis imposed various laws barring Jews from most professions and driving them out of public life, and after Kristallnacht made clear that Jews would not be allowed to live peacefully in

Hitler's German Reich, the British did not budge on their determination to limit Jewish immigration to Palestine. Already in December 1938, the British Mandatory government rejected an urgent plea that ten thousand Jewish children be allowed to immigrate to Palestine from central Europe.[28] No one then knew what would be the full extent of Nazi savagery, but there was no doubt that the British government knew that it was condemning these children to lives of unfathomable misery.

The British would not relent. On September 25, 1939, just over three weeks after World War II began, the British government determined that it would offer no aid to Jews trying to leave Nazi domains. It rejected an offer from the Italian government, which would before too long end up allied with the Nazis itself, to help the British enable German Jews to escape Europe by allowing them to use Italian ports to do so.[29]

The British compelled the government of Greece to prohibit the merchant marine from transporting Jewish refugees out of Europe, and in December 1939 called on the Turkish government to follow suit. Noting an increase in illegal Jewish immigration to Palestine, the British Foreign Office concluded during a December 29, 1939 meeting that "the only hope is that all the German Jews will be stuck at the mouth of the Danube for lack of ships to take them."[30]

The grand mufti was, as ever, unmoved by all this anxiousness to appease him. In October 1939, he wrote to Hitler to congratulate him "on the occasion of the great political and military triumphs which [the Führer] has just achieved through his foresight and great genius." He assured Hitler that "the Arab nation everywhere feels the greatest joy and deepest gratification on the occasion of these great successes.... The Arab people...confidently expect the result of your final victory will be their independence and complete liberation.... [T]hey will [then] be linked to your country by a treaty of friendship and collaboration."[31]

Al-Husseini may have considered himself to have good cause to give up on the British and cast the Arabs' lot with the Nazis. British

Prime Minister Winston Churchill continued to champion the Zionist cause, as he had ever since he penned his own white paper in 1922 calling for support for a Jewish national home in Palestine. Churchill wrote in October 1941: "If Britain and the United States emerge victorious from the war, the creation of a great Jewish state in Palestine inhabitated [sic] by millions of Jews will be one of the leading features of the Peace Conference discussions."[32]

U.S. president Franklin Roosevelt, meanwhile, despite his misgivings about igniting a "holy jihad," promised in May 1944 that "full justice will be done to those who seek a Jewish national home, for which our Government and the American People have always had the deepest sympathy and today more than ever in view of the tragic plight of hundreds of thousands of homeless Jewish refugees."[33] Roosevelt, however, temporized as much as the British. In March 1945, however, he assured Saudi King Ibn Saud that he would support "no action…that would prove hostile to the Arab people."[34]

Zionism Resurgent

As the war drew to a close, however, and the full shocking extent of the Nazi atrocities against the Jews of Europe became widely known, these hesitations and semiassurances appeared to be examples not of careful statecraft but of weakness in the face of an urgent humanitarian necessity.

Roosevelt died on April 12, 1945; the new president, Harry S. Truman, was much less inclined than his predecessor had been to take the advice of State Department "experts," who were solidly anti-Zionist. Truman later recounted that he was "skeptical" about "some of the views and attitudes assumed by the 'striped-pants boys' in the State Department. It seemed to me that they didn't care enough about what happened to the thousands of displaced persons who were involved. It was my feeling that it would be possible for us to watch out for the long-range interests of our country while at the same time helping these unfortunate victims of persecution to find a home."[35]

On July 24, 1945, Truman wrote to Churchill, asking that the British government "take steps to lift the restrictions of the White Paper into Palestine."[36] Churchill, however, was defeated in an election held just two days later. The new prime minister, Clement Attlee, was strongly anti-Zionist and continued prewar policies of restricting Jewish immigration to Palestine, even returning Jewish refugees to Europe and cracking down hard on Jewish military organizations that had begun to fight back against Arab violence.

No Compromise

The Arab Muslims, however, were as usual not placated. They grew even more enraged upon the release of the May 1, 1946, report of the Anglo-American Committee of Inquiry, which had been appointed in late 1945 to study the plight of the surviving Jews of Europe. While noting that some Jews would continue to live in Europe, the committee's report recommended that "100,000 certificates be authorized immediately for the admission into Palestine of Jews who have been the victims of Nazi and Fascist persecution."[37]

This was hardly adequate to meet the need. The committee itself acknowledged that "the number of Jewish survivors of Nazi and Fascist persecution with whom we have to deal far exceeds one hundred thousand; indeed there are more than that number in Germany, Austria and Italy alone."[38] Nor did it represent a tipping of the demographic balance in Palestine.

The committee also recommended "that Jew shall not dominate Arab and Arab shall not dominate Jew in Palestine," and "that Palestine shall be neither a Jewish state nor an Arab state.... Thus Palestine must ultimately become a state which guards the rights and interests of Moslems, Jews and Christians alike."[39]

The report rebuked both sides for the increasing violence in Palestine:

We have reached the conclusion that the hostility between Jews and Arabs and, in particular, the determination of each to achieve domination, if necessary by violence, make it almost certain that, now and for some time to come, any attempt to establish either an independent Palestinian state or independent Palestinian states would result in civil strife such as might threaten the peace of the world. We therefore recommend that, until this hostility disappears, the Government of Palestine be continued as at present under mandate pending the execution of a trusteeship agreement under the United Nations.[40]

This moral equivalence and assumption that both sides were trying to "achieve domination, if necessary by violence," were unwarranted. Certainly the Irgun and other Jewish groups had adopted some of the tactics of their Arab foes, even at times targeting civilians, and thereby drawing opposition from Jewish leaders. However, Zionist leaders had never stated that an Arab state in Palestine, along with a Jewish state, was unacceptable to them, while Arab Muslim leaders had many times insisted that they would never agree to a Jewish state of any kind. Ben-Gurion, Weizmann, and others had repeatedly acquiesced to a partitioning of Palestine, despite the fact that the size of the Jewish national home had already been substantially dimished when the British removed Transjordan from the area of the Mandate. Arab leaders, however, had never accepted any partition plan, as to have done so would have been to accept a Jewish state.

It was therefore no surprise that in response to this call to end the hostility, Jamal al-Husseini, vice-chairman (the grand mufti, Hajj Amin al-Husseini, was the chairman) of the Arab Higher Executive (renamed the Arab Higher Committee the following year), made sure that the world knew that the hostility would continue indefinitely. In a furious rage, Jamal al-Husseini wrote to Clement Attlee, declaring that the committee's recommendations not only were unacceptable but "would threaten the existence and national life of the Arab nation."[41]

That was not all. Al-Husseini told the British prime minister in no uncertain terms that the Arab Higher Executive "confirms the

Arab people's determination—in Palestine—to defend their country by all means in their power."[42] He gave Attlee an ultimatum: if the British didn't abandon the idea of a Jewish national home altogether and support an Arab state in Palestine, there would be jihad.[43]

This was a word that would be heard again and again, though most only dimly understood, at best, what it meant and what it entailed. British diplomat Hugh Stonehewer Bird used a word that was much more familiar to the British in a May 9, 1946, report to the Foreign Office, when he summarized a call for jihad that had appeared in a Baghdad newspaper: "The Arabs must proclaim a crusade to save the Holy Land from western gang which understands only the language of force."[44]

Though crusades have far shallower roots in Christian theology than jihad has in Islamic theology and law, Stonehewer Bird was right that the Arabs' objection to the Anglo-American Committee report was ultimately not because the terms were unacceptable to them and could be adjusted to be more to their liking, but because their theological beliefs and assumptions made it impossible for them to budge even an inch on the question of Jewish settlement in Palestine or a Jewish national home.

The concept of jihad underlies why the British had been unable to come to any solution acceptable to the Arabs during the period of the Mandate. Finally, on February 14, 1947, they gave up. Attlee's foreign minister, Ernest Bevin, who had been quite solicitous of the Arabs, complained: "The Arabs, like the Jews, refused to accept any of the compromise proposals that HMG [His Majesty's Government] had put before both parties."[45] There could be no compromise on what were for the Muslims religious principles, although then as now, the non-Muslim parties involved took scant note of this, and for the most part did not take it seriously.

The British turned the problem over to the new United Nations, which set up a Special Committee on Palestine (UNSCOP) to study the situation. On August 31, 1947, the UNSCOP issued two reports, a majority report and a minority report. The majority report called for a two-state solution: "Palestine was to be constituted into an Arab State, a Jewish State and the City of Jerusalem. The Arab and Jewish States would become independent after a transitional period of two years beginning on September 1, 1947."[46] Before they could be granted independence, however, they would have to meet certain conditions, including making "to the United Nations a declaration containing certain guarantees."[47]

The Arab Higher Committee was not any more disposed at that point than Arab leaders had ever been to compromise, conciliate, or guarantee anyone anything. It did not, however, find the minority report to be much more to its liking, despite the fact that the minority group criticized the majority's recommendations not only as, once again, impracticable but also as anti-Arab.[48] The minority report called for the creation of "an independent federal state of Palestine" that would be a double-headed beast: "The independent federal state would comprise an Arab State and a Jewish State. Jerusalem would be its capital."[49]

So the two-state solution and the one-state solution, both of the options being bruited about today as the only sensible possibilities ahead, were proposed in 1947 and before that. They have never had the effects that their modern-day proponents insist they can and will have, and that is because, proponents maintain, they have never been properly implemented.

Maybe. But the UNSCOP's minority report, like so many British government white papers before it, tried to placate the Arabs by limiting Jewish immigration into Palestine, stipulating that such immigration could continue only "for a period of three years from the beginning of the transitional period Jewish immigration would be permitted into the Jewish State in such numbers as not to exceed its absorptive capacity, and having due regard for the rights of the existing population within the State." The "absorptive capacity" of the land would be determined by a panel of experts made up of an equal number of Jewish and Arab representatives.

Partition and Escalation

Neither report was acceptable to the Muslim leaders. Expecting the United Nations to act without their approval and declare the partitioning of Palestine, paving the way for the creation of a Jewish state, they prepared for war: in October 1947, the Arab League Council told its member nations to send troops to the borders of Palestine.[50] On November 29, 1947, their fears came true: the UN General Assembly voted 32 to 13 for a partitioning of Palestine, and the stage was set for the jihad against the Jews in Palestine to take on a new virulence, in an attempt to destroy the Jewish state before it was even born.

The British helped. As all this was happening, they remained steadfast in preventing new Jewish immigration to Palestine and restricted Jews from obtaining weapons, even denying them permission to establish a militia and halting the activities of the active Jewish paramilitary organizations whenever they found them. The Jews managed to obtain a small quantity of rifles and machine guns from Czechoslovakia.[51]

British officials were not nearly so strict with the Arabs, selling weapons in large quantities to Transjordan and Iraq even when it was clear that those weapons would be used against the Jews of Palestine. The Arab Legion, commanded by British lieutenant-general John Bagot Glubb (who was known as "Glubb Pasha" as a result of his deep affection for the Muslim Arabs) and staffed with other British officers, was the most successful fighting force on the Arab side in the 1948 war. And as the British began to evacuate Palestine, they would notify Arab leaders just before they left particular areas, so that military installations, police stations and the like could be occupied by Arabs rather than Jews.[52]

The Muslims quickly showed how they would repay this confidence. Demonstrators in Damascus called for jihad and demanded weapons; in response, Syrian Prime Minister Jamil Mardam Bey promised that the Syrian government would "comply and be in the forefront of the liberation of Palestine."[53] Arab Muslims burned down eleven synagogues and three hundred Jewish homes in Aleppo. In Aden, Muslims murdered seventy-six Jews. In Palestine itself, Arabs attacked Jewish quarters in Jerusalem, Haifa, and Jaffa.[54] The Arab countries neighboring Palestine began planning to invade Palestine and drive the Jews out.

What is regarded now as Israel's war for independence began simply as a struggle for survival against relentless Arab Muslim attacks designed to drive them out of the region altogether.

Independence

Instead, on May 14, 1948, the targets of those attacks took a decisive step: the State of Israel declared its independence. The new state's Proclamation of Independence made it clear that what was being established was a homeland for the Jews: "We hereby proclaim the establishment of the Jewish State in Palestine, to be called Medinath Yisrael (The State of Israel)."[55]

The Proclamation of Independence set forth a simple historical case for this: "The Land of Israel was the birthplace of the Jewish people. Here their spiritual, religious and national identity was formed. Here they achieved independence and created a culture of national and universal significance. Here they wrote and gave the Bible to the world."[56] After centuries of exile, "in the year 1897, the First Zionist Congress, inspired by Theodor Herzl's vision of the Jewish State, proclaimed the right of the Jewish people to national revival in their own country."[57]

At the same time, the new state declared its readiness to accept the UN's moribund partition plan, and even to help implement it: "The State of Israel will be ready to co-operate with the organs and representatives of the United Nations in the implementation of the Resolution of the Assembly of November 29, 1947, and will take steps to bring about the Economic Union over the whole of Palestine."[58]

What's more, the Jews of Israel were not founding a state characterized by the "domination" that the British had warned against so many times. The Proclamation of Independence declared: "In the midst of wanton aggression, we yet call upon the Arab inhabitants of the State of Israel to preserve the ways of peace and play their part in the development of the State, on the basis of full and equal citizenship and due representation in all its bodies and institutions— provisional and permanent."[59]

The same conciliatory hand was offered to the new state's neighbors: "We extend our hand in peace and neighborliness to all the neighboring states and their peoples, and invite them to co-operate with the independent Jewish nation for the common good of us all. The State of Israel is prepared to make its contribution to the progress of the Middle East as a whole."[60]

Jihad

That extended hand was batted back in contempt. Egypt, Transjordan, Iraq, Syria, and Lebanon, along with volunteers from other Muslim countries, including Saudi Arabia, Yemen, and even far-off Pakistan, immediately invaded the Jewish state, intending to destroy it quickly, before it had a chance to get on its feet.

This was a religious war, a jihad, animated by Islamic principles. The Arab states neighboring Israel were frequently said to be motivated by a feeling of solidarity with their fellow Arabs in Palestine, but that could not be said of the Pakistani volunteers, who traveled from their native land only because the Qur'an commanded them to "drive them out from where they drove you out." (2:191)

Arab leaders likewise made it clear to their own people that this was an Islamic conflict. Nor was this anything new. As far back as March 1936, Sa'id al-Haj Thabit, the speaker of Iraq's Parliament, visited Palestine and repeatedly called upon the local Muslims to wage jihad against the Jews.[61] Two years later, the Muslim Brotherhood proclaimed that such a jihad was an "inescapable obligation on every Muslim."[62] In 1943, Ibn Saud, the king of Saudi Arabia, explained to Franklin D. Roosevelt that there was "religious hostility…between the Moslems and the Jews from the beginning of Islam…which arose from the treacherous conduct of the Jews toward Islam and the Moslems and their prophet."[63] Accordingly, the king was happy to discuss proposals for peace in Palestine with "anyone of religion except (repeat except) a Jew."[64]

Amid the Arab rage after the UN partition vote late in 1947, the ulema (Islamic religious scholars) of Cairo's venerable al-Azhar, the foremost institution in Sunni Islam, declared that "the liberation of Palestine" was "a religious duty for all Moslems without exception, great and small. The Islamic and Arab Governments should without delay take effective and radical measures, military or otherwise."[65] They declared that any Muslim who dealt with Jews (even in such trivial matters as "buying their produce") "is a sinner and criminal... who will be regarded as an apostate to Islam." This would carry serious consequences: "He will be separated from his spouse. It is prohibited to be in contact with him."[66]

In April 1948, Sheikh Muhammad Mahawif, the mufti of Egypt, issued a fatwa stating that jihad against the Jews in Palestine was an obligation incumbent upon all Muslims, because the Jews were working "to take over...all the lands of Islam."[67]

This language about the "liberation" of Palestine from the Jews' being an "obligation incumbent upon all Muslims," an "inescapable obligation on every Muslim," was rooted in Islam's theology of jihad. A manual of Islamic law certified by al-Azhar as conforming to "the practice and faith of the orthodox Sunni Community" stipulates that "when non-Muslims invade a Muslim country or near to one," then "jihad is personally obligatory upon the inhabitants of that country," and indeed, obligatory upon everyone "able to perform it, male or female, old or young," when "the enemy has surrounded the Muslims."[68] The Jews may not have surrounded the Muslims in the military sense, but they could be found everywhere in Palestine, and Muslim leaders considered them to be hostile invaders. Hence every Muslim was obligated to wage jihad against them.

When Israel declared its independence, Arab Muslim leaders likewise framed the conflict in exclusively Islamic terms. Addressing the Arab Legion on May 14, 1948, King Abdullah of Jordan promised that "he who will be killed will be a martyr; he who lives will be glad of fighting for Palestine.... I remind you of the Jihad and the martyrdom of your great-grandfathers."[69]

Muhammad Mamun Shinawi, the rector of Al-Azhar University, addressed Egyptian troops preparing to invade Israel on May 15, 1948: "The hour of 'Jihad' has struck," he told them. "A hundred of you will defeat a thousand of the infidels."[70]

Shinawi was referering to a promise from the Qur'an: "O Prophet, urge the believers to battle. If there are among you twenty steadfast, they will overcome two hundred. And if there are among you one hundred steadfast, they will overcome a thousand of those who have disbelieved because they are a people who do not understand." (8:65)

The Muslim cleric reminded the troops of inducements that had inspired Muslims to fight valiantly since the early days of the religion: "This is the hour in which...Allah promised paradise... "[71] If that wasn't enough of a goad, Shinawi offered more prosaic concerns as well: "Fighters, this is a war there is no avoiding, to defend your women, homes, and the fatherland of your fathers and forefathers."[72]

This wasn't true. The Jews of Palestine weren't threatening the women, homes, or fatherland of the Arabs. They were ready and willing to live together with them in peace. This readiness, however, was not reciprocated. Instead, Arab leaders called upon Muslims to leave Israel, which they did, thereby laying the foundation of the myth that the Muslims had been driven out, and so had to drive the Jews out, as Allah had commanded.

"Drive Them out From Where..." They Left Voluntarily

"Drive them out from where they drove you out," as mentioned several times previously, is a Qur'anic imperative, and it is a staple of the Palestinian case against Israel that the Palestinians were driven out of the land. The fact is, however, that the Israelis did not actually drive the Arab Muslims out.

This fact is ultimately immaterial to the Palestinian jihad, but it is true. In reality, the Arabs for the most part left Israel because they were ordered to do so by Muslim Arab leaders. Contrary to the contention of the Palestinians and their allies today, the Arab Higher Committee actually exhorted Arabs to leave the new State of Israel, and they obeyed in large numbers.

This action had been contemplated for a considerable period: in May 1946, fully two years before the State of Israel proclaimed its independence, Abdul Rahman Hassan Azzam, secretary-general of the Arab League, stated that "Arab circles proposed to evacuate all Arab women and children from Palestine and send them to neighboring countries, to declare 'Jehad' and to consider Palestine a war zone."[73]

When the war came, many of the Arab Muslims left of their own accord, to the consternation of others who were determined to wage jihad. The Arab newspaper *Ash Sha'ab*, based in Jaffa, lamented on January 30, 1948 that "the first group of our fifth column consists of those who abandon their houses and businesses and go to live elsewhere.... At the first sign of trouble they take to their heels to escape sharing the burden of struggle [jihad]."[74]

Others left because the plan to get the Arabs out of harm's way until the Jews were destoyed and Israel was defeated was being implemented. *The Economist* magazine reported on October 3, 1948:

> *Of the 62,000 Arabs who formerly lived in Haifa not more than 5,000 or 6,000 remained. Various factors influenced their decision to seek safety in flight. There is but little doubt that the most potent of the factors were the announcements made over the air by the Higher Arab Executive, urging the Arabs to quit.... It was clearly intimated that those Arabs who remained in Haifa and accepted Jewish protection would be regarded as renegades.*[75]

The Jordanian daily *Falastin* complained on February 19, 1949, that "the Arab state which had encouraged the Palestine Arabs to leave their homes temporarily in order to be out of the way of the

Arab invasion armies, have failed to keep their promise to help these refugees."[76]

The Near East Arabic Broadcasting Station confirmed this on April 3, 1949: "It must not be forgotten that the Arab Higher Committee encouraged the refugees' flight from their homes in Jaffa, Haifa, and Jerusalem."[77] The Egyptian daily *Akhbar el Yom* on October 12, 1963, reported that the grand mufti had issued the same call to Arabs to leave: "The 15th May, 1948, arrived.... On that day the mufti of Jerusalem appealed to the Arabs of Palestine to leave the country, because the Arab armies were about to enter and fight in their stead."[78]

The Jordanian daily *Al Urdun* reported on April 9, 1953: "For the flight and fall of the other villages it is our leaders who are responsible because of their dissemination of rumors exaggerating Jewish crimes and describing them as atrocities in order to inflame the Arabs.... By spreading rumors of Jewish atrocities, killings of women and children etc., they instilled fear and terror in the hearts of the Arabs in Palestine, until they fled leaving their homes and properties to the enemy."[79]

This was supposed to be a temporary displacement. The Melkite Greek Catholic bishop of Galilee, George Hakim, explained in August 1948: "The refugees were confident that their absence would not last long, and that they would return within a week or two. Their leaders had promised them that the Arab Armies would crush the 'Zionist gangs' very quickly and that there was no need for panic or fear of a long exile."[80]

According to the Lebanese journalist Habib Issa in 1951, the secretary-general of the Arab League, Abdul Rahman Hassan Azzam, who was popularly known as Azzam Pasha, "assured the Arab peoples that the occupation of Palestine and of Tel Aviv would be as simple as a military promenade.... Brotherly advice was given to the Arabs of Palestine to leave their land, homes and property and to stay temporarily in neighboring fraternal states, lest the guns of the invading Arab armies mow them down."[81]

The Beirut weekly *Kul-Shay* asked on August 19, 1951: "Who brought the Palestinians to Lebanon as refugees, suffering now from the malign attitude of newspapers and communal leaders, who have neither honor nor conscience? Who brought them over in dire straits and penniless, after they lost their honor? The Arab states, and Lebanon amongst them, did it."[82]

In 1955, the secretary of the Office of the Arab League in London, Edward Atiyah, admitted this:

This wholesale exodus was due partly to the belief of the Arabs, encouraged by the boasting of an unrealistic Arab press and the irresponsible utterances of some of the Arab leaders that it could be only a matter of some weeks before the Jews were defeated by the armies of the Arab States and the Palestinian Arabs enable to re-enter and retake possession of their country.[83]

Among the Arab leaders who encouraged the departure of the Arabs was none other than the grand mufti. American journalist Kenneth Bilby, who covered Palestine during the Israeli war for independence, recounted that "the Arab exodus, initially at least, was encouraged by many Arab leaders, such as Haj Amin el Husseini, the exiled pro-Nazi Mufti of Jerusalem, and by the Arab Higher Committee for Palestine. They viewed the first wave of Arab setbacks as merely transitory. Let the Palestine Arabs flee into neighboring countries. It would serve to arouse the other Arab peoples to greater effort, and when the Arab invasion struck, the Palestinians could return to their homes and be compensated with the property of the Jews driven into the sea."[84]

In the same vein, Iraqi Prime Minister Nuri al-Said boasted: "We will smash the country with our guns and obliterate every place the Jews seek shelter in. The Arabs should conduct their wives and children to safe areas until the fighting has died down."[85]

When the fighting did die down, of course, the Israelis had defeated the Arabs, who ever since then have been repeating the myth that the Israelis drove them from their homes. Not only does this gain the sympathy of the world, and has won the Palestinians numerous allies, but it also recalls that Qur'anic imperative that Muslims believe is an eternal command of Allah.

Why the UN Partition Plan Failed

All this makes clear that the UN partition plan failed for one reason only: the Muslim Arabs of Palestine and the surrounding Arab countries were never going to accept a Jewish state in any form. That refusal, moreoever, is rooted in Islamic concepts and commands, most notably the Qur'anic command to "drive out those who drove you out" and its underlying assumption that any land that has been ruled by the Muslims at any time belongs to the Muslims forever, and can never be ruled by anyone else.

Those who tout the two-state solution today seem to think that somehow, in the decades since the tumultuous period following the end of World War II, this situation has changed. But it has not, and will not. Islam is still Islam. Its Qur'an has not changed; neither has its theology. The imperatives that led the Muslim Arabs to reject a two-state solution in 1947, and to go to war to destroy the nascent Jewish state in 1948, still exist, and are still believed by millions of Muslims worldwide. It is only by ignoring this, or by remaining in blissful willful ignorance of it, that diplomats and presidents and kings could ever have thought that a negotiated agreement could be hit upon that would enable Israelis and Palestinians to lay down their arms and live side by side in peace.

This is a distasteful conclusion for many people, which is one reason why so few policymakers from any country that has ever been involved in the Israeli-Palestinian conflict have ever acknowledged it. Americans in particular like problems with solutions, and don't like to accept the possibility that there are some problems that simply cannot be solved.

That is not to say that the Israeli-Palestinian problem cannot be managed such that there is a minimum of bloodshed on both sides. But to think that a peace accord can be hit upon that will induce

Muslims in the Middle East and around the world to give up Islam's doctrines of jihad, its deeply rooted anti-Semitism, and its supremacist political ideology, is a position that could only be held by the willfully ignorant and historically uninformed.

But there has never been a shortage of the willfully ignorant and historically uninformed. As a result, the 1947–1948 efforts regarding a two-state solution were just the beginning of the "peace process."

CHAPTER FOUR

The Palestinians Are Invented

An Absent People

The State of Israel now established, there were no significant efforts to make peace for the next two decades. This was not, however, because peace had been established in the region. The Arab Muslim states neighboring Israel, although defeated in their effort to destroy the Jewish state in 1948, never accepted its existence. And in 1963, the foes of Israel hit upon a new strategy that would turn the tide of international public opinion against Israel and give new impetus to the jihad against it.

By now the attentive reader will have noticed a curious absence from the drama surrounding Jewish settlement in Palestine, the rise of Zionism, and the establishment of the Jewish state: through it all, the "Palestinians," named as such, are nowhere to be seen.

It is no accident that neither Mark Twain, nor any of the series of English travelers who visited the area, nor anyone else who traveled through desolate Palestine over the centuries ever mentioned the "Palestinian" people. They spoke of encountering Muslim Arabs, as well as Jews, Christian Arabs, and others, but no one, among multitudes of people who wrote about Palestine, ever refers to any Palestinians. Nor do the many British white papers and other documents the British government produced during the Mandate period ever mention the Palestinians. The opposing factions in those documents are the Jews and the Arabs.

There is a very simple reason for this: there were no Palestinians.

An uncomfortable fact for those who advance the claim that the Palestinians are the indigenous people of the area is that they have no history: there was never a state of Palestine, never a king or president of Palestine, never (until quite recently) a Palestinian flag, and nothing that distinguishes the Palestinians culturally, linguistically, or otherwise from the other Arabs of the region.

During the Mandate period, the Arabs of Palestine generally considered themselves to be Syrians, and Palestine to be Southern Syria. Early in 1919, Arab Muslims in fourteen Palestinian municipalities, calling themselves the Muslim-Christian Association, presented a petition to the Paris Peace Conference, which was deliberating about the postwar fate of Syria, Palestine, and other former Ottoman possessions.

The petitioners insisted that Southern Syria—that is, Palestine—be considered "inseparable from the independent Arab Syrian government," for it was "nothing but part of Arab Syria and it has never been separated from it at any stage." Arabs in Palestine, they said, had "national, religious, linguistic, moral, economic, and geographic bonds" with Syria, and therefore insisted that Palestine must be "undetached from the independent Arab Syrian Government."[1] Palestine "should be part of Southern Syria, provided the latter is not under foreign control."[2]

Likewise in March 1919 in far-off San Salvador: a group of people who identified themselves as "Syrian Palestinians" called on the world's powers to establish "no separation between Syria and Palestine," and hoped that "Syria and Palestine remain united." This unity was important, they explained, for "we trust that if Syria and Palestine remain united, we will never be enslaved by the Jewish yoke."[3] The president of the Muslim-Christian Association, Arif Pasha ad-Dajjani, declared that "Palestine or Southern Syria—an integral part of the one and indivisible Syria—must not in any case or for any pretext be detached."

Those who were making these demands would all today be considered Palestinians. Yet they would have been baffled beyond measure if they could have been transported a century ahead and made to listen to today's rhetoric about the Palestinians, the indigenous people of Palestine. So would Musa Kazim al-Husayni, who as head of the Jerusalem Town Council declared in October 1919: "We demand no separation from Syria."[4]

Even Ahmad Shukairy, who in the 1960s was president of the Palestine Liberation Organization, conceded that at the close of World War I, no one was talking about the rights of the Palestinian people; instead, what was in the air was union of the Arabs of Palestine with the Arabs in Syria: the slogan went "Unity, Unity, From the Taurus [Mountains] to Rafah [in Gaza], Unity, Unity."[5]

In February 1920, a group of Palestinian Arabs held a congress in order to emphasize that call for unity between Syria and Palestine. It passed a resolution stating that "it never occurred to the peoples of Northern and Coastal Syria that Southern Syria (or Palestine) is anything but a part of Syria." Another resolution called for Palestine "not to be divided from Syria" and demanded "the independence of Syria within its natural borders."[6]

The following month, the grand mufti of Jerusalem, Hajj Amin al-Husseini, who was to emerge in the ensuing years as the leader of the Arabs' violent opposition to the Jews in Palestine, lent his signature to a petition to the British military governor of Palestine, demanding that Palestine be included within the borders of Syria, and that any border between Syria and Palestine be removed. In April 1920, however, at the San Remo conference, the British and French decided to treat Syria and Palestine as separate entities. Even at this point, however, there were no widespread protests against this from Palestinian Arabs; there was no surge of Palestinian nationalism.

In fact, the word "Palestinians" was more often applied to Jews than to Muslim Arabs. During the Mandate period, some Arabs rejected the term, explaining: "We are not Palestinians, we are Arabs. The Palestinians are the Jews."[7]

Auni Bey Abdul-Hadi, an Arab Muslim leader, regarded the term with the same disdain, telling the Peel Commission in 1937: "There is no such country as Palestine! 'Palestine' is a term the Zionists invented! There is no Palestine in the Bible. Our country was for centuries part of Syria."[8]

In 1946, the Arab American historian Philip Hitti testified before the 1946 Anglo-American Committee of Inquiry: "There is no such thing as Palestine in history, absolutely not"—meaning that there had never been a nation bearing this name.[9]

After World War II, this situation hadn't changed. In May 1947, a representative of the Arab Higher Committee declared before the United Nations General Assembly that "Palestine was part of the Province of Syria...politically, the Arabs of Palestine were not independent in the sense of forming a separate political entity."[10] On April 12, 1948, King Abdullah of Transjordan stated at a meeting of the Arab League that "Palestine and Transjordan are one."[11]

Inventing a People

By the early 1960s, however, the situation had changed, and changed drastically. The 1963 draft constitution of the Palestine Liberation Organization refers matter-of-factly to "Palestinians," as if they were a distinct and readily identifiable people. "All the Palestinians," it states, "are natural members in the Liberation Organization exercising their duty in their liberation of their homeland in accordance with their abilities and efficiency."[12]

There were, however, still traces in this document of the fact that Palestine had always been the name of a region, never that of a nation. "The Palestinian people," it said, "shall form the larger base for this Organization."[13] Very well, but in the same sentence the term for the people changes: "and the Organization, after its creation, shall work closely and constantly with the Palestine people for the sake of their organization and mobilization so they may be able to assume their responsibility in the liberation of their country."[14]

The terms "Palestinian people" and "Palestine people" may appear interchangeable, but the latter gives the distinct impression of referring to the people who inhabit a particular area, as opposed to people of a distinct ethnicity and nationality.

The "Palestinian people" were a propaganda invention. In the 1960s, in order to counter the image of the tiny Jewish state standing virtually alone against the massive Muslim Arab nations surrounding it, the KGB (the Soviet Committee for State Security) invented the "Palestinians," an even smaller people who were, the propaganda insisted, oppressed by a powerful and ruthless Israel.[15] The French historians Guy Millière and David Horowitz, authors of the book *Comment le peuple palestinien fut inventé* (*How the Palestinian People Were Invented*), explain that the Palestinians were invented in order to "transform a population into a weapon of mass destruction against Israel and the Jewish people, to demonize Israel, and to give totalitarianism and anti-Semitism renewed means of action."[16]

A nation and a people need a distinct identity, and so one was constructed for the Palestinians. For a national flag, the new Palestinians appropriated the banner of the ill-fated Arab Federation of Iraq and Jordan, the short-lived 1958 union between those two nations.

But a nation and a people also need a founding father. There being no Palestinian history, and thus no great Palestinian historical figures, someone more contemporary would have to serve this purpose. That would be Yasser Arafat, who was even less of a Palestinian than his people. According to Ion Mihai Pacepa, who had served as acting chief of Cold War–era Communist Romania's spy service, Arafat was one of the multitudes of the indigenous people of Palestine who was actually from somewhere else: "the KGB destroyed the official records of Arafat's birth in Cairo, and replaced them with fictitious documents saying that he had been born in Jerusalem and was therefore a Palestinian by birth."[17]

Inventing a History

There were also efforts to fit out the new people with a history. The Palestinian daily *Al-Ayyam* reported on December 4, 1998, that the chairman of the history department at Gaza's Khan Yunis Educational College, Dr. Yussuf Alzamili, "called on all universities and colleges to write the history of Palestine and to guard it, and not to enable the [foreign] implants and enemies to distort it or to legitimize the existence of Jews on this land."[18]

Alzamili may have revealed more than he had intended. Universities and colleges were not only to "guard" the history of Palestine but to "write" it. Had it not already been written? Was this a tacit admission that the Palestinians were not a people and had no history, and so this history had to be fabricated, as was the nationality itself?

In any case, the effort was undertaken, and a notable ancestral hero was chosen: Jesus Christ. On Christmas Day in 2017, the Palestinian Authority's minister of education, Sabri Saidam, posted on his Facebook page: "To the authentic Palestinian, Jesus, and to the members of the [Palestinian] people—happy holidays."[19]

All Christians know this about Jesus, according to Fatah Central Committee member Abbas Zaki in April 2017: "The Christians know that Jesus Christ was a Palestinian. He really was from Jerusalem, and his resurrection was from Jerusalem."[20]

An official daily newspaper of the Palestinian Authority, *Al-Hayat Al-Jadida*, reminded its readers on November 18, 2005: "We must not forget that Messiah [Jesus] is a Palestinian, the son of Mary the Palestinian."[21] Everything about him was Palestinian, such that, as Palestinian politician Azzam al-Ahmed said on December 19, 2018, "Christmas is one of the permanent Palestinian symbols." Jesus as a Palestinian was central to Palestinian claims of victimhood. Al-Ahmed was speaking in the disputed Bedouin village of Khan Al-Ahmar, where Israeli officials had determined that the Bedouins were illegally squatting and had to be evicted. Despite the fact that Israel was providing the Bedouins with a home nearby, Palestinian leaders were accusing Israel of a war crime for moving them.

This meant that the people of Khan Al-Ahmar were like Jesus. Al-Ahmed added: "The children of Khan Al-Ahmar are happy about the lighting of this tree, as it is the symbol of the first Palestinian, Jesus, peace be upon him. We, the members of the Palestinian people, are celebrating Christmas together with everyone in the land of Palestine."[22]

A member of the Palestinian Authority's Parliament, Mustafa Barghouti, added on the same occasion: "Jesus, who was born on this land, was a Palestinian and defeated his suffering. This tree hints at an additional victory that the members of our people will achieve at Khan Al-Ahmar."[23]

A picture of Jesus as a victimized Palestinian also appeared in the rhetoric of Laila Ghannam, the district governor of Ramallah and El-Bireh. On July 31, 2017, she attended mass at Holy Family Roman Catholic Church in Ramallah, and told the priest, Father Ibrahim Shoumali: "The integration of all residents of the district"—that is, both Muslims and Christians—"brings everyone pride. Jesus is a Palestinian, and the occupier's bullets do not differentiate between one Palestinian and another. We are all partners to the struggle, building, and making decisions."[24]

In pursuing this notion of Palestinian victimhood being embodied in Jesus the Palestinian, *Al-Hayat Al-Jadida*'s editor in chief, Mahmoud Abu Al-Hija, in an editorial published on February 19, 2017, departed from Islamic orthodoxy, which holds that Jesus was a prophet of Allah, not the savior or redeemer of the world, and conveniently forgot about the hatred and genocidal incitement that are routinely featured in Palestinian media: "Palestine has never brought anything to the entire world but this message, the message of love, tolerance, and peace. There is no better and clearer proof of this than the message of the righteous Palestinian Jesus Christ, peace be upon him, who bore his cross while the crown of thorns wounded his forehead. He walked through the Via Dolorosa, bore the suffering of this path, and became the savior of all mankind and its redeemer from the injustices of hate and its destructive ailments."[25]

Similarly, despite the fact that the Qur'an states that Jesus was neither killed nor crucified (4:157), Fatah Central Committee member Tawfiq Tirawi declared him the first Palestinian martyr: "For Christmas, the birthday of Jesus the first Palestinian and the first Martyr (*Shahid*), peace be upon him, we will surely stop the path of suffering [that is, referring to the Via Dolorosa, which Christians believe to be the path Jesus walked on his way to being crucifixion] and go up to the free Palestine, happy New Year."[26]

A September 2016 editorial in *Al-Hayat Al-Jadida* was a bit more careful not to contravene Qur'anic claims regarding the crucifixion: "Jesus, Issa son of Maryam, peace be upon him, was the first Palestinian Martyr (*Shahid*), who was crucified by the Jews, or they think they crucified him."[27]

In an op-ed published in *Al-Hayat Al-Jadida* on May 16, 2015, columnist Omar Hilmi Al-Ghoul directly equated the sufferings of Jesus with the sufferings of the Palestinians, both, he said, at the hands of the Jews: "the messenger of peace and love, Jesus, may he rest in peace...suffered from the injustice of the first Jews...in the same way his people, the Palestinians, have suffered from the Zionist Jews in the past and in the present...for the delay in doing them [the Palestinians] justice through restoring some of their rights."[28]

On Christmas Day in 2014, Al-Ghoul wrote in *Al-Hayat Al-Jadida*: "My lord Jesus, peace be upon you, those who crucified you 2,000 years ago [that is, the Jews] have returned to crucify your people, of different religions, without distinguishing Christians from Muslims. They spread their poison in every part of your homeland—where your churches, and the mosques of your successor, Prophet Muhammad son of Abdullah of the Quraysh tribe, peace be upon him, were built—to spread destruction, strife and discord.... Jesus, the man of peace and love, rest in peace, for your people, the

Canaanites, stand firm on the ground, holding onto their rights, determined to protect their land."[29]

Perhaps Palestinian officials believed in the totalitarian dictum that once the big lie was frequently enough repeated, it would be generally accepted as true.

Fakery in Plain Sight

In the early days of the existence of the Palestinians, the fact of their nonexistence in history was much more widely known than it is today. In 1969, Israeli Prime Minister Golda Meir stated that "there was no such thing as Palestinians…. It was not as though there was a Palestinian people in Palestine considering itself as a Palestinian people and we came and threw them out and took their country away from them. They did not exist."[30] In fact, she noted, an "independent Palestinian people with a Palestinian State" had never existed.[31]

The Arab Muslims of Palestine knew this as well. Syrian President Hafez Assad once told Yasser Arafat: "You do not represent Palestine as much as we do. Never forget this one point: There is no such thing as a Palestinian people, there is no Palestinian entity, there is only Syria. You are an integral part of the Syrian people, Palestine is an integral part of Syria. Therefore it is we, the Syrian authorities, who are the true representatives of the Palestinian people."[32]

Prince Hassan of the Jordanian National Assembly put it simply on February 2, 1970: "Palestine is Jordan and Jordan is Palestine; there is only one land, with one history and one and the same fate."[33] In a 1977 interview with the Dutch newspaper *Trouw*, PLO executive committee member Zahir Muhsein likewise acknowledged that the Palestinian people were a propaganda invention:

The Palestinian people does not exist. The creation of a Palestinian state is only a means for continuing our struggle against the state of Israel for our Arab unity. In reality today there is no difference between Jordanians, Palestinians, Syrians and Lebanese. Only for political and tactical reasons do we speak today about the existence of a Palestinian people, since Arab national interests demand that we posit the existence of a distinct "Palestinian people" to oppose Zionism.

For tactical reasons, Jordan, which is a sovereign state with defined borders, cannot raise claims to Haifa and Jaffa, while as a Palestinian, I can undoubtedly demand Haifa, Jaffa, Beer-Sheva and Jerusalem. However, the moment we reclaim our right to all of Palestine, we will not wait even a minute to unite Palestine and Jordan.[34]

Abdul Hamid Sharif, the Prime Minister of Jordan, would have agreed. He said in 1980: "The Palestinians and Jordanians do not belong to different nationalities. They hold the same Jordanian passports, are Arabs and have the same Jordanian culture."[35]

King Hussein of Jordan put it most succinctly of all in 1981: "The truth is that Jordan is Palestine and Palestine is Jordan."[36]

Even Yasser Arafat himself admitted this, saying in 1993: "The question of borders doesn't interest us.... From the Arab standpoint, we mustn't talk about borders. Palestine is nothing but a drop in an enormous ocean. Our nation is the Arabic nation that stretches from the Atlantic Ocean to the Red Sea and beyond it.... The P.L.O. is fighting Israel in the name of Pan-Arabism. What you call 'Jordan' is nothing more than Palestine."[37]

Despite the now universal acceptance of the distinct nationality of the Palestinians, traces of their newly minted status sometimes appear in sources that would never admit that the entire Palestinian identity is an exercise in mummery. The Institute for Middle East Understanding, in a 2006 article entitled "Palestinian Social Customs and Traditions," stated matter-of-factly that "Palestinian social customs and traditions are similar to those of other Arab countries."[38] The Palestinian values noted—family solidarity, hospitality, honor—are elements of Muslim culture all over the world; there is absolutely nothing specifically Palestinian about them.

Likewise the Excellence Center in Palestine acknowledged that "the Culture of Palestine is closely related to those of its nearby countries such as Lebanon, Syria, and Jordan."[39] Indeed. By now it is commonplace to see traditional Arab dress, food, and customs described as "Palestinian," with no acknowledgment that they are just as Syrian, and Lebanese, and Jordanian as they are Palestinian. The propaganda creation has taken on a life of its own. The existence of the Palestinians is taken for granted.

The Palestinians Strike Back

There are, however, still occasional dissenting voices. Late in 2011, former House speaker Newt Gingrich, who was then a strong contender for the Republican Party's 2012 presidential nomination, dared to inject a note of historical realism into the campaign. "Remember," he told an interviewer, "there was no Palestine as a state. It was part of the Ottoman Empire.... I think that we've had an invented Palestinian people who are in fact Arabs and who were historically part of the Arab community. And they had a chance to go many places, and for a variety of political reasons we have sustained this war against Israel now since the 1940s, and it's tragic."[40] The Palestinians, said Gingrich, had "an enormous desire to destroy Israel."[41]

In response, the Prime Minister of the Palestinian Authority, Salam Fayyad, affected dismay, demanding that Gingrich "review history" and claiming: "The Palestinian people inhabited the land since the dawn of history."[42] Fayyad added: "From the beginning, our people have been determined to stay on their land. This, certainly, is denying historical truths."[43] Palestinian politician Hanan Ashrawi charged that Gingrich had "lost touch with reality" and that he questioned the reality of the Palestinian nationality only as "a cheap way to win [the] pro-Israel vote."[44] A Hamas spokesman declared that Gingrich's remarks were "shameful and disgraceful" and demonstrated "genuine hostility toward Palestinians."[45]

None of the reporters who interviewed Fayyad, Ashrawi, or the Hamas spokesman had the historical knowledge or temerity to confront them with the statements of Yasser Arafat, Zahir Muhsein, or any of the other Arab leaders who had denied that there was any such thing as a Palestinian people.

Hussein Ibish of the American Task Force on Palestine went even further than his allies, charging that denying the reality of the Palestinian people was just an attempt to divert attention away from the fact that the Israelis were a newly minted people as well: "To call the Palestinians 'an invented people' in an obvious effort to undermine their national identity is outrageous, especially since there was no such thing as an 'Israeli' before 1948."[46]

Ibish was being disingenuous. It is hard to go anywhere in Israel, from the Negev to the Golan Heights—including Judea and Samaria, known today as the West Bank and a center of Palestinian settlement—without encountering archeological sites that testify to the ancient Jewish presence in the land. There most certainly were "Israelis" before 1948; in English Bible translations they are known as "Israelites," but they are the same people, and they had lived continuously in Eretz Israel for several thousand years.[47] There is, in contrast, no evidence of Arabs in the area before the seventh century of the common era.

Nonetheless, the myth has taken hold, and it is now widely taken for granted, in our age that has little historical memory and scant interest in gaining more, that the Palestinians are a genuine nationality and are the indigenous people of the land that Israel illegally occupies.

This is a propaganda success that Josef Goebbels and the editors of *Pravda* would have envied, and it became the foundation for more. Having established the Palestinians as a tiny indigenous people whose land had been stolen by rapacious, well-heeled, and oppressive foreigners, it was time to return to the negotiating table—not in order to achieve any genuine accord with Israel, but to exploit the victimhood status of the new tiny people they had invented in order to win valuable concessions from the Israelis.

The story of the Israeli-Palestinian "peace process" henceforth universally refers to the Muslim Arabs of Palestine as Palestinians, and almost always also adopts the Jordanian term "West Bank" for Judea and Samaria. For the sake of convenience, this book will from this point forward also use these terms, while accepting neither the reality of a distinct "Palestinian" people nor the erasure of the historical reality that the "West Bank" is the ancient land of the Jewish people.

CHAPTER FIVE

Seeds of the "Peace Process"

The term "peace process" is generally applied to the Oslo Accords of 1993 and the Israeli-Palestinian negotiations that followed it. However, initiatives to achieve a negotiated peace began long before 1993. After Israel won its war for independence, there was no large-scale effort to make peace between it and its neighbors until the much-heralded Camp David Accords of 1978. However, there were other abortive attempts between 1948 and 1978 to pacify the situation, usually following the British pattern of favoring the Muslim Arabs and requiring the Jews to make concessions.

The Suez Crisis

A premier example of this came right after the State of Israel was founded. After Israel won its war for independence, the world powers assumed that the blockade on Israeli ships passing through the Suez Canal would end. On July 26, 1949, Dr. Ralph Bunche stated before the UN Security Council that "there should be free movement for legitimate shipping and no vestiges of the wartime blockade should be allowed to remain, as they are inconsistent with both the letter and spirit of the Armistice Agreement."[1] On September 1, 1951, the United Nations Security Council passed Resolution 95, calling upon Egypt to "terminate the restrictions on the passage of international commercial ships and goods through the Suez Canal, wherever bound, and to cease all interference with such shipping."[2] And not only that: the government of Egypt had pledged in an agreement it signed in 1888 to keep the canal open to vessels of all nations.

But the Egyptian government of 1888 hadn't counted on the existence of the State of Israel. Egypt blockaded the Suez Canal and wouldn't let Israeli ships through. In July 1954, the British, true to what was its established practice by then, concluded a treaty with Egypt that recognized this blockade as legitimate. Israel protested, but none of the great powers were much interested in coming to its aid. When an Israeli freighter tested the blockade and was seized by Egyptian forces, the United Nations did nothing.

Meanwhile, Egyptian President Gamal Abdel Nasser began a massive arms buildup, obtaining a huge quantity of weaponry from the Soviet Union. The Israelis were thoroughly alarmed, and became even more so when Nasser in August 1955 began launching raids of Muslim Arab guerrillas (*fedayeen*) across the border, usually targeting Israeli civilians. Two hundred Israeli civilians were killed or wounded in these raids during the summer of 1955.[3]

Israeli forces began a series of reprisal attacks. The situation didn't fully boil over, however, until Nasser nationalized the Suez Canal on July 26, 1956. Britain and France subsequently began planning operations to seize the canal and overthrow the Nasser regime; they reluctantly included Israel in their plans, and ultimately it was decided that Israel would invade first, which it did on October 29, 1956. Within just a few days, Israeli forces had taken the Gaza Strip and most of the Sinai Peninsula.

The British and French then began their own military operations and were also successful, but the operation proved wildly unpopular internationally. In an age of receding colonialism, the British and French actions against Egypt were widely viewed as the reassertion of a dead, discredited ideology. The British and French governments, thoroughly embarrassed and risking a significant loss of international prestige, began to back away.

The Israelis, however, had their own reasons for the attack, although lamentably, they had, in the words of Israeli diplomat Abba Eban, "appeared before the whole world as tools of the imperialists."[4] They hoped to stop the Egyptian raids and murders of Israeli civilians, and open up the Suez Canal to Israeli shipping. Eban also told U.S. secretary of state John Foster Dulles of another possible benefit: "As a result of what Israel has done, Nasser is going to lose all his credit. A more moderate government will replace his. Possibly Israel and other countries will be able to make peace at last in the Middle East."[5]

The Americans, who had been Israel's closest and most reliable allies, were unmoved. President Dwight Eisenhower warned of the end of "friendly cooperation between our two countries."[6] The U.S. even sponsored a UN resolution calling upon Israel to withdraw from the Sinai, although the British and French vetoed it. Nonetheless, the Israelis, almost friendless in the world, had to relent. The Israeli government withdrew its forces from the Sinai, after obtaining Eisenhower's promise that the U.S. would ensure that its ships could make use of the Suez Canal.

Meanwhile, Israel still had troops in Gaza, which had been occupied by Egypt since 1948. Another Israeli diplomat, Golda Meir, pleaded Israel's case before the UN General Assembly:

> It is inconceivable to my government that the nightmare of the previous eight years should be reestablished in Gaza with international sanction. Shall Egypt be allowed once more to organize murder and sabotage in this strip? Shall Egypt be allowed to condemn the local population to permanent impoverishment and block any solution of the refugee problem?[7]

That is exactly what Egypt wanted to do. The Palestinian refugees, supposedly people who had been driven from their homes by the Israelis in 1948, were not offered Egyptian citizenship, or citizenship in any other Muslim Arab state except Jordan. The strategy was clear: the Palestinian refugees would be kept as refugees, and any alleviation of their plight resisted, so that by their very existence they could serve as a permanent rebuke to the State of Israel, and a potent weapon in attempts to discredit and destroy that state.

Meir also criticized the idea of putting international peacekeeping forces in the Sinai and Gaza: "It must be admitted that any international force would be powerless to prevent…the recrudescence of fedayun activities."[8] The Israelis nonetheless had to withdraw, and UN Expeditionary Force troops replaced the Israeli forces.

The disaster was not total. Meir's dark prophecy proved at least partly incorrect: the *fedayeen* raids did indeed drop significantly, and the Suez Canal was open to Israeli shipping for more than a decade following the conflict. Israel went into Egypt not to conquer territory but to secure those two goals, and it did so.

However, 1956 would by no means be the last time that Israel gave up territory won in war and, according to the ancient laws of nations, therefore belonging to them by right of conquest, in exchange for promises. Certainly no nation in the world, not even the United States, was willing in 1956 to recognize Israel's right to annex the Sinai and Gaza, which Israeli Prime Minister David Ben-Gurion had hinted he might do. And the promises made to Israel at that time did not prove entirely empty, as other promises would prove to be more than once in the future.

Nonetheless, in the Suez Crisis, Israel was forced by international pressure to give up what it had for what it might receive, and to abandon tangible military gains in exchange for intangible assurances. A bad precedent had been set that would be reinforced many times in later years, when the Israeli-Palestinian "peace process" was in high gear.

The Six-Day War

The fragile peace established after the Suez Crisis lasted eleven years. It was, however, merely the absence of outright military hostilities.

The jihad goal of the total elimination of Israel remained the same. On March 8, 1965, Nasser made it clear that the shooting war would someday resume: "The liquidation of Israel will be liquidation through violence. We shall enter a Palestine not covered with sand, but soaked in blood."[9] Four months later, he declared that "the final account with Israel will be made within five years if we are patient. The Moslems waited seventy years until they expelled the Crusaders from Palestine."[10] He maintained that the ultimate destruction of Israel was "immutable as a permanent interest."[11]

He backed up these words with a military buildup that he thought was ready two years later to destroy the Jewish state once and for all. Meanwhile, the new Palestine Liberation Organization and others were launching regular jihad terror attacks against Israeli civilians: there were thirty-five terror raids in 1965, forty-one in 1966, and thirty-seven in just the first half of 1967.[12] Syria, meanwhile, was shooting at Israeli civilians from the Golan Heights.

On Israel's twentieth Independence Day, May 15, 1967, Nasser began to amass troops on Egypt's border with Israel. The next day, Nasser ordered the UN forces that had been there since 1956 to leave the Sinai; they completed their withdrawal two days later. The Voice of the Arabs radio station gleefully proclaimed: "As of today there no longer exists an international emergency force to protect Israel. We shall exercise patience no more. We shall not complain any more to the UN about Israel. The sole method we shall apply against Israel is total war, which will result in the extermination of Zionist existence."[13] Syrian defense minister Hafez Assad was just as confident: "Our forces are now entirely ready not only to repulse the aggression, but to initiate the act of liberation itself and to explode the Zionist presence in the Arab homeland. The Syrian army with its finger on the trigger is united. I, as a military man, believe that the time has come to enter into a battle of annihilation."[14]

On May 22, Nasser closed the Strait of Tiran, Israel's means of access to trade partners in Africa and Asia, to Israeli ships. On May 25, he told the Egyptian Parliament: "The problem presently before the Arab countries is not whether the port of Eilat should be blockaded or how to blockade it—but how totally to exterminate the State of Israel for all time."[15] Posters calling on all Arabs to wage jihad against Israel began appearing. On June 3, Egypt's Sinai commander, General Mohsin Murtagi, told his officers: "The eyes of the whole world are on you…. Reconquer the stolen land with God's help and the power of justice and with the strength of your arms and your united faith."[16]

The PLO's Ahmad Shukairy told reporters that the Palestinians were ready to "march to liberate the country—our country." Asked what would be the fate of the citizens of Israel if the attack succeeded, Shukairy replied: "Those who survive will remain in Palestine. I estimate that none of them will survive."[17]

The writing was on the wall. The Israelis on June 5 launched a preemptive strike against Egypt, after which Syria and Jordan attacked Israel. Six days after that, on June 10, it was all over, with Israel having thoroughly routed the forces of all three countries and taken possession of the Sinai, Judea, and Samaria (known to the Jordanian government that had occupied that land since 1948 as the West Bank), including East Jerusalem, and the Golan Heights.

No Negotiations

On June 12, 1967, Israeli Prime Minister Levi Eshkol told the Knesset: "Let this be said—there should be no illusion that Israel is prepared to return to the conditions that existed a week ago…. We have fought alone for our existence and our security, and we are therefore justified in deciding for ourselves what are the genuine and indispensable interests of our State, and how to guarantee its future."[18]

This meant that this time, the territories that Israel won would not simply be handed back. Israel wanted a genuine peace agreement with its neighbors; failing that, it would hold what it needed for its own security. It placed the West Bank, Gaza Strip, and Sinai under military rule in anticipation of future negotiations.

There would, however, be no negotiations, and no lasting peace. On September 1, 1967, at an Arab League summit meeting in Khartoum, the principal belligerents in the Six-Day War—Egypt, Syria, and Jordan—along with Algeria, Iraq, Kuwait, Lebanon, and Sudan, passed the Khartoum Resolution, which stated flatly: "The Arab Heads of State have agreed to unite their political efforts at the international and diplomatic level to eliminate the effects of the aggression and to ensure the withdrawal of the aggressive Israeli forces from the Arab lands which have been occupied since the aggression of June 5. This will be done within the framework of the main principles by which the Arab States abide, namely, no peace with Israel, no recognition of Israel, no negotiations with it, and insistence on the rights of the Palestinian people in their own country."[19]

Once again the Arab states had enunciated the intransigence and undying hatred of Israel that were the inevitable result of Islam's teachings regarding the Jews and the need for Muslims to dominate, not be dominated, in any society. Abba Eban, by this time Israel's foreign minister, quipped after the Khartoum Resolution was published that the Six-Day War was "the first war in history in which the victor sued for peace and the loser called for unconditional surrender."[20] But that was the nature of jihad warfare throughout history: never to relent, never to surrender, never to give up, but to keep on pressing relentlessly, inexorably, forward.

Resolution 242

The United Nations, heedless of or indifferent to the principles of jihad warfare, continued to hold out hope for a negotiated peace. On November 22, 1967, the UN Security Council unanimously (that is, including Israel's only friend in the world, the United States) adopted Resolution 242, which was offered in the hope of its becoming the framework for lasting peace between Israel and its neighbors, as well as with the Palestinians.

The resolution began by "*emphasizing* the inadmissibility of the acquisition of territory by war and the need to work for a just and lasting peace in which every State in the area can live in security," and then made what appeared to be evenhanded calls to both sides. It called for "withdrawal of Israeli armed forces from territories occupied in the recent conflict," as well as the "termination of all claims or states of belligerency and respect for and acknowledgement of the sovereignty, territorial integrity and political independence of every State in the area and their right to live in peace within secure and recognized boundaries free from threats or acts of force."[21]

The framers of this resolution appeared to have envisioned the Arab Muslim states dropping their belligerent stance as Israel divested itself of the territory it had just won. But it was not a completely naïve document. It was, in fact, very carefully worded.

A draft resolution introduced by several Latin American countries had called upon Israel to "withdraw all its forces from all territories occupied by it as a result of the recent conflict."[22] Resolution 242, by contrast, did not say that. Its primary architect was Hugh M. Foot, Lord Caradon, British permanent representative to the United Nations. He later explained just how precisely the document had been crafted, and made clear that the resolution did not call upon Israel to withdraw from all the territories it had won in the Six-Day War. Referring to the call for the "withdrawal of Israeli armed forces from territories occupied in the recent conflict," Caradon explained: "Much play has been made of the fact that we didn't say 'the' territories or 'all the' territories. But that was deliberate. I myself knew very well the 1967 boundaries and if we had put in the 'the' or 'all the' that could only have meant that we wished to see the 1967 boundaries perpetuated in the form of a permanent frontier. This I was certainly not prepared to recommend."[23]

In 1974, Caradon reiterated that Resolution 242 did not mean that Israel must abandon everything it had gained: "It would have been wrong to demand that Israel return to its positions of 4 June 1967 because those positions were undesirable and artificial. After all, they were just the places the soldiers of each side happened to be the day the fighting stopped in 1948. They were just armistice lines.

That's why we didn't demand that the Israelis return to them and I think we were right not to."[24]

Then in a 1976 interview, Caradon was asked: "The basis for any settlement will be United Nations Security Council Resolution 242, of which you were the architect. Would you say there is a contradiction between the part of the resolution that stresses the inadmissibility of the acquisition of territory by war and that which calls for Israeli withdrawal from 'occupied territories,' but not from 'the occupied territories'?"[25]

Caradon answered:

> *I defend the resolution as it stands. What it states, as you know, is first the general principle of inadmissibility of the acquisition of territory by war. That means that you can't justify holding onto territory merely because you conquered it. We could have said: well, you go back to the 1967 line. But I know the 1967 line, and it's a rotten line. You couldn't have a worse line for a permanent international boundary. It's where the troops happened to be on a certain night in 1948. It's got no relation to the needs of the situation.*
>
> *Had we said that you must go back to the 1967 line, which would have resulted if we had specified a retreat from all the occupied territories, we would have been wrong.... So what we stated was the principle that you couldn't hold territory because you conquered it, therefore there must be a withdrawal to—let's read the words carefully—"secure and recognized boundaries." They can only be secure if they are recognized. The boundaries have to be agreed; it's only when you get agreement that you get security. I think that now people begin to realize what we had in mind—that security doesn't come from arms, it doesn't come from territory, it doesn't come from geography, it doesn't come from one side domination [sic] the other, it can only come from agreement and mutual respect and understanding.*[26]

Caradon's insistence that the UN was not requiring Israel to return to the 1947 partition lines or 1948 borders after the war of independence was well taken. Abba Eban famously once referred to those borders as "Auschwitz borders"; leaving Israel only eight miles wide at one point, they kept the Jewish state extremely vulnerable and in danger of extinction in an area where its neighbors had repeatedly made clear their desire to destroy it utterly.

However, the resolution's declaration of the "the inadmissibility of the acquisition of territory by war" and Caradon's statement that it was a "principle that you couldn't hold territory because you conquered it" were odd. The resolution stated this in a preamble, and preambular language in UN documents is not binding, but it was nonetheless a strange assertion, placed in the document in order to please the Arab states that had just lost the war. If the United Nations were consistent in applying that principle, not just Israel but quite a few other countries would have to give up territory. Britain itself had acquired territory by conquest all over the world, although by 1967 the sun had largely set on the British Empire. The United States acquired California and the vast territories of the American Southwest after defeating Mexico in war.

The most precise analogies for Israel's territorial gains as a result of the Six-Day War, however, are the Soviet Union's territorial expansion in Eastern Europe and Poland's gains of former German territory in the aftermath of World War II. Germany had started an aggressive and unnecessary war; no one questioned the fact that after the war, it should suffer a substantial loss of territory. Nations that lost wars, particularly when the wars were the result of their own aggression, had lost territories throughout history. The Soviet Union and Poland, meanwhile, had suffered grievously at the hands of Germany; no one likewise questioned the right of each to claim German territories as its own. Königsberg, which had been a German city for a thousand years, became Russian. Other areas that had been German since time immemorial became Polish.

The same situation prevailed at the end of the Six-Day War. Egypt, Syria, and Jordan had waged an aggressive war against Israel, intending to destroy it utterly and commit (if Ahmad Shukairy is to be believed) a genocide of its people. Israel had existed for nearly two decades with borders that were well-nigh indefensible, as well as with a capital divided between it and a hostile power. It had a chance to take control of territories that would allow it to live with greater security—and with a unified capital.

The right of conquest had been taken for granted since wars between human beings began. The United Nations never questioned the Soviet Union's postwar territorial expansion, or any other territorial gain at the expense of a defeated aggressor. But after the Six-Day War, suddenly it was instead taking for granted "the inadmissibility of the acquisition of territory by war."

Israel did not give up the territories, at least not immediately, as the Arab Muslim states did not give up their threats and fulminations against Israel. Resolution 242 is also noteworthy, however, in that it once again called upon Israel to surrender tangible assets—the territories it had taken during the Six-Day War—in exchange for promises: some kind of assurance, presumably, from Egypt, Syria, Jordan, and the rest that they would terminate all "claims or states of belligerency" and express their "respect for and acknowledgement of the sovereignty, territorial integrity and political independence of every State in the area," including Israel.

The Yom Kippur War

Egypt and Syria, along with expeditionary forces from Algeria, Iraq, Jordan, Libya, Morocco, Saudi Arabia, and Tunisia, as well as Cuba, started another war against Israel on Yom Kippur, October 6, 1973. By this time, the conflict between Israel and the Arab Muslim states had been almost entirely subsumed into the Cold War machinations of the United States and the Soviet Union. The Soviets were supporting the Arabs, which was why their fellow communists, the Cubans, sent forces, and the United States was supporting Israel. The oil-producing Muslim Arab nations, meanwhile, began an oil embargo directed at the United States and other nations that supported Israel.

U.S. secretary of state Henry Kissinger, however, on October 25, 1973, as he was pressing both sides to accept a ceasefire, suggested that Israel could not take American support for granted in the future. "Our position," he explained, "is that…the conditions that produced this war were clearly intolerable to the Arab nations and that in the process of negotiations it will be necessary to make substantial concessions. The problem will be to relate the Arab concern for the sovereignty over the territories to the Israeli concern for secure boundaries. We believe that the process of negotiations between the parties is an essential component of this."[27]

The Watergate scandal overwhelmed and destroyed the administration of which Kissinger was a part, but there would, before too very long, be those negotiations, and Israel would indeed be pressured to make "substantial concessions."

The Beginning of the "Peace Process"

On October 22, 1973, as the Yom Kippur War was still raging, the UN Security Council passed Resolution 338, not only calling upon all the belligerents to "cease all firing and terminate all military activity immediately, no later than 12 hours after the moment of the adoption of this decision, in the positions they now occupy," but requiring that "immediately and concurrently with the ceasefire, negotiations start between the parties concerned under appropriate auspices aimed at establishing a just and durable peace in the Middle East."[28]

The "appropriate auspices" were beginning to appear. The Israelis had long asked their Muslim Arab neighbors to sit down with them and come to a negotiated settlement, but they had always refused, as the Khartoum Resolution avowed emphatically in 1967: "No peace with Israel, no recognition of Israel, no negotiations with it."[29]

But now it was not just the Americans and the UN but the Soviet Union also, which had protected and aided Egypt and its allies against Israel, that wanted to see negotiations. Even before the October 1973 war, in a February 1973 Politburo meeting, Soviet leader Leonid Brezhnev said: "Let [Egyptian President Anwar] Sadat think about what the end of the war in Vietnam means for him. Andropov and Gromyko are assigned to look for new ways to establish contact with Israel. Past attempts were unsuccessful. To just sit there with severed relations—that is not a policy."[30]

Sadat was not born to the role of peacemaker with Israel. As a youth he had revered Hitler; in 1953, when rumors swept Egypt that the Führer was still alive, a Cairo newspaper asked the young colonel Anwar Sadat to write the German dictator a letter. Sadat wrote:

My Dear Hitler,

I admire you from the bottom of my heart. Even if you appear to have been defeated, in reality you are the victor. You have succeeded in creating dissension between 4the old man Churchill and his allies, the sons of Satan.[31]

By the "sons of Satan" Sadat likely meant the Jews, as it was partly the British authorities' worry about German and Italian influence in the Arab Muslim world that led them to back away from the Balfour Declaration and start working against Jewish interests in Palestine. Although he acknowledged in his letter to Hitler that the Nazi leader "did some mistakes," he doesn't seem to have meant to include the Holocaust among them, as he quickly avowed that "our faith in your nation has more than compensated for them."[32]

Sadat's anti-Semitism ran deep. He once said: "I knew that a Jew would do anything if the price was right."[33] But if Sadat carried these views into the 1970s, the harsh realities of Egypt's geopolitical situation were forcing him to moderate them, at least publicly. At the end of the Yom Kippur War, Brezhnev was emphatic about the need for Egypt to agree to participate in negotiations. Sadat had expelled all Soviet advisers and begun moving closer to the United States in 1972, but the Soviets were still very much in the picture, and during the Yom Kippur War, Sadat had appealed for their help, even including asking for Soviet troops to move against Israel.

The Soviets had refused this, and now wanted Sadat to try a different approach. Referring to the Israeli-Palestinian conflict, Soviet foreign minister Andrei Gromyko asked him: "Leonid, what are we going to do?"[34] Brezhnev responded with a three-point plan:

1. We will participate in negotiations, and we will do it persistently and everywhere. We have a right and duty to do this.

2. We will participate in guaranteeing the borders. And Israel's borders too, because that is what we are talking about. They are the apple of discord.

3. At the appropriate time we will restore diplomatic relations with Israel.

On our own initiative! Yes, that's right.[35]

Gromyko warned: "But the Arabs will get upset, they'll make a fuss."[36] Brezhnev revealed his frustration at dealing with Muslim Arab recalcitrance as he shot back:

They can go to hell! We have offered them a sensible way for so many years. But no, they wanted to fight. Fine! We gave them technology, the latest, the kind even Vietnam didn't have. They had double superiority in tanks and aircraft, triple in artillery, and in air defense and anti-tank weapons they had absolute supremacy. And what? Once again they were beaten. Once again they scrammed. Once again they screamed for us to come save them. Sadat woke me up in the middle of the night twice over the phone, "Save me!" He demanded to send Soviet troops, and immediately! No! We are not going to fight for them. The people would not understand that. And especially we will not start a world war because of them. So that's that. We will act like I said.[37]

Cornered, Sadat saw an opportunity. Henry Kissinger was renowned for his diplomatic skills and ability to bring recalcitrant parties to agreement; for this, he was celebrated throughout the Western world as a peacemaker. Sadat determined to become a peacemaker as well, and give the UN and the world what it wanted:

negotiations with the Israelis. During them, Kissinger and the Americans, anxious for an agreement, would pressure the Israelis for concessions, and Egypt would win at the peace table what it could not win with the force of arms. Sadat would give his Soviet allies what they wanted, negotiations with Israel, and in doing so, move closer to the world's other great power, the United States. After all, he asked rhetorically, "What other country can force Israel to withdraw?"[38]

The United States could, and would. Kissinger and U.S. President Richard Nixon compelled Egypt and Israel to commit to peace talks in Geneva in December 1973. When the Israelis showed reluctance, Nixon was as truculent as Brezhnev had been about Sadat. He told a group of American governors: "The only way we're going to solve the crisis is to end the oil embargo, and the only way we're going to end the embargo is to get the Israelis to act reasonable. I hate to use the word blackmail, but we've got to do some things to get them to behave."[39]

He did. The Israelis duly appeared in Geneva, although the Syrians did not, and no agreement was reached. However, the Geneva conference started the "peace process" rolling. In 1974 and 1975, Egypt and Israel signed two agreements providing for a partial withdrawal of Israeli troops from the Sinai, and the deployment of UN peacekeeping forces between the Egyptian and Israeli forces there. In the second of these agreements, signed in Geneva on September 4, 1975, Egypt and Israel stipulated that "the conflict between them and in the Middle East shall not be resolved by military force but by peaceful means."[40]

Sadat in Jerusalem

Sadat's star rose with these agreements internationally, except in the Islamic world, which looked on with suspicion as he began negotiating with Israel. That suspicion turned to alarm on November 9, 1977, when Sadat announced: "Israel will be surprised to hear me say that I am willing to go to their parliament, the Knesset itself, and debate with them."[41]

The Israelis, as delighted as they were stunned, quickly accepted, and Sadat made plans to arrive in Jerusalem on November 19, 1977. King Khalid of Saudi Arabia was appalled: "I have always before gone to the Kaaba to pray for somebody, never to pray against anyone. But on this occasion I found myself saying, 'Oh God, grant that the airplane taking Sadat to Jerusalem may crash before it gets there, so that he may not become a scandal for all of us.'"[42]

The prayer wasn't answered; Sadat arrived on schedule. As he toured the ancient sites of Jerusalem, Palestinian protesters denounced him and cried: "Sadat, what do you want from us? We are against you. We don't want you here."[43]

Their anxiety, and King Khalid's, was misplaced. Sadat had no intention of betraying them. However, when he addressed the Knesset on November 20, he did sound numerous conciliatory notes.

You want to live with us in this part of the world. In all sincerity, I tell you, we welcome you among us, with full security and safety. This, in itself, is a tremendous turning point; one of the landmarks of a decisive historical change.

We used to reject you. We had our reasons and our claims, yes. We used to brand you as "so-called" Israel, yes. We were together in international conferences and organizations and our representatives did not, and still do not, exchange greetings, yes. This has happened and is still happening.[44]

His speech was not all conciliation. On the demands that Arab leaders had made since the Six-Day War, he showed no sign of yielding an inch, saying: "There are Arab territories which Israel has occupied by armed force. We insist on complete withdrawal from these territories, including Arab Jerusalem."[45] He claimed that this issue was so clear as to be beyond discussion or argument:

Let me tell you, without the slightest hesitation, that I did not come to you under this dome to make a request that your troops evacuate the occupied territories. Complete withdrawal from the Arab territories occupied in 1967 is a logical and undisputed fact. Nobody should plead for that. Any talk about permanent peace based on justice, and any move to ensure our coexistence in peace and security in this part of the world, would become meaningless, while you occupy Arab territories by force of arms. For there is no peace that could be in consonance with, or be built on, the occupation of the land of others. Otherwise, it would not be a serious peace.[46]

Sadat similarly declared that "nobody in the world could accept, today, slogans propagated here in Israel, ignoring the existence of the Palestinian People, and questioning their whereabouts. The cause of the Palestinian People and their legitimate rights are no longer ignored or denied today by anybody. Rather, nobody who has the ability of judgment can deny or ignore it."[47]

The Egyptian president also hinted at a desire for Islamic rule over the land of Israel when he said: "Instead of awakening the prejudices of the Crusaders, we should revive the spirit of Umar ibn el-Khattab and Saladin, namely the spirit of tolerance and respect for rights."[48] Umar and Saladin were Islamic rulers, in whose domains Jews and Christians were subjugated and denied basic rights.

In a final insult, Sadat told the Knesset: "I shall not indulge in past events since the Balfour Declaration sixty years ago. You are well acquainted with the relevant facts. If you have found the legal and moral justification to set up a national home on a land that did not all belong to you, it is incumbent upon you to show understanding of the insistence of the People of Palestine on establishing, once again a state on their land."[49]

Sadat garlanded his intransigence with quotes from the Bible and Qur'an and invocations of grieving mothers, which had their desired effect: his insults and lack of any hint of genuine conciliation went unnoticed. So did the tie featuring a series of interlocking swastikas that he wore as he sat between Israeli Prime Minister Menachem Begin and foreign minister Moshe Dayan at a state dinner held in his honor on November 21, 1977.[50]

The Egyptian president went home thinking that the Israelis would be so overwhelmed at being treated with kindness and respect by a Muslim Arab leader that they would quickly give the Arab Islamic world everything it wanted: he told a group of reporters in Cairo that "all you journalists are going to find yourselves with nothing to do. Everything has been solved. It's all over."[51] When they asked him about the West Bank, Gaza, and Jerusalem, he replied: "In my pocket!"[52]

Not quite. But he was now an international hero, a warrior for peace. A fond and trusting new American president would soon help him attain some of his goals, and would tell him that he was "probably the most admired statesman in the United States."[53]

He may well have been. *Time* magazine exclaimed: "It was as if a messenger from Allah had descended to the Promised Land."[54] And thanks to that naïve president, his star would continue to rise.

CHAPTER SIX

"Poor Naïve Carter"

Jihad Against Sadat

Many Muslims were enraged at Anwar Sadat for breaking ranks and negotiating with the Israelis. Sadat and his allies became new jihad targets. On February 18, 1978, the PLO murdered Sadat's friend Youssef el-Sebai, the editor of the Egyptian newspaper *Al-Ahram*, who had gone with Sadat to Jerusalem. The killers vowed: "Everyone who went to Israel with Sadat will die, including Sadat."[1]

Israelis would die as well. As if to emphasize that they would have nothing to do with any negotiated settlement, on March 11 Palestinian jihadis landed a boat on a beach north of Tel Aviv and went on a killing spree, murdering thirty-eight Israeli Jews.

Sadat was undaunted. When U.S. President Jimmy Carter sent him a handwritten invitation to join him and Israeli Prime Minister Menachem Begin at the presidential retreat of Camp David in September 1978, he readily accepted. "What we are after," he explained to his aides, "is to win over world opinion. President Carter is on our side. This will end in Begin's downfall!"[2]

A Man of Faith

He was right about Carter. Jimmy Carter had been elected President of the United States as an outsider, unfamiliar with the corruption and venality of Washington. He was, famously, a man of faith, giving the appearance of being scrupulously honest and aboveboard in all his dealings, and he appeared to assume that others would be also. After Sadat's trip to Jerusalem, Carter seemed convinced that Sadat was a visionary, as well as a fellow man of faith, given the abundance of biblical and Qur'anic quotes in his Knesset speech, and the U.S. president apparently determined to do everything he could to be of service to the great man.

Carter, thoroughly entranced with his Egyptian counterpart, referred to Sadat as "a great and good man" and "my wonderful friend."[3] Carter told Sadat: "I will represent your interests as if they were my own. You are my brother."[4] Carter was anxious for Sadat to see him as trustworthy, telling the Egyptian president: "I hope I will never let you down."[5]

Carter never lavished such praise on Begin, nor did he give him any such assurances. In fact, Carter's national security adviser, Zbigniew Brzezinski, observed that Carter's relationship with Begin was "icy, and even mutual praise was formalistic and devoid of any personal feeling."[6]

From the very beginning of the Camp David summit, Carter's affinity for Sadat was clear. It would have enormous consequences.

"Exert Pressure on Begin"

Carter was true to his word to Sadat. The day after the Egyptian president arrived, Sadat and Carter had a private meeting, at which Carter listened thoughtfully to Sadat's "Framework for the Comprehensive Peace Settlement of the Middle East Problem." Sadat demanded that Israel withdraw from all the territories it had occupied in the Six-Day War, including East Jerusalem; dismantle all Israeli settlements in those territories; and return to its precarious original boundaries,

Abba Eban's "Auschwitz borders." The framework stipulated: "The Palestinian peoples shall exercise their fundamental right to self-determination and shall be enabled to establish their national entity. Egypt and Jordan by virtue of their responsibility in the Gaza Strip and the West Bank, shall recommend that the entity be linked with Jordan as decided by their peoples."[7]

While this Palestinian entity was being established, "Palestinian refugees and displaced persons shall be enabled to exercise the right of return and receive compensation in accordance with relevant United Nations resolutions."[8] That "right of return" would overwhelm the Jewish population of Israel with Palestinian "refugees" of the second and third generation, ultimately destroying Israel's character as a Jewish state. Sadat's framework did not, of course, make any mention of a "right to return" for the nine hundred thousand Jews who had been expelled from Muslim lands after the establishment of the State of Israel.

Sadat's plan also mandated that Israel "pay full and prompt compensation for the damage which resulted from the operations of its armed forces against the civilian populations and installations, as well as its exploitation of natural resources in occupied territories."[9]

In return for all these concessions, Israel would get a statement of both nations' "determination to reach a comprehensive settlement of the Middle East problem through the conclusion of peace treaties on the basis of full implementation of Security Council Resolutions 242 and 338 in all their parts."[10]

After unstinting, relentless hostility to Jewish settlement in Palestine from the very beginning of the Zionist project, that wasn't nothing, but it also wasn't much. Israel would be retreating to barely defensible borders, while all the Arab Muslim states that had made war against the Jewish state and tried to destroy it before were just as hostile as they always had been, with the lone exception of Egypt. And Egypt would be getting everything that it had tried to gain militarily in the Yom Kippur War, except by peaceful means, just as Sadat had hoped, without making any substantial concessions to Israel.

Sadat's foreign minister, Mohamed Ibrahim Kamel, praised the proposal but advised him to reveal this "Framework for Peace" after the summit had been going on for a while, "so as to assess the attitude of President Carter, ascertain how far he is prepared to move, and expose Begin's position."[11]

Sadat, however, was determined to introduce his terms at the earliest possible opportunity. "Why go round in circles?" he asked Kamel. "Since you say the project is well constructed and may be easily defended, I intend, from the very outset, to lay the project before Carter and Begin. In the end, all depends on whether Carter is really ready to undertake the role of full partner he has accepted, and exert pressure on Begin."[12]

Sadat told the president that if the summit failed, it wouldn't be his fault but Begin's, because of his obstinacy and stubbornness.

When Sadat rejoined his aides, he was ebullient, and regaled them with the details of his meeting with the man he referred to as "poor naïve Carter."[13]

Carter had manifested the same impatience with Begin before. In July 1977, Begin visited Carter at the White House and brought along one of his advisers, Samuel (Shmuel) Katz, a historian who possessed encyclopedic knowledge of the circumstances of Israel's founding, the Palestine situation before the advent of Zionism, and related issues. Katz began a presentation to Carter about the desolation of nineteenth-century Palestine and the falsity of the claim that the Israelis had driven the Arabs out of the land in 1948. Carter's tense, irritated expression, however, led Begin to cut the presentation short and change the subject.[14] What Katz was telling Carter was entirely accurate, and important to know in order to understand contemporary crises more comprehensively, but the president did not have the patience or goodwill to sit still for it.

"Sadat Insists"

Begin had also met privately with Carter on the night before. In contrast to his attentiveness and solicitude toward Sadat, with Begin the American president was peremptory, faithfully conveying the Egyptian president's demands, adding to them the weight of his own authority: "The United States," said Carter, "expects Israel to put an end to the settlements in the occupied territories."[15] He also made it clear that Sadat was the one who was dictating the terms, telling Begin: "Sadat insists that Israel accept the principle that no land be taken by force," a principle derived from the UN Security Council Resolution 242's statement about the "inadmissibility of the acquisition of territory by war."[16]

Begin replied: "Security Council Resolution 242 does not say that. It says land is not to be taken by war. Mr. President, the difference is significant. There are defensive wars, too. It's not so simple."[17]

Carter and Sadat continued throughout the summit to maintain that it was indeed just that simple, and the language and interpretation of Resolution 242 continued to be a point of contention.

The auspices were not good for the Israelis.

"You Roared Like a Lion"

Later, after Sadat, Begin, and Carter met, the Egyptian president had another story for his advisers: "I wish you could have heard President Carter say to me after the tripartite meeting: 'You roared like a lion when you told Begin in front of me that neither yourself nor he, nor even King Hussein [of Jordan], can claim sovereignty over the West Bank and Gaza, and that the Palestinian people were alone entitled to do so.'"[18] Carter later recounted that during the same meeting, as they discussed Sadat's framework, "I tried to break the tension by telling Begin that if he would sign the document as written, it would save us all a lot of time."[19]

Sadat grew so used to Carter's obsequiousness that when Carter, in an opening speech the first night of the summit, praised him and Begin on roughly equal terms for being men who had the courage and vision to try to make peace, Sadat was annoyed. "It was I," he said stiffly, "who made the peace initiative." He didn't mention the Soviet pressure. "Had Begin really desired peace, we would have had it for some time now. And there would have been no cause for our presence here now."[20]

At that point one of Sadat's aides, Hassan el-Tohamy, addressed Carter himself, claiming that "one of Begin's inner circle" had told him while Sadat and his entourage were in Jerusalem: "Why have you come to Jerusalem? We are satisfied with the present situation and our occupation of the land we have liberated. Peace at present is not in our interest!"[21] Carter brushed this aside, but Tohamy's unfortunate interruption precluded any response from Carter to Sadat's ungracious self-aggrandizement and belittling of the Israeli prime minister. Not that it is likely that "poor naïve Carter" would have had a word of protest for this "great and good man."

Nothing Left to Concede

A bit later on in the summit, Sadat went for a walk with Kamel and spoke to him in terms that made it clear that he understood his dealings with the Israelis in light of the Qur'an's frequent condemnations of Jews: "We are dealing with the lowest and meanest of enemies. The Jews even tormented their Prophet Moses, and exasperated their God!"[22] He was silent for a time, and then said: "I pity poor Carter in his dealings with Begin, with his stilted mentality."[23] Kamel then asked Sadat if he thought Carter would put pressure on Begin. "Of course he will," Sadat replied.[24] "Otherwise the Conference will flounder, and that will affect Carter's position. I have made it clear to him that I have offered everything in order to bring about a peace which the Israelis could never have imagined in their wildest dreams, and I told him there was nothing left for me to concede."[25]

But Sadat had actually conceded absolutely nothing, unless the act of concluding a peace treaty with the State of Israel, rather than remaining in a state of perpetual war, could be considered a concession.

Moments after Sadat railed against the Jews as "the lowest and meanest of enemies," he and Kamel ran into Israeli defense minister Ezer Weizman, who asked Sadat if he could talk with him that day.

Suddenly the new, charming, peacemaking Sadat reappeared. "Of course!" he told Weizman. "It's always a pleasure to talk to you!"[26]

"I Became Angry, and Almost Shouted"

The primary acolyte of Sadat the peacemaker, Jimmy Carter, was ready to press Begin for concessions. On the summit's third day, when Carter and Begin met, Begin took issue with the references to the "Palestinians" in Sadat's framework. "Palestinians!" Begin exclaimed. "This is an unacceptable reference. Jews are also Palestinians. He must mean 'Palestinian Arabs.'"[27] Carter recounted: "This was to develop into a difficult issue later on, which could be resolved only by special footnote entries in the signed agreement."[28] Regardless of the footnote entries, however, the main Camp David documents referred to the "Palestinians," a significant concession on Begin's part to the propaganda initiative to invent a nationality that had begun less than two decades before.

Carter quickly came to the heart of the matter, asking Begin: "Are you willing to withdraw from the occupied territories and honor Palestinian rights, in exchange for adequate assurances for your security, including an internationally recognized treaty of peace? If not, Egypt will eventually turn away from the peace process, and the full power of the Arabs, and perhaps world opinion, will be marshaled against you."[29]

That was what Israel was being offered: land for assurances. Given the Islamic imperative to "drive them out from where they drove you out," however, it was an open question as to how ironclad those assurances could be. And even if they were ironclad on Sadat's part, there were many other Muslims for whom they would never be acceptable and who would never honor them.

Tensions ran high between Carter and Begin. At one point, Carter recalled, "I became angry, and almost shouted" at the Israeli prime minister.[30] Carter also asked Begin to make "a generous concession that would respond to Sadat's trip to Jerusalem."[31] Begin replied that Sadat had been given a rapturous welcome in Jerusalem, and that was a fitting enough response to Sadat's overture. As they went on to discuss Sadat's framework, Begin said that it would turn the Jews into a minority in Israel, and likened it to the Treaty of Versailles, which had ended World War I, with Israel cast as Germany and with the defeated party making enormous concessions to the victors. He said that Sadat wanted a peace treaty that would not only weaken Israel but put it on the path to total destruction.[32]

When the three again met, Begin insisted that there could be no Palestinian state. "We will not allow," he said, "the establishment of a base for Yasser Arafat's murderers within our borders, including the redivision of Jerusalem. There can be no agreement on the basis of these demands."[33]

Sadat replied: "No! I said yesterday that there is no need to divide Jerusalem."[34] This was true, but only partially. His framework directed that "Israel shall withdraw from Jerusalem to the demarcation lines of the Armistice Agreement of 1949 in conformity with the Principle of the inadmissibility of the acquisition of territory by war. Arab sovereignty and administration shall be restored to the Arab sector." However, the city would not technically be divided, since "a joint municipal council composed of an equal number of Palestinian and Israeli members" would be created in order to regulate and supervise public utilities, public transportation, the postal service and utilities.[35]

Begin then told Sadat: "You address us as if we were a defeated nation. You demand we pay compensation for damages incurred by Egyptian civilians. I would like you to know that we also claim damages from you."[36] This enraged Sadat, who launched into a litany of grievances, concluding petulantly, "I thought that after my initiative there would be a period of goodwill. We are giving you peace and you want territories."[37] As the atmosphere grew even more heated, Sadat shouted, "Premier Begin, you want land!"[38] and "Security, yes! Land, no!" He insisted that Egyptian territory must be "clean-shaved" of any Israeli presence.[39] Sadat was furious at Begin's unwillingness to make concessions: "Minimum confidence does not exist anymore," he lamented, "since Premier Begin has acted in bad faith."[40]

Neither Sadat nor Carter was willing to consider the possibility that Israel needed land in order to ensure its security. Promises and even treaties would not by themselves give Israel the land, or the security, it needed. While Sadat may have been willing to give up the jihad imperative to "drive them out from where they drove you out," if he wasn't simply working toward attaining it by different means from those that Muslim Arabs had employed previously, other Muslim Arabs in the countries neighboring Israel were more committed to jihad than ever, and were determined to destroy the Jewish state.

But at Camp David, despite Begin's best efforts, these concerns were never seriously or adequately addressed. Begin pointed out that Sinai had been the base of attacks on Israel from Egypt in 1948, 1967, and 1973, the last one initiated by Sadat himself. He maintained that Israel needed to keep the Sinai and maintain Israeli settlements there as a matter of national security. "Never!" Sadat shot back. "If you do not agree to evacuate the settlements, there will be no peace."[41] He complained: "I have tried to provide a model of friendship and coexistence for the rest of the Arab world leaders to emulate. Instead, I have become the object of extreme insult from Israel, and scorn and condemnation from other Arab leaders."[42]

The summit several times came close to breaking down. Carter met with the Egyptian delegation and told them: "I know you are all very discouraged."[43] On the Sinai settlements, "our position is that they are illegal and should be removed. On this, your views and ours are the same."[44] Addressing "my good friend Jimmy," Sadat reiterated his position and declared: "The man is obsessed, he's a hopeless case, he keeps citing European precedents, but we have not been defeated. Begin haggles over every word. Begin is making withdrawal conditional on land acquisition. Begin is not ready for peace."[45] Carter then, unusually, defended Begin, but Sadat wouldn't budge: "It was I who made the peace initiative. If Begin had really desired peace, we would have had it for some time now."[46] And he insisted that not only must he get his way regarding the Sinai but he "must have also a resolution of the West Bank and Gaza."[47]

After this stalemate lasted a bit longer, Carter told Secretary of State Cyrus Vance: "I think we ought to get tough on the Israelis, and the time has come to let them know this."[48] After another tense and fruitless meeting with Begin, Carter drank mint tea with Sadat and proposed a joint Egyptian-American agreement, even if the Israelis refused to be a party to it. Sadat was happy. "You write it," he told Carter, like a superior giving orders to a trusted underling. "You know the issues that are important to me. I will support any reasonable document you put forth."[49]

"The Americans Have Simply Copied the Egyptian Plan"

When Carter presented his proposals to Begin, they got into yet another argument over the meaning of Resolution 242. Carter asked Begin: "Do you reject United Nations Resolution 242?" Referring to Begin's objection to the clause about the "inadmissibility of acquisition of territory by war," Carter said: "To delete this phrase would mean that we have no basis for negotiation now or in the future. What you say convinces me that Sadat was right—what you want is land!"[50]

Carter never gave any indication that he understood or appreciated the fact that Begin wanted security, and that security could only be obtained by means of holding on to certain territories, as nations had done throughout history. When Begin told him that his interpretation of Resolution 242 "has been our position for eleven years," Carter replied acidly: "Maybe that's why you haven't had peace for eleven years."[51]

Begin explained: "You should know, Mr. President, that in all the wars we were the victims of Arab aggression."[52]

Carter was unmoved; the phrase would remain, despite the fact that it stripped Israel of its right to claim territory conquered in wartime in order to strengthen its own defenses. "Mr. Prime

Minister," he told Begin, "that is not only the view of Sadat, it is also the American view—and you will have to accept it."[53] Angrily he repeated, "You will have to accept it."[54]

Wearily, Begin replied, "Mr. President. No threats, please."[55]

Grimly, Begin reported back to his advisers: "Gentlemen, the Americans have simply copied the Egyptian plan."[56]

At one point, Carter told Begin, "Listen, we're trying to help you bring peace to your land. You would have us feel that we are going out of our way deliberately to be as unfair to Israel as possible."[57] Well, yes. Boiling over in frustration at Begin's refusal to make vast concessions, Carter told his wife, Rosalynn, that the Israeli prime minister was a "psycho."[58]

Still, the talks continued. At one point Sadat hinted to Carter that he would allow Israel to play a role in deciding which Palestinians could be allowed to settle in the West Bank. This was a significant development, as it might open the way for Israel to agree to withdraw from that area. But then Osama al-Baz, one of the Egyptian delegates, told Carter just the opposite: that Sadat would never agree to such a thing. When Baz reported all this back to his boss, Sadat responded: "You're right. It is impossible for me to agree to an article like that. But you know my strategy, Osama. We want to gain Carter for our side. I know he's a weak man, but let's be patient."[59]

Sadat's patience paid off. A compromise was hit upon: the question of whether or not Israel would dismantle its settlements in the occupied territories was left to the Knesset. And glossing over what had repeatedly been a point of contention, the documents stated: "The agreed basis for a peaceful settlement of the conflict between Israel and its neighbors is United Nations Security Council Resolution 242, in all its parts."[60] But what exactly Resolution 242 meant regarding the need for Israel to withdraw from territories it had won in the Six-Day War was not discussed. Jerusalem was not mentioned except in reference to "the historic initiative of President Sadat in visiting" it.[61]

There was also no talk of compensation for Palestinians or Egyptians. Aware that the Palestinians were an invented people, Begin had wanted the documents to refer to "Palestinian Arabs," but Carter dismissed this as meaningless nitpicking. In most respects, the final "Framework for Peace in the Middle East" was substantially like Sadat's "Framework for the Comprehensive Peace Settlement of the Middle East Problem."

As for the West Bank and Gaza, there would be "a peaceful and orderly transfer of authority" that would ultimately "provide full autonomy to the inhabitants" and would involve the withdrawal of "the Israeli military government and its civilian administration."[62]

The accompanying "Framework for the Conclusion of a Peace Treaty between Egypt and Israel" announced that Egypt and Israel agreed to "the full exercise of Egyptian sovereignty up to the internationally recognized border between Egypt and mandated Palestine" and "the withdrawal of Israeli armed forces from the Sinai."[63] That doomed the Israeli settlements there, which could not exist without Israeli military protection. Egypt and Israel, pledged to resolve their differences through peaceful means, would establish full diplomatic relations.

The Signing

On September 17, 1978, the "Framework for Peace in the Middle East" and the "Framework for the Conclusion of a Peace Treaty between Egypt and Israel" were signed. Carter, Sadat, and Begin all spoke on this happy occasion, in that order. Carter praised "the courage and wisdom of these two leaders," noting that both of them, "through 13 long days at Camp David," had displayed "determination and vision and flexibility which was needed to make this agreement come to pass."[64] Carter added: "All of us owe them our gratitude and respect. They know that they will always have my personal admiration."[65]

Carter announced that "these negotiations will be based on all the provisions and all the principles of the United Nations Security Council Resolution 242," including, though this was not emphasized, its rejection of the acquisition of territory by war.[66] "And it provides," Carter said, "that Israel may live in peace within secure and recognized borders."[67] For this, Carter praised Sadat effusively: "This great aspiration of Israel has been certified without constraint with the greatest degree of enthusiasm by President Sadat, the leader of one of the greatest nations on earth."[68] He had no words of specific praise for Begin, whom he did not mention by name.

Sadat addressed his remarks to Carter, whom he called his "dear friend."[69] He did not refer to Begin in the same way, or at all (although he did address him as "my dear friend the Prime Minister" at a joint press conference with Begin in Haifa on September 5, 1979).[70] But at the September 1978 signing, Sadat slyly reiterated before the world his earlier claim to have been the originator of the entire rapprochement, thanking Carter, who had invited him and Begin to Camp David, for joining him in his initiative: "You made a commitment to be a full partner in the peace process. I am happy to say that you have honored your commitment."[71]

Begin himself, on the other hand, was the most lavish in his praise of his two counterparts. "The Camp David conference," he declared, "should be renamed. It was the Jimmy Carter Conference. The President took an initiative most imaginative in our time and brought President Sadat and myself and our colleagues and friends and advisers together under one roof. In itself it was a great achievement."[72] What Carter had done was world-historical: "Mr. President," Begin told him, "you inscribed your name forever in the history of two ancient civilized peoples, the people of Egypt and the people of Israel."[73]

Then Begin turned to Sadat, to whom he referred as his friend three times in four sentences: "I would like to say a few words about my friend, President Sadat. We met for the first time in our lives last November in Jerusalem. He came to us as a guest, a former enemy, and during our first meeting, we became friends. In the Jewish teachings, there is a tradition that the greatest achievement of a human being is to turn his enemy into a friend, and this we do in reciprocity."[74]

Was Sadat really Begin's friend? Had he had a change of heart since his pre–Camp David confidence that the summit would be "Begin's downfall"? Had he softened since the early days of the summit, when he had characterized the Israelis as the "lowest and meanest of enemies"?

And does it even matter? Sadat may well have despised Begin personally, but he nonetheless made peace, and isn't that what counts? What's more, he paid the ultimate price for this accord with Israel. Islamic jihadis, enraged that Sadat had abandoned the jihad and come to an accord with Israel, assassinated him in Cairo on October 6, 1981. The mastermind of the murder, the Egyptian army lieutenant Khalid al-Islambouli, is revered as a martyr for Islam throughout the Islamic world; jihad groups as far off as Chechnya name themselves after him.[75]

Maybe the fact that Sadat was willing to make peace at all, and gave his life for doing so, is all that counts, and establishes Sadat as a martyr for peace. But Sadat obtained that peace without making any significant concessions to the Israelis, who gave up a great deal for that peace with Egypt. The Camp David summit wasn't Adolf Hitler browbeating Czechoslovakia's Emil Hácha into submission, but neither was it a summit of three people who respected one another as equals. Neither Carter nor Sadat had any respect for Begin. Sadat had scant respect for Carter, either, but cultivated his friendship as useful. Carter had boundless admiration and regard for Sadat, bordering on hero worship, and Carter and Sadat were in substantial agreement about what had to be done. All this put Begin and the Israelis at a decided disadvantage.

The speeches at the signing are important for what they show about Sadat and Carter's closeness. They also reveal that in this group, Begin was an outsider, whose repeated affirmations that Sadat was his friend may have betrayed an intense desire that it be so, more than it was in reality. Could Begin and the Israelis have accepted the uneven terms both Sadat and Carter insisted they take at Camp

David simply out of a desire finally not to be hated, to be accepted in the community of nations as equals, and even indeed as friends?

"Mr. President, I Believe My Assignment Has Been Carried Out Satisfactorily. You Will Be Pleased."

The same dynamic played out again in March 1979, when Carter traveled first to Jerusalem and then to Cairo to hammer out the details of the Egypt-Israel peace treaty. In Jerusalem, Carter once again played the role of messenger, relaying Sadat's demands. Then in Cairo, Carter recounted his meeting with Begin to Sadat as if he were an underling reporting to his superior: "Mr. President, I believe my assignment has been carried out satisfactorily. You will be pleased."[76] Sadat was ready with praise for his subordinate: "Marvelous."[77] Carter then told Sadat: "For the first two days Begin behaved the way he does normally. He was unpleasant, interrupted me. But then the moderates began to convince him to be more constructive."[78]

In a private meeting with several of his aides later, Carter, according to Zbigniew Brzezinski, "made earthy comments about Begin personally."[79]

A "Surrenderist Agreement"

The reaction to the Camp David Accords in the Arab and Islamic world was mixed but generally negative. Some hailed the fact that for the first time, the Israelis had recognized the existence of "the Palestinian people." However, the Accords' ambiguous acknowledgment of the "legitimate rights of the Palestinian people," wording that Begin had questioned, raised eyebrows. The political analyst Fayez A. Sayegh asked in the *Journal of Palestine Studies*: "Where indeed is the line of demarcation to be drawn, as between the 'legitimate' and the 'not-so-legitimate' or perhaps 'illegitimate' rights of the Palestinian people?"[80]

The PLO, which the Israelis for all their concessions had not recognized as the legitimate representative of the Palestinian people, condemned the Camp David Accords as a "surrenderist agreement…a de facto sanctification of the occupation with a new guise."[81] Sadat, the PLO charged, had taken a "capitulationist road" that meant "nothing but the granting of a legal character and consecration of the action of occupying our land and swallowing it."[82] The PLO called the idea of Palestinian administration in Gaza and the West Bank a "very filthy project among the politically naïve and the opportunists among our fellow citizens."[83] Only the total destruction of Israel would do.

The Arab League likewise condemned the agreement and condemned Egypt as well, for entering into it. The Arabs' struggle against Israel, it said, was "a battle of destiny and civilization," a "fateful struggle" that needed the support of "all the forces of peace and justice throughout the world."[84] Reflecting the view of the conflict as between the Arabs in their totality and the Israelis, the understanding that had prevailed before the Palestinian people were invented, the league reaffirmed that its "conflict with the Zionist enemy goes beyond the struggle of the countries whose territories were occupied in 1967 and involves the entire Arab nation."[85]

The Organization of the Islamic Conference was also enraged, condemning all negotiations with Israel and suspending Egypt's membership in the organization for entering into talks with the Zionists.[86]

On the other hand, the Camp David Accords were generally popular in Israel, but there were some dissenters. Shmuel Katz, the Begin adviser who had tried to explain the realities of the Israeli-Palestinian conflict to Carter the year before, resigned in protest against the many concessions the Israeli prime minister had made.[87] Katz would have agreed with the PLO that the Camp David Accords were a "surrenderist agreement," but would have insisted that the ones doing the surrendering were actually the Israelis. They had recognized the fiction of the "Palestinian people," given up the Sinai, and agreed to Palestinian administration of the West Bank and Gaza in exchange for what has proved to be an exceedingly cold peace with Egypt.

It may be, however, that Israel had no choice but to accept what the American president wanted it to. And so the Camp David Accords, with their one-sided concessions, set yet another bad precedent. Camp David became the paradigm of Israeli-Palestinian negotiations in which American presidents press the Israelis for concessions while asking little to nothing of the Palestinians, such that the overall outcome is a weakened Israel.

Even in the warm glow of the aftermath of Camp David, Carter kept the pressure up on Begin. When the Israeli government on October 26, 1978, accompanied acceptance of the Egypt-Israel peace treaty with a decision to expand Israeli settlements in Judea and Samaria, Carter was enraged. "At a time when we are trying to organize the negotiations dealing with the West Bank and Gaza," he wrote to Begin, "no step by the Israeli government could be more damaging." On this typed letter he added a handwritten note: "I have to tell you with gravest concern and regret that taking this step at this time will have the most serious consequences for our relationship."[88]

But Carter never really had a friendly relationship with the man he had once called a "psycho." Carter and Begin attended Sadat's funeral; they did not speak to each other.[89] Carter in his dotage has hardened into a vociferous foe of Israel, which he now accuses of apartheid. He has been frequently accused, not without justification, of anti-Semitism. His views since Camp David may not so much have evolved as become more explicitly articulated.

CHAPTER SEVEN

Hudaybiyya Revisited

Refusing Israel

The Camp David Accords' "Framework for Peace in the Middle East" declared that "Egypt, Israel, Jordan and the representatives of the Palestinian people should participate in negotiations on the resolution of the Palestinian problem in all its aspects."[1]

This posed an insuperable problem from the moment that Anwar Sadat, Menachem Begin, and Jimmy Carter signed the documents. While the Arab League accepted the PLO as the "sole legitimate representative of the Palestinian people," and the United Nations likewise saw it as "the representative of the Palestinian people," the government of Israel refused to accept it.[2]

There was a very simple reason for this: the PLO refused to accept Israel.

The Palestine Liberation Organization's Palestinian National Charter, adopted in May 1964 and revised in July 1968, declared that "Palestine, with the boundaries it had during the British Mandate, is an indivisible territorial unit," and that "the partition of Palestine in 1947 and the establishment of the state of Israel are entirely illegal...."

The Balfour Declaration, the Mandate for Palestine, and everything that has been based upon them, are deemed null and void."[3] What's more, "claims of historical or religious ties of Jews with Palestine are incompatible with the facts of history and the true conception of what constitutes statehood."[4]

Consequently, "the Arab Palestinian people, expressing themselves by the armed Palestinian revolution, reject all solutions which are substitutes for the total liberation of Palestine and reject all proposals aiming at the liquidation of the Palestinian problem, or its internationalization."[5]

If Palestine was indivisible and partition illegitimate, the State of Israel illegal and "the total liberation of Palestine" the goal, then the PLO, which had a better claim than any other group to be "the representatives of the Palestinian people," was committed to Israel's complete destruction. If the PLO rejected "all proposals aiming at the liquidation of the Palestinian problem," there was no point in Israel's opening up any negotiations with the group, and no desire among the Palestinian leadership for negotiations anyway.

Thus the Camp David Accords' determination to resolve "the Palestinian problem in all its aspects" was a dead letter. Making matters worse was the fact that the Palestinians and their allies continued jihad terror attacks against Israeli civilians, culminating in the First Intifada of 1987–1991, during which the United Nations began its now well-established practice of condemning Israel without taking into account Palestinian actions or Israel's security requirements.

However, the intifada and the rise of a murderous new jihad group led to a new round in the "peace process."

"Israel Will Rise and Will Remain Erect Until Islam Eliminates It"

With the intifada in full swing, a new group arose that thoroughly alarmed the Israelis and drastically altered the course of the "peace process": the Islamic Resistance Movement, Harakat al-Muqawamah al-Islamiyyah, known by its Arabic acronym, Hamas.

Hamas was founded in August 1988 as an Islamic alternative to the PLO's secularism and willingness to negotiate. The Hamas Charter criticized the PLO (whose own charter makes no reference to Islam at all) for forsaking Islam under the sway of foreign influences: "Under the influence of the circumstances which surrounded the founding of the PLO, and the ideological confusion which prevails in the Arab world as a result of the ideological invasion which has swept the Arab world since the rout of the Crusades, and which has been reinforced by Orientalism and the Christian Mission, the PLO has adopted the idea of a Secular State."[6]

Such a state, in Hamas's view, must be rejected; only an Islamic state would suffice for Palestine: "Secular thought is diametrically opposed to religious thought. Thought is the basis for positions, for modes of conduct and for resolutions. Therefore, in spite of our appreciation for the PLO and its possible transformation in the future, and despite the fact that we do not denigrate its role in the Arab-Israeli conflict, we cannot substitute it for the Islamic nature of Palestine by adopting secular thought. For the Islamic nature of Palestine is part of our religion, and anyone who neglects his religion is bound to lose."[7] The charter followed this with a quotation from the Qur'an: "And who forsakes the religion of Abraham, except him who makes a fool of himself?" (2:130)

Hamas opened the door to a future accord with the PLO, but only if the PLO came around to accepting the centrality of Islam: "When the PLO adopts Islam as the guideline for life, then we shall become its soldiers, the fuel of its fire which will burn the enemies."[8]

Hamas identified itself in the charter as "one of the wings of the Muslim Brothers in Palestine. The Muslim Brotherhood Movement is a world organization, the largest Islamic Movement in the modern era. It is characterized by a profound understanding, by precise notions and by a complete comprehensiveness of all concepts of Islam in all domains of life: views and beliefs, politics and economics, education and society, jurisprudence and rule, indoctrination and teaching, the arts and publications, the hidden and the evident, and all the other domains of life."[9]

The Muslim Brotherhood is a global movement that originated in Egypt with the determination of restoring the Islamic caliphate and imposing the rule of Sharia wherever and whenever possible. It was founded by Hasan al-Banna, who was quoted in the Hamas charter: "Israel will rise and will remain erect until Islam eliminates it as it had eliminated its predecessors."[10]

In keeping with this guiding idea that Islam must, and will, be the force that ultimately eliminates Israel, and that Islamic principles must rule all aspects of life, Hamas stated its membership and its mission in the broadest possible terms, complete with copious quotes from the Qur'an: "The Islamic Resistance Movement consists of Muslims who are devoted to Allah and worship Him verily [as it is written]: 'I have created Man and Devil for the purpose of their worship' [of Allah].... They have raised the banner of Jihad in the face of the oppressors in order to extricate the country and the people from the [oppressors'] desecration, filth and evil. 'Nay, but we hurl the true against the false; and it does break its head and lo! it vanishes' Sura 21 (the Prophets), verse 18."[11]

Hamas's goal was avowedly religious. "As the Movement adopts Islam as its way of life, its time dimension extends back as far as the birth of the Islamic Message and of the Righteous Ancestor. Its ultimate goal is Islam, the Prophet its model, the Quran its Constitution."[12]

As Islam is a universal religion, proclaiming itself to be the guiding belief system for all mankind, so Hamas declared that its mission was not restricted to Israel only: "Its spatial dimension extends wherever on earth there are Muslims, who adopt Islam as their way of life; thus, it penetrates to the deepest reaches of the land and to the highest spheres of Heavens.... By virtue of the distribution of Muslims, who pursue the cause of the Hamas, all over the globe, and strive for its victory, for the reinforcement of its positions and for the encouragement of its Jihad, the Movement is a universal one."[13]

The Hamas Charter rejected the "peace process" as inimical to Islamic principles: "[Peace] initiatives, the so-called peaceful solutions, and the international conferences to resolve the Palestinian problem, are all contrary to the beliefs of the Islamic Resistance Movement. For renouncing any part of Palestine means renouncing part of the religion; the nationalism of the Islamic Resistance Movement is part of its faith, the movement educates its members to adhere to its principles and to raise the banner of Allah over their homeland as they fight their Jihad: 'Allah is the all-powerful, but most people are not aware.'"[14]

The intifada led many Israeli leaders to the conclusion that the status quo in Gaza and the West Bank could not be preserved, and that the time had come to implement the Camp David Accords' directive that an autonomous Palestinian governing organization be established. The rise of Hamas at the same time led some Israeli leaders to believe that the best hope for peace lay in negotiations with a group they had previously referred to only as a terrorist organization that must be defeated, not as a "peace partner": the Palestine Liberation Organization (PLO).

"Faith in Political and Diplomatic Struggle as Complements"

The PLO was willing to play this new role. As far back as 1974, PLO chairman Yasser Arafat had affirmed his willingness to negotiate, although he made it clear that he saw negotiations the way Sadat did, as a means to obtain what one could not get by force of arms. He told the UN General Assembly that he had "faith in political and diplomatic struggle as complements, as enhancements of our armed struggle."[15]

At that time, however, Arafat was referring to talks with other governments of the world, not with Israel, as the PLO was still committed to rejecting all negotiations with the Israelis and pursuing the Jewish state's total destruction. On June 8, 1974, the Palestine National Council adopted a Political Program that stated: "The

Palestine Liberation Organization will employ all means, and first and foremost armed struggle, to liberate Palestinian territory and to establish the independent combatant national authority for the people over every part of Palestinian territory that is liberated."[16] This struggle would advance in stages, and "any step taken towards liberation is a step towards the realization of the Liberation Organization's strategy of establishing the democratic Palestinian State specified in the resolutions of the previous Palestinian National Councils." The goal was "completing the liberation of all Palestinian territory," that is, completely destroying Israel.

In a political communiqué issued by the Palestine National Council, meeting in Algiers on November 15, 1988, the PLO reaffirmed that goal, stating that its "national program" was "aimed at the termination of the occupation and the achievement of our people's right to return, self-determination, and statehood."[17] The ending of the "occupation" would mean either Israel's withdrawal to indefensible borders or its total eradication, depending on how the word was defined, and if anything of Israel remained as a Jewish state, the "right of return" would finish it off.

But a hint that the PLO's stance was changing came on the same day, in, paradoxically enough, its Declaration of Palestinian Independence, which stated: "Despite the historical injustice inflicted on the Palestinian Arab people resulting in their dispersion and depriving them of their right to self-determination, following upon U.N. General Assembly Resolution 181 (1947), which partitioned Palestine into two states, one Arab, one Jewish, yet it is this Resolution that still provides those conditions of international legitimacy that ensure the right of the Palestinian Arab people to sovereignty."[18]

This was momentous, since for four decades before this declaration, Arab Muslim leaders, both before and after they became "Palestinian," had adamantly rejected Resolution 181 and any partitioning of Palestine. Now the PLO was invoking Resolution 181 as the basis for the "international legitimacy" of a sovereign Palestinian

Arab state. It did not include any acceptance of a Jewish state, but there did appear to be a tiny opening of the door.

"Reach Out to the Palestinians"

Then in December 1988, against the backdrop of the intifada and the rise of Hamas, Arafat flung the door wide open, proclaiming that the PLO "accepted the existence of Israel as a state in the region" and "declared its rejection and condemnation of terrorism in all its forms."[19]

At a subsequent press conference, Arafat went even further in contradicting the Palestinian National Charter, saying: "We accept two states, the Palestine state and the Jewish state of Israel."[20] Addressing the United Nations on December 13, 1988, Arafat repeated that the Palestine National Council had "reaffirmed its rejection of terrorism in all its forms, including state terrorism.... This position, Mr. President, is clear and free of all ambiguity. And yet, I, as chairman of the Palestine Liberation Organization, hereby once more declare that I condemn terrorism in all its forms."[21]

UN secretary-general Javier Pérez de Cuéllar was thrilled, asserting that these statements offered "fresh opportunities...for fresh progress toward peace."[22] Israeli foreign minister Shimon Peres, however, dismissed Arafat's words as a "cunning exercise in public relations" and called on the PLO leader to end the Palestinians' violence against Israelis.[23] Coming after so much of that violence, which continued, Arafat's words were greeted with considerable skepticism, both within Israel and elsewhere.

Yet Arafat persisted. Early in May 1989, during a trip to France, he told reporters: "As for the 25-year-old Palestinian National Charter, I believe you have an expression in French, 'C'est caduc,' it's null and void."[24]

The United States, which had been engaging in discussions with the PLO for several years, signaled that as far as it was concerned, this was sufficient. On May 22, 1989, during an address to the American Israel Public Affairs Committee (AIPAC), Secretary of State James

Baker called on the Israeli government once again to make concessions in order to obtain peace: "For Israel, now is the time to lay aside, once and for all, the unrealistic vision of a greater Israel. Israeli interests in the West Bank and Gaza—security and otherwise—can be accommodated in a settlement based on Resolution 242. Forswear annexation. Stop settlement activity. Allow schools to reopen. Reach out to the Palestinians as neighbors who deserve political rights."[25]

The rapid ascendancy of Hamas turned the apparent willingness of the PLO to enter into negotiations into a message that the Israeli government, under the leadership of the leftist Labor Party Prime Minister Yitzhak Rabin, very much wanted to hear. On September 29, 1989, while he was Israel's defense minister, Rabin said: "The reality today is that the only partner with whom Israel can, perhaps, enter into a political process is the Palestinians...and whoever does not see this is not reading the map correctly."[26] Returning to the prime minister's office (he had previously served as prime minister from 1974 to 1977), Rabin began moving toward a new round in the "peace process," although he emphasized in his inaugural speech to the Knesset on July 13, 1992, that "when it comes to security, we will concede nothing. From our standpoint, security takes preference even over peace."[27]

He thought, however, that the time was auspicious for a peace settlement: "No longer are we necessarily a 'people that dwells alone,' and no longer is it true that 'the whole world is against us.' We must overcome the sense of isolation that has held us in its thrall for almost half a century. We must join the international movement towards peace, reconciliation and cooperation that is spreading all over the entire globe these days—lest we be the last to remain, all alone, at the station. The new Government has accordingly made it a central goal to promote the making of peace and take vigorous steps that will lead to the end of the Arab-Israeli conflict."[28]

Had Anwar Sadat lived to hear these words, he might have chuckled to his aides about "poor naïve Rabin," and all the more so in light of the fact that in the same speech, Rabin noted that "a number of countries in our region have recently stepped up their efforts to develop and produce nuclear arms.... The possibility that nuclear weapons will be introduced in the Middle East in the coming years is a very grave and negative development from Israel's standpoint.... [T]his situation requires us to give further thought to the urgent need to end the Arab-Israeli conflict and live in peace with our Arab neighbors."[29]

To obtain this peace, Rabin was prepared to make significant concessions: "As a first step toward a permanent solution we shall discuss the institution of autonomy in Judea, Samaria, and the Gaza District.... As a first step, to illustrate our sincerity and good will, I wish to invite the Jordanian-Palestinian delegation to an informal talk, here in Jerusalem, so that we can hear their views, make ours heard, and create an appropriate atmosphere for neighborly relations."[30]

Once again, the gestures of goodwill and conciliation, desires for friendly relations and substantive concessions came from only the Israeli side.

"In the Line of Fire Against the Danger of Fundamentalist Islam"

That Rabin thought the Arab-Israeli conflict could be definitively ended by means of negotiations shows that he didn't understand the root causes of that conflict at all, but he did have some understanding of the resurgent Islamic jihad and its significance. In December 1992, Rabin addressed the Knesset after having deported several leaders of Hamas and another jihad group that was set against Israel, Islamic Jihad, to Lebanon:

> *Our struggle against murderous Islamic terror is also meant to awaken the world which is lying [in] slumber. We call on all nations and all people to devote their attention to the great danger inherent in Islamic fundamentalism. That is the real and serious danger which threatens the peace of the world in the forthcoming years. The*

danger of death is at our doorstep. And just as the state of Israel was
the first to perceive the Iraqi nuclear threat, so today we stand in the
line of fire against the danger of fundamentalist Islam.[31]

Rabin saw the growing popularity of these groups among the
Palestinian Arabs, and thought it placed Israel in a race against time.
He noted in December 1992 that "today Iran is the leading dissem-
inator of fundamentalist Islam in the region.... Within seven years
from today, this will be the threat in the Middle East. We have this
time to resolve problems. I believe we will succeed."[32] He thought a
lasting peace was attainable well within that seven-year time span; in
September 1992, he declared: "I believe that we are on a path of no
return...to reach peace, even if it takes another year or two years."[33]

With Hamas and its allied groups advocating all-out jihad against
Israel, the Israelis would turn to the secular PLO. In November 1992,
Rabin said in a speech at Tel Aviv University:

I believe that among the leadership of the territories and outside of
the territories, maybe even in [PLO headquarters in] Tunisia, there
are today Palestinian leaders who have wised up, and they under-
stand that they cannot repeat the mistakes of the past.... There are
many among them who understand that it is better to establish the
nucleus of a Palestinian entity, even if it is administrative.[34]

Rabin was saying that there existed Palestinian leaders who were
willing to enter into negotiations with the Israelis and establish a
Palestinian administrative authority for Gaza and Judea and Samaria,
even if it fell short of being an actual independent Palestinian state.

The Israeli leadership quietly began communicating with Yasser
Arafat and the rest of the Palestinian leadership, and found them
receptive to the possibility of negotiations. Those negotiations were
held in secret in Oslo, Norway. By September 1993, the two sides
had agreed to a peace accord, known as the Declaration of Principles on Interim Self-Government Arrangements, which began by
stating that "the Government of the State of Israel and the PLO team

(the 'Palestinian Delegation'), representing the Palestinian people, agree that it is time to put an end to decades of confrontation and conflict, recognize their mutual legitimate and political rights, and strive to live in peaceful coexistence and mutual dignity and security and achieve a just, lasting and comprehensive peace settlement and historic reconciliation through the agreed political process."[35]

They agreed to begin negotiations "within the current Middle East peace process" in order to "establish a Palestinian Interim Self-Government Authority" in the West Bank and Gaza.[36] Israel would withdraw from some areas, which would come under direct Palestinian control. Over a period of years, the Israelis would withdraw from more territories, and the scope of that Palestinian control would expand. The Oslo Accords paved the way for the establishment in May 1994 of the Palestinian Authority, the self-governing entity of which Arafat appointed himself the first president.

"The PLO Recognizes the Right of the State of Israel to Exist in Peace and Security"

But before that could be done, the sticking point of the Palestinian National Charter's statements supporting the total destruction of Israel had to be addressed. Accordingly, four days before the Declaration of Principles was formally adopted by the government of Israel and the PLO, Yasser Arafat addressed a portentous letter to Israeli Prime Minister Yitzhak Rabin:

> *The signing of the Declaration of Principles marks a new era.... I would like to confirm the following PLO commitments: The PLO recognizes the right of the State of Israel to exist in peace and security. The PLO accepts United Nations Security Council Resolutions 242 and 338. The PLO commits itself...to a peaceful resolution of the conflict between the two sides and declares that all outstanding issues relating to permanent status will be resolved through negotiations.... [T]he PLO renounces the use of terrorism and other acts of violence and will assume responsibility over all PLO elements and personnel*

in order to assure their compliance, prevent violations and discipline violators.... [T]he PLO affirms that those articles of the Palestinian Covenant which deny Israel's right to exist, and the provisions of the Covenant which are inconsistent with the commitments of this letter are now inoperative and no longer valid. Consequently, the PLO undertakes to submit to the Palestinian National Council for formal approval the necessary changes in regard to the Palestinian Covenant.[37]

Arafat's letter did not go as far as his 1988 statements. At that time, he had said: "We accept two states, the Palestine state and the Jewish state of Israel." Now, however, he was recognizing only "the right of the State of Israel to exist in peace and security." He made no mention of recognizing Israel as a "Jewish state." If, as he demanded, Palestinians were to be granted a "right of return" to Israel, they could in a short time overwhelm the Jewish population of Israel, and transform the nation into something quite different from a Jewish state.

Arafat spoke about this more clearly on September 8, 1993, five days before he signed the Oslo Accords, when he said: "In the future, Israel and Palestine will be one united state in which Israelis and Palestinians will live together."[38] That cast his recognition of Israel's right to exist in a vastly different light from what most people assumed at the time. Given the nature of Islamic teachings, a united state composed of both "Israel and Palestine" would inevitably be ruled by Palestinians, with Jews relegated to the second-class status mandated in the Qur'an. Israel, or Palestine, or whatever it would be renamed, would indeed no longer be a Jewish state.

If Rabin had any misgivings, however, about Arafat's intentions, he did not show them. He responded reciprocally on the same day:

In response to your letter of September 9, 1993, I wish to confirm to you that, in light of the PLO commitments included in your letter, the Government of Israel has decided to recognize the PLO as the representative of the Palestinian people and commence negotiations with the PLO within the Middle East peace process.

The First Step?

On Sunday, September 12, 1993, U.S. President Bill Clinton announced the imminent signing of the Declaration of Principles during his weekly radio address: "We're living in truly revolutionary times. On Monday, Israel and the P.L.O. will come to the White House to sign a courageous and historic peace accord, the first step in replacing war with peace and giving the children of the Middle East a chance to grow up to a normal life."[39]

"The first step in replacing war with peace"? Clinton's very words of triumph were an admission of the failure of the "peace process." Only in 1993 were the Israelis and Palestinians making a first step toward peace? Had Clinton forgotten about the Camp David Accords? Or had they failed so abysmally to heal the Israeli-Palestinian conflict that by a decade and a half later, it was more convenient for the Democratic Party's first president since Jimmy Carter to pretend they never existed?

In any case, the *New York Times* the next day portrayed the signing as a world-historical event, taking place as "three thousand witnesses watched in amazement, including former Presidents Jimmy Carter and George Bush."[40]

Rabin's words at the signing ceremony reflected Israel's war-weariness: "We the soldiers who have returned from the battle stained with blood, we who have fought against you, the Palestinians, we say to you today in a loud and clear voice: 'Enough of blood and tears! Enough!'"[41] Arafat asserted: "Our two peoples are awaiting today this historic hope, and they want to give peace a real chance."[42] Clinton praised both for their "brave gamble that the future can be better than the past."[43]

"Statesman and Peacemaker"

The previous day, Elaine Sciolino of the *New York Times* had excitedly offered a suggestion of how the "peace process" could be made to work this time: all it needed was a good picture. "A photograph of

Mr. Arafat," she wrote, "shaking hands with, perhaps embracing, the Israeli leader and President Clinton on the South Lawn of the White House would be one of the most dramatic images in the history of Middle East peacemaking. That image will transform Mr. Arafat into a statesman and peacemaker. Their presence would seal the accord with their commitments to make it work and help rob its enemies of the opportunity to sabotage it."[44]

Sciolino got her photograph. There was no embrace, but there was a handshake, and that had to be coaxed from Rabin and Arafat by Bill Clinton. According to *The Times*, repeatedly taking care to note that Rabin was the reluctant party, Clinton "took Mr. Arafat in his left arm and Mr. Rabin in his right arm and gently coaxed them together, needing to give Mr. Rabin just a little extra nudge in the back. Mr. Arafat reached out his hand first, and then Mr. Rabin, after a split second of hesitation and with a wan smile on his face, received Mr. Arafat's hand. The audience let out a simultaneous sigh of relief and peal of joy, as a misty-eyed Mr. Clinton beamed away."[45]

Forced, but good enough. It was splashed across the front page of the *New York Times* the next day, Rabin with a pinched half smile and a dark suit and a grinning Arafat in a military jacket and keffiyeh, shaking hands as an avuncular Clinton stands behind them with his arms outstretched, looking toward Arafat as if to say, "There, that wasn't so hard, now, was it?"

Arafat was now a statesman and a peacemaker, as the *Times* had hoped he would be.

Yet as the world rejoiced over the photograph of Rabin and Arafat shaking hands and ushering in a new era of peace, Arafat's sincerity was still an open question. But to understand why, the world leaders and opinion-makers of the day would have had to be familiar with the early history of Islam, and they weren't.

Oslo: A New Treaty of Hudaybiyya

The PLO had denounced the Camp David Accords and excoriated Anwar Sadat as a sellout, but now Yasser Arafat was cast in Sadat's role. The academic Edward Said, a Christian Arab who had served on the Palestine National Council, furiously characterized the Declaration of Principles as "an instrument of Palestinian surrender, a Palestinian Versailles."[46] Hamas denounced the accords as contrary to Islam, although Hamas granted that there would sometimes be tactical reasons to make a temporary truce with the non-Muslim enemy, as Muhammad, the prophet of Islam, himself had done in his Treaty of Hudaybiyya with the pagan Quraysh of Mecca.[47]

Arafat's own thinking was in line with this view. The Oslo Accords were his golden opportunity to play on the world stage the part that had been taught him by Romanian dictator Nicolae Ceausescu fifteen years before.

Long after the Declaration of Principles had been signed, Romanian spy service operative Ion Mihai Pacepa explained that the entire foundation of the Oslo Accords, the PLO's recognition of Israel and renunciation of terrorism, was a ruse: "In March 1978, I secretly brought Arafat to Bucharest for final instructions on how to behave in Washington. 'You simply have to keep on pretending that you'll break with terrorism and that you'll recognize Israel—over, and over, and over,' Ceausescu told him [Arafat].... Ceausescu was euphoric over the prospect that both Arafat and he might be able to snag a Nobel Peace Prize with their fake displays of the olive branch.... Ceausescu failed to get his Nobel Peace Prize. But in 1994 Arafat got his—all because he continued to play the role we had given him to perfection. He had transformed his terrorist PLO into a government-in-exile (the Palestinian Authority), always pretending to call a halt to Palestinian terrorism while letting it continue unabated."[48]

Even as the negotiations were reaching their final stages, Arafat placed the Oslo Accords within the context of the PLO's 1974 Political Program, which articulated its determination to work toward the destruction of Israel in stages. He stated on Radio Monte Carlo on September 1, 1993, that the accords would be "a basis for an independent Palestinian state in accordance with the Palestinian National Council resolution issued in 1974.... The PNC resolution issued in

1974 calls for the establishment of a national authority on any part of Palestinian soil from which Israel withdraws or which is liberated."[49]

Speaking in Johannesburg, South Africa, in May 1994, Arafat also suggested that the whole exercise had been an elaborate ruse, explaining the strategy he was employing and arguing that Muslims should not be angry over the Oslo Accords, even if they considered them unfavorable to their cause. Hamas had granted that Muslims should follow the example of Muhammad's treaty with the Quraysh, and now Arafat was saying that was exactly what he had done: "This agreement, I am not considering it more than the agreement which had been signed between our Prophet Muhammad and Quraish, and you remember the Caliph Omar had refused this agreement and considered it 'Sulha Dania' [a despicable truce]. But Muhammad had accepted it and we are accepting now this [Oslo] peace accord."[50] He amplified this at a Gaza rally on April 16, 1995, saying: "We signed that agreement in Oslo, and if any of you has one objection to it, I have one hundred objections."[51]

But that was all right, as Muhammad also had agreed to an unfavorable treaty for tactical reasons. The treaty between Muhammad and the Quraysh, the Treaty of Hudaybiyya, became the template in Islamic law for all treaties between Muslims and infidels. In the year 628, Muhammad and the Quraysh concluded a ten-year truce (*hudna*), because Muhammad wanted to make the pilgrimage to Mecca but the Quraysh were hostile to the Muslims.

Muhammad was willing to make concessions to the Quraysh to be allowed to make the pilgrimage, and he did so. When the time came for the agreement to be written, Muhammad called for one of his most fervent followers, Ali ibn Abi Talib, and told him to write, "In the name of Allah, the Compassionate, the Merciful."[52] But the Quraysh negotiator, Suhayl bin 'Amr, stopped him: "I do not recognize this; but write 'In thy name, O Allah.'"[53] Muhammad agreed, telling Ali to write the treaty as Suhayl had directed.

Muhammad then continued, directing Ali to write: "This is what Muhammad, the apostle of God, has agreed with Suhayl bin

Amr."[54] But then Suhayl protested again. "If I witnessed that you were God's apostle," Suhayl told Muhammad, "I would not have fought you. Write your own name and the name of your father."[55] Again Muhammad told Ali to write the document as Suhayl wished.

The treaty they finally agreed on read this way:

This is what Muhammad b. Abdullah has agreed with Suhayl b. Amr: they have agreed to lay aside war for ten years during which men can be safe and refrain from hostilities on condition that if anyone comes to Muhammad without the permission of his guardian he will return him to them; and if anyone of those with Muhammad comes to Quraysh they will not return him to him. We will not show enmity one to another and there shall be no secret reservation or bad faith. He who wishes to enter into a bond and agreement with Muhammad may do so and he who wishes to enter into a bond and agreement with Quraysh may do so.[56]

Muhammad shocked his men by agreeing that those fleeing the Quraysh and seeking refuge with the Muslims would be returned to the Quraysh, while those fleeing the Muslims and seeking refuge with the Quraysh would not be returned to the Muslims.

Yet Muhammad insisted that the Muslims had been victorious despite all appearances to the contrary, and Allah confirmed this view in a new revelation: "Indeed, We have given you a clear conquest" (Qur'an 48:1). As if in compensation, Allah promised new spoils to the Muslims: "Allah has promised you much booty that you will take and has hastened this for you this and withheld the hands of people from you—that it may be a sign for the believers and He may guide you to a straight path." (Qur'an 48:18–20)

Soon after this promise was made, a woman of the Quraysh, Umm Kulthum, joined the Muslims in Medina; her two brothers came to Muhammad, asking that she be returned "in accordance with the agreement between him and the Quraysh at Hudaybiya."[57] But Muhammad refused. He was following Allah's orders: "O you who have believed, when the believing women come to you as emigrants, examine them. Allah is most knowing as to their faith. And if you know them to be believers, then do not return them to the disbelievers; they are not lawful for them, nor are they lawful for them. But give the disbelievers what they have spent. And there is no blame upon you if you marry them when you have given them their due compensation. And hold not to marriage bonds with disbelieving women, but ask for what you have spent and let them ask for what they have spent. That is the judgment of Allah; He judges between you. And Allah is Knowing and Wise." (Qur'an 60:10)

In refusing to send Umm Kulthum back to the Quraysh, Muhammad broke the treaty, claiming that the treaty stipulated that the Muslims would return to the Quraysh any *man* who came to them, not any *woman*.[58] However, Muhammad soon began to accept men from the Quraysh as well, thus definitively breaking the treaty.[59]

By invoking Hudaybiyya to justify Oslo, Arafat was saying that despite appearances, he had actually conceded nothing. Muhammad had undertaken the treaty of Hudaybiyya so that he could make the pilgrimage to Mecca, and so that the Muslims could recover their strength after a series of costly battles with the Quraysh. When the Muslims were strong enough to fight again and defeat the Quraysh, he broke the treaty. Arafat was telling Muslim audiences, who would have been familiar with the Treaty of Hudaybiyya, that he had entered into the treaty with Israel not as a retreat from the Palestinian jihad against the Jewish state but as a tactical move to further the aims of that jihad. And when the Palestinians were strong enough not to need the treaty anymore, he would, like Muhammad, break it.

"Like Rats Abandoning a Sinking Ship"

On September 18, 2018, in an article noting the twenty-fifth anniversary of the Oslo Accords, Palestinian journalist Abd Al-Bari Atwan lamented that they had ever been signed: "A quarter of a century ago today, the PLO leadership and the Palestinian people walked into the biggest trap in modern Arab history, set for them by the Israelis and their Western allies and some Arabs [as well]. They walked into it with their eyes open, believing the lie of peace and of the establishment of an independent Palestinian state—a lie exposed later by the facts on the ground."[60]

In the same article, however, Atwan said he had written critically at the time about the Oslo Accords, and that in response, Arafat had taken him for a walk in the neighborhood of his headquarters in Tunis, Tunisia. Once they were away from the listening devices, Atwan said that Arafat told him: "I want to tell you something that I ask that you not mention or attribute to me until after my death. I am going to Palestine through the Oslo gate, despite my reservations [about this path], in order to bring back to there [that is, to Palestine] the PLO and the resistance. I promise you that the Jews will leave Palestine like rats abandoning a sinking ship. This will not come true in my lifetime, but it will in your lifetime."[61]

Atwan added: "He told me that he did not trust the Israelis at all."[62] According to Atwan, Arafat "maintained that the Oslo track, whose architect was Mahmoud Abbas [who would succeed him as president of the Palestinian Authority], could protect the PLO, extricate it from its isolation, bring it back into the international arena and plant in it the first seeds of the Palestinian state."[63]

All that it certainly accomplished, along with significant Israeli withdrawals from much of the territory it had occupied after the Six-Day War and the establishment of a Palestinian governing entity that would end up being recognized as the government of a sovereign state by many nations around the world.

Land for No Peace

In return for all its concessions, Israel got a renunciation of terrorism from the PLO. And while it had entered into the entire negotiating process in the first place in order to strengthen the PLO against Hamas, the Oslo Accords were so unpopular among the Palestinians that if Israel had hoped that they would lead the Palestinian people to rally around the PLO and forsake Hamas, those hopes would come to naught. Oslo ended up only strengthening Hamas, as many

Palestinian Arabs came to see it and other groups such as Islamic Jihad as embodying the properly Islamic hard line against Israel, as opposed to the PLO's conciliation and capitulation.

On the White House lawn as the Oslo Accords were signed on September 13, 1993, Yitzhak Rabin again reached out to the Palestinians: "Enough of blood and tears. Enough. We harbor no hatred towards you. We have no desire for revenge. We, like you, are people who want to build a home, plant a tree, love, live side by side with you—in dignity, in empathy, as human beings, as free men. We are today giving peace a chance and saying to you: Enough. Let's pray that a day will come when we all will say: Farewell to arms."[64]

No one on the Palestinian side was willing to echo Rabin's words sincerely.

Hamas and Islamic Jihad did not consider themselves bound to the PLO's renunciation of terrorism. Hamas murdered eight Israelis and wounded forty-four more with a car bomb in Afula in April 1994. That same month, Hamas murdered five Israelis and injured twenty-eight in a bus bombing in Hadera. In October 1994, Hamas murdered twenty-three more Israelis in another bus bombing, this time in Tel Aviv. Three months later, Islamic Jihad murdered twenty-one Israelis in Beit Lid.[65] In all, jihadis murdered around 120 Israelis between the signing of the Oslo Accords in September 1993 and January 1995.[66] Pacepa noted in 2003: "Two years after signing the Oslo Accords, the number of Israelis killed by Palestinian terrorists had risen by 73 percent."[67]

Yasser Arafat did not repudiate Hamas, despite its continuing jihad terror attacks on Israeli civilians. In a 1994 letter to Hamas's leader, the Muslim cleric Sheikh Ahmed Yassin, and to jihad terrorist Sheikh Abdelhadi Hunam, who in 1989 murdered fourteen Israelis on a bus: "My brother, Sheikh Yassin, my brother the holy Sheikh Abdelhadi Hunam, I recognize your participation in the struggle to free Palestine. Because of you, Palestine is free."[68] In January 1996, Arafat hailed the mastermind of the Hamas jihad suicide bombing, Yihye Ayyash, as a martyr.[69]

On May 27, 1994, Jibril Rajoub, whom Arafat appointed as the head of the new Palestinian Preventative Security Force, said in a speech at Bethlehem University that those who opposed the Oslo Accords were perfectly free to continue their acts of violence against Israelis: "We sanctify the weapons found in the possession of the national factions which are directed against the occupation.... If there are those who oppose the agreement with Israel, the gates are open to them to intensify the armed struggle."[70] There is no indication that Arafat ever rebuked him for violating the Oslo pledge to renounce terrorism.

Indeed, Arafat and other PLO leaders disregarded this Oslo promise almost immediately, repeatedly calling upon their people to commit acts of violence against Israelis. Speaking on Jordanian TV on September 13, 1993, the very day that the Oslo Accords were signed, the man who told the UN in 1988 that the Palestinians had renounced terrorism "in all its form" issued a sly call for violence: "Palestine is only a stone's throw away for a small Palestinian boy or girl."[71] Three years later, on October 21, 1996, he was more direct, telling a group from Hebron: "Have you run out of stones in Hebron? Prepare the stones."[72]

"War Is Deceit"

PLO official Faisal Husseini assured the Palestinians on November 22, 1993, that "everything you see and hear today is for tactical and strategic reasons. We have not given up the rifle. We still have armed gangs in the areas and if we do not get our state we will take them out of the closet and fight again."[73]

Speaking from Algiers on Voice of Palestine on December 31, 1993, Arafat proclaimed: "It is a revolution until victory, until victory, until victory."[74] This revolution was a violent one. Far from renouncing violence, Arafat said during a Gaza speech on January 7, 1994: "The heroic intifada, which has entered its seventh year, is an extension of the 29-year-old Palestinian revolution and will go on relentlessly.... It is continuing, continuing, continuing."[75]

Arafat also emphasized that the Palestinians' violent struggle was intrinsically Islamic; it was a jihad. Speaking on May 10, 1994, at a mosque in Johannesburg, he declared: "The jihad will continue.... You have to understand our main battle is Jerusalem.... You have to come and to fight a jihad to liberate Jerusalem, your precious shrine.... No, it is not their capital. It is our capital."[76] At a rally in Gaza on November 22, 1994, he expressed his confidence that "our people will continue with its jihad."[77]

Then on December 10, 1994, Arafat (along with fellow winners Rabin and Israeli foreign minister Shimon Peres) picked up his Nobel Peace Prize in Oslo, and suddenly shifted gears, sounding as if Rabin had ghostwritten his speech: "Peace is in our interest: as only in an atmosphere of just peace shall the Palestinian people achieve their legitimate ambition for independence and sovereignty, and be able to develop their national and cultural identity, as well as enjoy sound neighborly relations, mutual respect and cooperation with the Israeli people."[78]

Arafat did not, of course, say anything about jihad in Oslo, but he hadn't had a change of heart; five days later he resumed his incitement to violence. Addressing the Organization of the Islamic Conference on December 15, 1994, he said: "The glorious Islamic solidarity together with our people's jihad is an additional inducement for the realization of our hopes."[79] On February 14, 1995, he told those attending a rally in Hebron: "Our nation is a nation of sacrifice, struggle and jihad."[80]

In calling for jihad, Arafat invoked the Qur'an. Speaking in Gaza on October 4, 1996, Arafat said: "They will fight for Allah, and they will kill and be killed," a quotation from the Qur'anic passage that guarantees Paradise to those who "kill and are killed" for Allah (9:111), thereby providing the impetus for suicide bombing.[81]

On June 19, 1995, Arafat spoke at Gaza's Al-Azhar University and again reiterated that the Israeli-Palestinian conflict was a jihad: "The commitment still stands and the oath is still valid: that we will continue this long jihad, this difficult jihad...via deaths, via sacrifices."

In this speech he went further, praising Dalal al-Maghrabi, a Palestinian woman and member of Fatah, a PLO faction. Al-Maghrabi was one of the jihad attackers who had murdered thirty-seven Israelis after hijacking a bus on Israel's Coastal Road. Said Arafat: "She was one of the heroes.... She commanded the group that established the first Palestinian republic in a bus.... This is the Palestinian woman... the woman we are proud of."[82]

Arafat praised another female PLO jihad murderer, Abir al-Wahidi, along with al-Maghrabi in a speech on September 3, 1995: "Yes, we are proud of the Palestinian girl, the Palestinian woman and the Palestinian child who fulfilled these miracles. The Palestinian woman participated in the Palestinian revolution. The Palestinian girl participated in the Palestinian revolution. Abir al Wahidi, commander of the central region and Dalal al-Maghrabi, Martryr of Palestine. I bow in respect and admiration to the Palestinian woman who receives her martyred son with joyful cheering. The soul and blood for you, O Palestine!"[83]

Another Martyr for Peace

Despite all this incitement from Arafat, Rabin flew to Washington in September 1995, where he and Arafat signed another agreement, which came to be known as Oslo II, increasing the area of Palestinian rule in the West Bank. Rabin took the occasion to urge Arafat to "prevent terrorism from triumphing over peace."[84] Two months later, on November 4, 1995, Rabin was shot dead by twenty-five-year-old Israeli Yigal Amir, who believed that the prime minister had severely compromised Israel's security by agreeing to the Oslo Accords.

Rabin, like Anwar Sadat before him, was revered in death as a hero, a martyr of the "peace process."

In his statement of condolence, Yasser Arafat referred to Rabin as his friend and then went back to calling for blood.[85] Despite having signed an agreement renouncing terrorism, Arafat felt free to threaten the Israelis with it: "The Israelis are mistaken if they think we do not have an alternative to negotiations. By Allah I swear they are wrong.

The Palestinian people are prepared to sacrifice the last boy and the last girl so that the Palestinian flag will be flown over the walls, the churches, and the mosques of Jerusalem."[86] On June 7, 1996, Arafat thundered: "If Israel rejects our demands there will be a reaction and we have a 30,000 man armed force."[87]

On October 21, 1996, Arafat declared: "We know only one word: jihad, jihad, jihad. When we stopped the intifada, we did not stop the jihad for the establishment of a Palestinian state whose capital is Jerusalem. And we are now entering the phase of the great jihad prior to the establishment of an independent Palestinian state whose capital is Jerusalem…. We are in a conflict with the Zionist movement and the Balfour Declaration and all imperialist activities."[88]

Arafat on November 11, 1995, spoke on Voice of Palestine and made it clear that, despite Oslo, he was still committed to the destruction of Israel: "The struggle will continue until all of Palestine is liberated."[89]

On January 13, 1998, Arafat wrote to Bill Clinton reaffirming that "all of the provisions of the Covenant," that is, the Palestinian National Charter, "which are inconsistent with the P.L.O. commitment to recognize and live in peace side by side with Israel are no longer in effect…. I can assure you on behalf of the PLO and the Palestinian Authority that all the provisions of the Covenant that were inconsistent with the commitments of

September 9/10, 1993 to Prime Minister Rabin have been nullified."[90]

As Muhammad, the prophet of Islam, said: "War is deceit."[91]

"They Think Arafat Is a Pussycat Who Will Be Nice if You Pat Him on the Head"

Assessing in 2016 the Oslo "peace process," historian Efraim Karsh said: "For Israel, it has been the starkest strategic blunder in its history, establishing an ineradicable terror entity on its doorstep, deepening its internal cleavages, destabilizing its political system, and weakening its international standing."[92]

Yet once the "peace process" had been set in motion, it didn't seem as if anything could stop it—not jihad terror attacks, not a murderous retaliatory attack at a mosque by an unbalanced Israeli named Baruch Goldstein, and not Arafat's manifest duplicity. And so Bill Clinton, Yasser Arafat, and Israeli Prime Minister Benjamin Netanyahu met for another summit in Wye River, Maryland, in October 1998, in order to continue to hammer out the details of the Israeli withdrawal from the West Bank and Gaza Strip.

In exchange for new Palestinian pledges to end jihad terrorism against Israel, Israel agreed to withdraw from more territory, handing it over to the Palestinian Authority. Israeli foreign minister Ariel Sharon said candidly that "the return of our historic land was a painful thing to do, very painful." Referring to one of the areas of withdrawal, he told an American interviewer: "Look, Rachel's tomb is here, Jews have worshiped here for four thousand years. Imagine if you had to give back Texas to Mexico or New York to Canada. But you know, after Oslo, this was inevitable. The only thing we could do was prepare against the dangers. On the one hand, we had to learn how to live with the Arabs, and on the other, we had to protect against them."[93]

Unusually for a participant in the "peace process," Sharon also noted that the Palestinians weren't keeping their word: "The Palestinians have not implemented most of their agreements, and there have to be some concrete moves; Israelis are being killed; thousands of illegal weapons remain uncollected."[94]

Sharon also opined that the Clinton administration, which was overseeing the negotiations, was naïve: "They think Arafat is a pussycat who will be nice if you pat him on the head, but they greatly underestimate him. The present 'intifada' in the West Bank is directly incited by Arafat…. I was asked over and over this time if Israel is looking for an excuse not to withdraw from more territory. Why does Israel have to constantly prove itself?"[95]

Why indeed? The answer, apparently, was because the Americans' naïveté was compounded by their concerns with other matters.

"There is a new Mideast order," said Sharon. "We used to be the major concern of America, but now we are just a small part of a larger game. We are a tiny country in the target area of Iraq and Iran, Syria and Lebanon, all hostile to us. This is why we must take a very hard line in protecting our territory. And this is why it is so frustrating that Washington does not seem to know that Arafat will not give up anything unless forced. He would not have even come to the negotiating table were it not for the growing communities the settlements in Judea and Samaria have become."[96]

So Arafat, like Sadat at Camp David, was coming to the negotiating table to obtain what he could not win by the force of arms: the lessening or full removal of the Israeli presence in Judea and Samaria, the West Bank.

"Mr. Arafat Is an Elusive Player"

When negotiations resumed, the Americans were no less naïve than they had been before. On July 11, 2000, Clinton convened the Camp David Summit along with Arafat and Israeli Prime Minister Ehud Barak. Clinton had raised the stakes simply by his choice of location: after the first Camp David Accords, Anwar Sadat had become an international hero and, after his assassination by a jihadi, an enduringly revered martyr for peace. Could a new Camp David gathering mint a new group of heroes of peace?

Barak gave his best effort to becoming a hero of peace, offering Arafat almost everything that he said he had always wanted: a full-fledged independent Palestinian state in Gaza and 92 percent of the West Bank, plus Palestinian sovereignty in East Jerusalem. Clinton offered Arafat a similar deal.

Arafat, however, was intransigent. He wanted all of the West Bank, not just almost all of it. He wanted the "right of return" for the Palestinian refugees, who were not just people who had actually left Palestine when the State of Israel was founded, but their children and grandchildren. The United Nations Relief and Works Agency for Palestine Refugees in the Near East (UNRWA) in 2000 classified, and still classify today, as Palestinian refugees not just "persons whose normal place of residence was Palestine during the period 1 June 1946 to 15 May 1948, and who lost both home and means of livelihood as a result of the 1948 conflict," but also "the descendants of Palestine refugee males, including adopted children."[97] Thus it is no surprise that "when the Agency began operations in 1950, it was responding to the needs of about 750,000 Palestine refugees. Today, some five million Palestine refugees are eligible for UNRWA services."[98]

Five million Palestinian refugees returning to Israel would have destroyed its character as a Jewish state, and of this Arafat was well aware. And so the deal was off. A chagrined Clinton announced on July 25, 2000, that no deal had been reached. For that, he blamed Arafat: "The true story of Camp David," he said hotly later in response to criticism of his role in Camp David II, "was that for the first time in the history of the conflict the American president put on the table a proposal, based on UN Security Council resolutions 242 and 338, very close to the Palestinian demands, and Arafat refused even to accept it as a basis for negotiations, walked out of the room, and deliberately turned to terrorism. That's the real story—all the rest is gossip."[99]

Ehud Barak was candid about his own willingness to let Arafat mislead him into thinking he wanted peace. He wrote in the *New York Times* on July 30, 2001, that "Mr. Arafat is an elusive player. It took me some time and cost a certain price to find this out."[100] He warned against further naïveté:

> *Mr. Arafat has violated almost every agreement he has signed with Israel in both letter and spirit. The Oslo accords assumed that the transfer of administrative responsibilities for the West Bank and Gaza to Mr. Arafat would encourage his transformation into a leader of a nation state. The utter failure of Mr. Arafat to live up to that assumption is the primary cause of our crisis today....*
>
> *Given the violence of the past ten months and Mr. Arafat's failure to stop the terrorism, the new governments in the United States and in Israel would be foolish to give him the benefit of the doubt...*[101]

It should have been clear to both Clinton and Barak that Arafat was never going to accept a negotiated settlement that would require Palestinians to live in peace with Israelis, no matter how favorable it was. For years he had been preaching jihad to his own people and calling upon them to continue to struggle until all of Palestine was liberated. For him to have accepted Barak's offer would have been seen among his own people as an even greater betrayal than the Oslo Accords, and could have even resulted in his being toppled from power or even assassinated like Sadat and Rabin, no matter how strenuously he insisted that it was just another Hudaybiyya-like treaty.

And so the jihad would continue.

The Al-Aqsa Intifada

The Arafat-directed intifada to which Sharon had referred in 1998 was a small matter compared to what was to come, and he himself would be blamed for the next round of violence. On September 28, 2000, Sharon, by this time the leader of the opposition Likud Party, visited the Temple Mount in Jerusalem. "I brought a message of peace," Sharon said later.[102]

He was not received in peace. Muslims screaming *"Allahu akbar"* ("Allah is greater"—that is, greater than other gods and all earthly authorities) and "With soul and blood we will redeem you, Al Aqsa!" tried to break through police lines and attack Sharon, and threw stones, chairs, and other hard objects at police.[103] Israeli Arab Knesset member Ahmad Tibi and other Muslim Arab Knesset members also dogged Sharon, following him as he walked around the Temple Mount area and screaming: "Murderer, get out!" and "Al Aqsa is Palestinian!"[104] The Muslims rioted, injuring twenty-five Israeli police officers; three Palestinian protesters were also wounded.

Sharon denied that he had any malign intentions in visiting the Temple Mount. "I believe that Jews and Arabs can live together. It was no provocation whatsoever. It's our right. Arabs have the right to visit everywhere in the Land of Israel, and Jews have the right to visit every place in the Land of Israel.... I'm sorry about the casualties, and I wish the wounded a speedy recovery, but a Jew in Israel has the right to visit the Temple Mount. The Temple Mount is still in our hands."[105]

Yasser Arafat, however, called the visit a "dangerous action" that threatened the two mosques on the Temple Mount, the al-Aqsa Mosque and the Dome of the Rock.[106] And the PLO's Faisal Husseini rejected Sharon's assertion that Israelis had any right to visit the Temple Mount: "Israel has no sovereignty here. They have military might, they have the power of occupation, but not sovereignty." He charged that Sharon's visit was "a direct attempt to derail the peace process and an attempt to inflame the whole region."[107]

That it did. Large-scale rioting began the next day in the West Bank and Gaza, and the Second Intifada, known as the al-Aqsa Intifada, had begun. It would continue for several years, with Palestinians continuing to blame it on Sharon's visit to the Temple Mount. On November 1, 2000, however, acting Israeli foreign minister Shlomo Ben-Ami appeared on *PBS NewsHour* with Jim Lehrer, where he told interviewer Ray Suarez that on the day Sharon went to the Temple Mount, "I happened to exchange a few words over the telephone with one of the chief security personnel guys in the Palestinian system, Jabril Rajoub, and he told me, if Ariel Sharon doesn't go into the mosques, but just visits the surface, nothing will happen. So that day—that precise day—was of no special significance. What happened was that a day or a couple of days later, groups of people were organized to come on the Temple Mount and stage these outbursts of violence. So I think that the whole thing was prepared in advance."[108]

It was prepared, said Ben-Ami, in order to intimidate the Israelis into giving in to all of Arafat's demands:

In 1993, through the Oslo Agreement, Arafat got a series of advantages. He got a quasi-Palestinian state, personal authority as a quasi-Palestinian state, a government, a parliament, an enormous amount of international aid. He got money from the European

Union, from this country, and a military sort of establishment; he has his own kind of military power. And all these were supposed to lead gradually to negotiations on the final status. But negotiations whose result is not known in advance—because this is an open-ended negotiation.

Now, what we see is that the moment Arafat doesn't reach the precise result of the negotiations that he wants, he breaks the rules of the game.

He got international aid, he got a dramatic shift in his strategic position, thanks to the Oslo Agreement. Seven years ago, he could not get a visa to America, now he's a frequent flyer to the White House—only thanks to Oslo. Now, he breaks the rules of the game just because he did not get the deal he thinks he should get. Which means a diktat—Israel should accept all these terms. And once he doesn't get it, he breaks the rules of the game.[109]

Arafat's duplicity, Ben-Ami noted with clear regret, had called into question the entire decades-long attempt to find a negotiated settlement that would allow Israelis and Palestinians to live side by side in peace:

Where do we stand now, after seven years of peace process? Because to some of us it means the collapse of the work of a lifetime. The peace camp in Israel is shattered to pieces—those who believe in generosity, flexibility, the creation of the Palestinian state—what is due to the Palestinians, because the Arab world, when they occupied these territories, never gave to the Palestinians any rights, let alone self-determination. Israel is ready for the creation of a Palestinian state friendly to Israel, not hostile. And now we see that the work of our life is under question.[110]

Muhamed al-Durah

It got even worse two days after Sharon's ill-fated visit to the Temple Mount. On September 30, 2000, a twelve-year-old Palestinian boy named Muhamed al-Durah joined a group of other Muslim men and boys who were throwing rocks and Molotov cocktails at an Israeli police station in Gaza. Talal Abu Rahma, a Palestinian photographer for France2, a French television network, caught the horrifying scene on video as al-Durah and his father were caught in a crossfire between Israelis and Palestinians, and young Muhamed was apparently shot dead by the Israeli Defense Forces. Muhamed al-Durah became a symbol of the intifada, with Palestinians furiously claiming that the Israelis had deliberately murdered the boy, and the violence got even worse.

However, oddities almost immediately began to appear in the story. France2 refused, without explanation, to release the entirety of the footage Talal Abu Rahma had shot that day. The photos of Muhamed al-Durah that his family provided after his apparent death don't look like they're of the same boy who was supposedly killed. There is no footage of an ambulance arriving, or of any ambulance carrying the boy arriving at the hospital.

What's more, Abu Rahma was the only cameraman who filmed the scene, an extremely unlikely occurrence in these days of twenty-four-hour news saturation, especially given the fact that Muslim Arabs were just beginning to riot over Sharon's Temple Mount visit, and the international media was out in force in Gaza and the West Bank.[111]

The most likely scenario is that the entire killing of Muhamed al-Durah was staged in order to stoke both Palestinian and international outrage against Israel, and force the Israelis to make more concessions in order to assuage their guilt.

It almost worked. Against the backdrop of ongoing Palestinian violence and shrill international condemnation of Israel, the "peace process" once again gathered steam. On December 23, 2000, the Israelis and Palestinians seemed on the verge of an agreement: a Palestinian state would be established in over 90 percent of the West Bank and all of Gaza.

Arafat, however, backed out at the last minute, once again insisting on the "right of return" that would destroy the Jewish state.[112]

The Israelis dodged a bullet. A Palestinian state of that size, established under those circumstances, would certainly have become a new jihad base for renewed attacks against Israel, as the great majority of its citizens would never have taken seriously the Palestinian recognition of Israel, or considered that it applied to Israel as a Jewish state.

"Never Been Closer"

But few analysts, if any, at the dawn of the twenty-first century saw the establishment of a Palestinian state as self-defeating and ultimately dangerous for Israel. And so the "peace process" rolled on.

Meeting again from January 21 to 27, 2001, at Taba in the Sinai, the Israelis and Palestinians found themselves at an impasse over the same issues that had derailed previous attempts to negotiate peace: the status of Jerusalem, the "right of return," and Israeli settlements on territory that Palestinians claimed as their own. Moreover, there was a new president in Washington and elections were looming in Israel, so neither side wanted to proceed with an agreement that might not be considered binding by new leaders.

The two sides, however, issued a joint statement affirming that progress had been made: "The sides declare that they have never been closer to reaching an agreement and it is thus our shared belief that the remaining gaps could be bridged with the resumption of negotiations following the Israeli elections."[113]

However, on February 8, 2001, the Israeli prime minister's office issued a statement saying that "in a letter to President George Bush, Prime Minister Barak stated that his government had done the utmost to bring about an end to the Israeli-Palestinian conflict, but that these efforts did not bear fruit, primarily because of a lack of sufficient readiness for compromise on the part of the Palestinian leadership."[114]

Even at this point, however, Barak had not given up hope that one day his intransigent peace partners would come around: "Prime Minister Barak expressed his hope that the peace process in the region will continue."[115]

Meanwhile, the al-Aqsa intifada raged on. Palestinians began frequent suicide bombings of Israeli civilians, enticing young Muslims to blow themselves up in Israeli restaurants or on buses and in other crowded places by reminding them of the Qur'an's guarantee of a place in Paradise for those who "kill and are killed" for Allah (9:111). More than one hundred Israelis were murdered in jihad suicide attacks during 2001.[116] In 2002, using both suicide bombings and more conventional methods, Palestinians murdered 184 Israeli civilians inside Israel proper and eighty-eight more in the West Bank and Gaza; in 2003, they murdered 104 additional civilians in Israel and twenty-five in the West Bank and Gaza; and in 2004, fifty-three more in Israel and fifteen more in the West Bank and Gaza.[117]

"The Palestinian Accounts Could Not Be Verified"

This ongoing carnage and targeting of noncombatants threatened to turn international public opinion against the Palestinians, and of that Palestinian leaders were well aware. It was time once again to implement Muhammad's dictum "war is deceit." On April 3, 2002, Israeli troops entered the Palestinian refugee camp of Jenin, charging that it was a staging ground for jihad suicide attacks. Palestinian leaders seized the opportunity to claim that the Israelis had committed war crimes inside Jenin: Palestinian negotiator Saeb Erekat, the PLO's chief negotiator for the Oslo Accords, announced: "People were massacred, and we say the number will not be less than five hundred."[118]

The media outcry against Israel was immediate and intense. The U.K.'s *Independent* declared: "A monstrous war crime that Israel has tried to cover up for a fortnight has finally been exposed." The *Independent*'s Phil Reeves quoted "a quiet, sad-looking young man called Kamal Anis," who led Reeves around the camp: "He suddenly stopped. This was a mass grave, he said, pointing. We stared at a mound of debris. Here, he said, he saw the Israeli soldiers pile thirty bodies beneath a half-wrecked house. When the pile was complete, they bulldozed the building, bringing its ruins down on the corpses. Then they flattened the area with a tank. We could not see the bodies. But we could smell them."[119]

Janine di Giovanni, a correspondent for the *Times* of London wrote: "The refugees I had interviewed in recent days while trying to enter the camp were not lying. If anything, they underestimated the carnage and the horror. Rarely, in more than a decade of war reporting from Bosnia, Chechnya, Sierra Leone, Kosovo, have I seen such deliberate destruction, such disrespect for human life."[120]

However, after reporting on what the Palestinian claimed about Jenin ("'It's a disaster,' said Ruba Al Ruzi, a young woman who watched the scene. 'I hope the Arab countries and the Americans who watched us being slaughtered will face the same situation.'"), the *New York Times* added a terse cautionary note: "The Palestinian accounts could not be verified."[121]

Indeed they couldn't. The *Washington Post* reported on the same day: "Interviews with residents inside the camp and international aid workers who were allowed here for the first time today indicated that no evidence has surfaced to support allegations by Palestinian groups and aid organizations of large-scale massacres or executions by Israeli troops."[122]

The *New York Times* and *Washington Post* were correct regarding the lack of evidence. Amnesty International and Human Rights Watch investigated and found no evidence of Israeli war crimes. The UN mounted an investigation of its own, finding that fifty-two people had been killed in Jenin and that almost all of those were Palestinian jihadis; it stated that no civilians had been deliberately killed in Jenin.[123]

On August 3, 2002, the *Independent*'s Reeves published an article entitled "Even Journalists Have to Admit They're Wrong Sometimes," in which he admitted that "the massacre allegations were false," although he still insisted, without a trace of evidence, that Israel's action in Jenin was an act of collective punishment against many innocent civilians."[124] Despite this, however, Reeves was singular in retracting his initial claims; Janine di Giovanni and the other journalists who revealed Israel's supposed atrocities in Jenin before a horrified world never did so.

But by that time the lie had done its job. Public opinion worldwide was turning decisively against Israel, and the pressure was increasing on Israel to make more concessions to the Palestinians, who by now were widely perceived in the West as intransigent terrorists but also as innocent victims of a merciless Israeli war machine.

Israel began the next round of the "peace process" more hated and derided worldwide than ever.

CHAPTER EIGHT

Road Map to Nowhere

"My Vision Is Two States, Living Side by Side in Peace and Security"

Israel's low standing in world opinion was reflected in President George W. Bush's June 24, 2002, speech announcing the beginning of yet another "peace process" initiative. Working with The Quartet of the U.S., Russia, the European Union, and the United Nations, Bush developed a comprehensive plan for peace in the Middle East, and unveiled it with great fanfare.

Throughout his speech, Bush assumed a complete equivalency between the Israeli and Palestinian sides, speaking as if both held equal responsibility for the failure to achieve peace thus far: "For too long," Bush said, "the citizens of the Middle East have lived in the midst of death and fear.... It is untenable for Israeli citizens to live in terror. It is untenable for Palestinians to live in squalor and occupation"—as if the alleged "squalor and occupation" in which Palestinians lived justified the relentless jihad against Israel.[1]

Bush lobbied strongly for the two-state solution: "My vision is two states, living side by side in peace and security. There is simply no way to achieve that peace until all parties fight terror."[2] The problem he saw was not the jihad ideology that would never allow the vast majority of Muslims to accept a Jewish state in Palestine (or anywhere else, for that matter); it was Yasser Arafat. The Palestinians simply needed new leadership: "Peace requires a new and different Palestinian leadership, so that a Palestinian state can be born. I call on the Palestinian people to elect new leaders, leaders not compromised by terror. I call upon them to build a practicing democracy, based on tolerance and liberty. If the Palestinian people actively pursue these goals, America and the world will actively support their efforts. If the Palestinian people meet these goals, they will be able to reach agreement with Israel and Egypt and Jordan on security and other arrangements for independence."[3]

Bush did have some strong words for the Palestinians, warning that "a Palestinian state will never be created by terror—it will be built through reform. And reform must be more than cosmetic change, or veiled attempt to preserve the status quo. True reform will require entirely new political and economic institutions, based on democracy, market economics and action against terrorism."[4] He implied that if the Palestinians didn't stop engaging in terrorism, support from the United States would be cut off: "Today, Palestinian authorities are encouraging, not opposing, terrorism. This is unacceptable. And the United States will not support the establishment of a Palestinian state until its leaders engage in a sustained fight against the terrorists and dismantle their infrastructure."[5] However, calling upon Palestinian leaders to "engage in a sustained fight against the terrorists" is not the same as saying that there could be no Palestinian state until jihad terrorism against Israel was completely ended; Bush was signaling that he would be satisfied with gestures and half measures, as long as he was satisfied that progress was being made.

For Israel's neighbors, Bush set the bar high—indeed, far too high for his conditions to have been meet, given the realities of Islamic jihad: "As we move toward a peaceful solution, Arab states will be expected to build closer ties of diplomacy and commerce with

Israel, leading to full normalization of relations between Israel and the entire Arab world."[6]

However, Bush reserved his strongest words for Israel, taking for granted that Israel was engaged in an occupation of land that was legitimately Palestinian, and lecturing Israel as if its occupation and refusal to allow a Palestinian state were responsible for Palestinian terrorism: "Permanent occupation threatens Israel's identity and democracy. A stable, peaceful Palestinian state is necessary to achieve the security that Israel longs for. So I challenge Israel to take concrete steps to support the emergence of a viable, credible Palestinian state."[7]

In pursuit of this elusive security, Israel would have to render itself less secure: "As we make progress towards security, Israel forces need to withdraw fully to positions they held prior to September 28, 2000."[8] September 28, 2000, was the date of Sharon's visit to the Temple Mount and the beginning of the Second Intifada. Bush was demanding that Israel withdraw all forces that had been deployed in order to counter the intifada and protect Israeli civilians.

Without any apparent awareness that Israeli security measures had been put into place as a response to jihad terror activity, Bush spoke of those measures as an obstacle to Palestinian economic development, and demonstrated American naïveté once again by calling upon the Israelis to dismantle them in good faith as terrorism levels decreased: "The Palestinian economy must be allowed to develop," Bush said, as if Israel had been deliberately hampering its development. "As violence subsides, freedom of movement should be restored, permitting innocent Palestinians to resume work and normal life. Palestinian legislators and officials, humanitarian and international workers, must be allowed to go about the business of building a better future. And Israel should release frozen Palestinian revenues into honest, accountable hands."[9]

It all sounded fine on paper, but it depended upon a vision of the Palestinian people as consisting of a vast majority of thoughtful, peaceful Jeffersonian democrats who had been held hostage by terrorists among them, and who were oppressed by Israeli overreaction to those terrorists. It was, once again, a naïve and ill-informed view of the situation, based on a lack of understanding of the depth of Arab Muslim hatred for Israel, and the roots of that hatred in Islamic anti-Semitism and supremacism.

Bush stated to "the Palestinian people": "[Y]our interests have been held hostage to a comprehensive peace agreement that never seems to come, as your lives get worse year by year. You deserve democracy and the rule of law. You deserve an open society and a thriving economy. You deserve a life of hope for your children. An end to occupation and a peaceful democratic Palestinian state may seem distant, but America and our partners throughout the world stand ready to help, help you make them possible as soon as possible."[10]

He took for granted that the great majority of the Palestinian people actually wanted democracy, the rule of any law other than Sharia, and an open society, but this was by no means self-evident or proven.

It was no surprise, in light of Bush's lack of understanding of the overall situation, that Bush also repeated demands that had been made upon the Israelis many times before, in other failed peace negotiations: "Israeli settlement activity in the occupied territories must stop."

The Israeli settlements in the West Bank and Gaza (the latter of which were ultimately dismantled) always had been a sticking point. They were on land that had been dedicated to a Jewish national home in the Balfour Declaration, and that belonged to the State of Israel by the right of conquest that had been universally recognized as a law of war except in regard to Israel. The land in question was, moreover, part of the ancient land of Israel. But it was a staple of the two-state solution that the West Bank and Gaza were lands that belonged by right to the Palestinians, and consequently that Israeli settlements were not just an obstacle to peace but illegal in and of themselves.

They also provided an easy way for Palestinian negotiators to continue participating in the "peace process" while blaming Israel for their failure, despite not ending jihad terror incitement or activity:

the problem was the Israeli settlements, and if they were dismantled, peace would dawn. No one involved seemed to realize that even if all the settlements were dismantled, there would be no peace, but only more Palestinian demands, until the ultimate goal, the total destruction of Israel, was realized.

Bush added:

Ultimately, Israelis and Palestinians must address the core issues that divide them if there is to be a real peace, resolving all claims and ending the conflict between them. This means that the Israeli occupation that began in 1967 will be ended through a settlement negotiated between the parties, based on U.N. Resolutions 242 and 338, with Israeli withdrawal to secure and recognize borders.

We must also resolve questions concerning Jerusalem, the plight and future of Palestinian refugees, and a final peace between Israel and Lebanon, and Israel and a Syria that supports peace and fights terror.[11]

Bush admitted it wouldn't be easy: "All who are familiar with the history of the Middle East realize that there may be setbacks in this process."[12] Nonetheless, he was hopeful: "If liberty can blossom in the rocky soil of the West Bank and Gaza, it will inspire millions of men and women around the globe who are equally weary of poverty and oppression, equally entitled to the benefits of democratic government."[13]

Bush concluded with praise for Muslims and Islamic culture:

I have a hope for the people of Muslim countries. Your commitments to morality, and learning, and tolerance led to great historical achievements. And those values are alive in the Islamic world today. You have a rich culture, and you share the aspirations of men and women in every culture. Prosperity and freedom and dignity are not just American hopes, or Western hopes. They are universal, human hopes. And even in the violence and turmoil of the Middle East, America believes those hopes have the power to transform lives and nations.[14]

Whatever the truth of these assertions, jihad also remained alive in the Islamic world, particularly the jihad against Israel, and so another round of the "peace process" would in time fail, as had all the others.

The Road Map to Peace

The Road Map to Peace developed out of Bush's recommendations in this speech. Its scope was ambitious: the plan was to settle the Israeli-Palestinian conflict and bring peace to the region by the end of 2005, accomplishing this in three phases. This would begin with the Palestinians ending terrorism. Phase I would involve Palestinian leadership issuing an "unequivocal statement reiterating Israel's right to exist in peace and security and calling for an immediate and unconditional ceasefire to end armed activity and all acts of violence against Israelis anywhere," as if Israel's defense measures were comparable to Palestinian jihad terrorism against Israeli civilians.[15] The plan added: "All official Palestinian institutions end incitement against Israel."[16]

However, continuing Bush's moral equivalence between the two sides, Phase I also required Israeli leadership to issue an "unequivocal statement affirming its commitment to the two-state vision of an independent, viable, sovereign Palestinian state living in peace and security alongside Israel, as expressed by President Bush, and calling for an immediate end to violence against Palestinians everywhere. All official Israeli institutions end incitement against Palestinians."[17] The document didn't offer any examples of Israeli incitement against Palestinians, and would have been hard-pressed to find one.

The road map demanded that words would have to be backed up with actions: "Palestinians declare an unequivocal end to violence and terrorism and undertake visible efforts on the ground to arrest, disrupt, and restrain individuals and groups conducting and planning violent attacks on Israelis anywhere."[18] It actually envisioned the Palestinian Authority's taking strong, decisive action against the jihadis targeting Israel: a "rebuilt and refocused Palestinian Authority security apparatus begins sustained, targeted, and effective operations aimed at confronting all those engaged in terror and dismantlement of terrorist capabilities and infrastructure. This includes commencing confiscation of illegal weapons and consolidation of security authority, free of association with terror and corruption."[19]

Meanwhile, continuing its careful equating of both sides, the road map specified that the government of Israel must take "no actions undermining trust, including deportations, attacks on civilians; confiscation and/or demolition of Palestinian homes and property, as a punitive measure or to facilitate Israeli construction; destruction of Palestinian institutions and infrastructure."[20]

Phase I also envisioned that Israel would immediately make numerous concessions, based solely on the Palestinian recognition of its right to exist: "Israel withdraws from Palestinian areas occupied from September 28, 2000 and the two sides restore the status quo that existed at that time, as security performance and cooperation progress. Israel also freezes all settlement activity."[21] Israel "immediately dismantles settlement outposts erected since March 2001" and "takes measures to improve the humanitarian situation."[22]

Phase II was to focus on "creating an independent Palestinian state with provisional borders and attributes of sovereignty, based on the new constitution, as a way station to a permanent status settlement." It specified that "this goal can be achieved when the Palestinian people have a leadership acting decisively against terror, willing and able to build a practicing democracy based on tolerance and liberty." Phase II "[starts] after Palestinian elections and ends with possible creation of an independent Palestinian state with provisional borders in 2003.... Quartet members promote international recognition of Palestinian state, including possible UN membership."[23]

Finally, in Phase III, "[p]arties reach final and comprehensive permanent status agreement that ends the Israel-Palestinian conflict in 2005, through a settlement negotiated between the parties based on UNSCR 242, 338, and 1397, that ends the occupation that began in 1967, and includes an agreed, just, fair, and realistic solution to the refugee issue, and a negotiated resolution on the status of

Jerusalem that takes into account the political and religious concerns of both sides, and protects the religious interests of Jews, Christians, and Muslims worldwide, and fulfills the vision of two states, Israel and sovereign, independent, democratic and viable Palestine, living side-by-side in peace and security."[24] UN Security Council Resolution 1397 called for an end to the violence and implementation of the two-state solution.

The Moderate Abbas

In line with Bush's call for the Palestinians to establish democratic institutions, and due to the refusal of both the United States and Israel to engage in further negotiations with Arafat, on March 19, 2003, Arafat, under heavy pressure, named Mahmoud Abbas Prime Minister of the Palestinian Authority. Abbas had a reputation as a moderate, was a principal architect of the Oslo Accords, and was believed to oppose the al-Aqsa intifada, so the Americans and Israelis had high hopes that he would be able to work well with them to implement the road map.

Belying Abbas's moderate reputation, however, was the fact that he was a Holocaust denier whose doctoral dissertation, written when he was studying at Moscow Oriental College in the Soviet Union, claimed that Zionists had collaborated with the Nazis so as to make the need to emigrate to Palestine appear more urgent. The dissertation, which was published in Arabic as a book in 1983 under the title *The Other Side: The Secret Relations Between Nazism and the Leadership of the Zionist Movement*, asserts: "A partnership was established between Hitler's Nazis and the leadership of the Zionist movement," and those Zionist leaders gave "permission to every racist in the world, led by Hitler and the Nazis, to treat Jews as they wish, so long as it guarantees immigration to Palestine."[25]

The Zionists, Abbas said, were so focused on establishing a Jewish state in Palestine that they wanted Jews to be killed so as to show the need for this state: "Having more victims meant greater rights and stronger privilege to join the negotiation table for dividing the spoils of war once it was over. However, since Zionism was not a fighting partner—suffering victims in a battle—it had no escape but to offer up human beings, under any name, to raise the number of victims, which they could then boast of at the moment of accounting."[26]

Abbas apparently believed that the Zionists hadn't gotten enough victims of which they could boast, so they had inflated the casualty count of the Holocaust in order to buttress their claim that Jews needed a state of their own: "Following the war, word was spread that six million Jews were amongst the victims and that a war of extermination was aimed primarily at the Jews.... The truth is that no one can either confirm or deny this figure. In other words, it is possible that the number of Jewish victims reached six million, but at the same time it is possible that the figure is much smaller—below one million."[27]

According to Abbas, the figure of six million Jews killed was put forward as part of a cynical political ploy: "It seems that the interest of the Zionist movement, however, is to inflate this figure so that their gains will be greater. This led them to emphasize this figure in order to gain the solidarity of international public opinion with Zionism. Many scholars have debated the figure of six million and reached stunning conclusions—fixing the number of Jewish victims at only a few hundred thousand."[28]

Despite all this, the Americans and Israelis thought that in Abbas they had the anti-Arafat: a colorless technocrat in a Western suit instead of a flamboyant, gun-toting militant in a uniform, a man who they thought was sincere in rejecting terrorism. Finally, someone with whom they could deal.

Road Map to Nowhere

However, the Road Map to Peace ran aground almost as soon as it began to be implemented. On June 3, 2003, Bush met with Abbas and the leaders of Egypt, Jordan, Saudi Arabia, and Bahrain; they all agreed to the Road Map provision that "Arab states cut off public and private funding and all other forms of support for groups supporting and engaging in violence and terror."[29] Two days later, Palestinians murdered two Israelis; on June 8, Hamas killed four Israeli soldiers; on June 11, a Palestinian jihad suicide bomber murdered seventeen people on an Israeli bus.[30]

This indicated that the Palestinian Authority was either not able or not willing to follow through on its Road Map commitment to end terrorism. Either it would not or could not compel Hamas and Islamic Jihad to lay down their arms, so one of the essential premises of the Road Map, that Palestinians would end terrorism, was impossible to fulfill from the start.

Hope was nevertheless rekindled on June 29, 2003, when Hamas and Islamic Jihad declared a three-month ceasefire, and the PLO's Fatah movement announced a six-month truce if Israel freed Palestinian prisoners from Israeli jails. Israel began withdrawing from the northern Gaza Strip and Bethlehem. But yet again the jihad did not stop: seventy-one more Israelis were murdered in jihad suicide bombings between the announcements of the ceasefire and the truce and the end of 2003.[31]

The Gaza Withdrawal

Ariel Sharon, however, who succeeded Ehud Barak as Prime Minister of Israel in 2001, was determined to proceed with Israeli withdrawals. On May 27, 2003, he declared that the "occupation" of Palestinian areas was "a terrible thing for Israel and for the Palestinians" that "cannot continue endlessly."[32] The following year, after more jihad attacks and abundant evidence that the Road Map to Peace was stillborn, Sharon on June 6, 2004, announced Israel's unilateral withdrawal from Gaza. Israeli settlements in the Gaza Strip, some of which had been there for thirty-seven years and which in total housed nearly nine thousand people, would be uprooted, by force if necessary. No Israeli presence at all would be left in the Gaza Strip. Sharon also declared that he was going to dismantle the settlements in the West Bank as well, beginning with four in the northern part of the territory.

Addressing the Knesset on October 25, 2004, about the disengagement from Gaza, Sharon explained: "I am firmly convinced and truly believe that this disengagement will strengthen Israel's hold over territory which is essential to our existence, and will be welcomed and appreciated by those near and far, reduce animosity, break through boycotts and sieges and advance us along the path of peace with the Palestinians and our other neighbors."[33]

Withdrawal from Gaza, Sharon said, was necessary due to demographic realities: "We have no desire to permanently rule over millions of Palestinians, who double their numbers every generation. Israel, which wishes to be an exemplary democracy, will not be able to bear such a reality over time. The Disengagement Plan presents the possibility of opening a gate to a different reality."[34]

And once again he turned in peace to those who had never reciprocated such gestures in the past: "Today, I wish to address our Arab neighbors. Already in our Declaration of Independence, in the midst of a cruel war, Israel, which was born in blood, extended its hand in peace to those who fought against it and sought to destroy it by force (and I quote): 'We appeal—in the very midst of the onslaught launched against us now for months—to the Arab inhabitants of the State of Israel to preserve peace and participate in the upbuilding of the State on the basis of full and equal citizenship and due representation in all its provisional and permanent institutions.'"[35]

George W. Bush expressed his approval of the withdrawal in an August 27, 2005, radio address: "Now that Israel has withdrawn, the way forward is clear. The Palestinians must show the world that they will fight terrorism and govern in a peaceful way. We will continue to help the Palestinians to prepare for self government and to defeat the terrorists who attack Israel and oppose the establishment of a peaceful Palestinian state."[36]

The withdrawal from Gaza was completed on September 12, 2005, and the four West Bank settlements were removed on September 22, 2005.

The Gaza Greenhouses: a Parable

Some thought that the unilateral Gaza withdrawal was an excellent opportunity for Israel to show yet again its goodwill toward those who wanted only its destruction. In Gaza, Israeli farmers had built and operated four thousand greenhouses that employed around 3,500 Palestinians and earned around one hundred million dollars a year. James Wolfensohn, former president of the World Bank, and a Middle East envoy for the Bush White House, approached Mortimer Zuckerman, publisher of the New York *Daily News*, and asked him to raise $14 million to buy the irrigation systems and other necessary equipment for the continued operation of the greenhouses, so that the Palestinians could keep on operating them and would immediately have an opportunity to establish a normal society, providing employment for some of their citizens who would presumably be turning away from terrorism now that the Israelis were leaving.

"Despite my skepticism," Zuckerman said in an August 2005 interview with the *New York Times*, "I thought to myself, 'This is perhaps the only illustration or symbol of what could be the benefits of a co-operational, rather than a confrontational attitude.'"[37] Leonard Stern, a wealthy real estate entrepreneur and former owner of the *Village Voice*, was one of the donors; he recounted that he got a phone call from Secretary of State Condoleezza Rice: "She said that she wanted to let me know that myself and every member of the group that helped make this possible had made a very positive contribution to the peace."[38]

The Palestinians did not receive this "contribution to the peace" in the way that was expected or intended. When the Israeli withdrawal was complete, Palestinians immediately looted and destroyed hundreds of the greenhouses, causing two million dollars in damage.[39] Police sometimes joined the looters.[40]

The destruction of the greenhouses was emblematic of the entire "peace process"—so much so that the entire greenhouse incident serves as a parable of the "peace process" itself. Throughout the process, Israelis would make gestures of goodwill that would not be reciprocated, or the Palestinian Arabs would say everything they were expected to say and then act as if they had meant none of it. Instead of calling the Muslims to account, however, the world powers—Britain first and then the United States, would put more pressure on Israel to make more concessions, as if some new manifestation of generosity would finally have the desired effect. Every one of Israel's concessions and goodwill gestures would be received in the same way, and yet the obvious lesson was never learned.

In fact, it was studiously avoided, although Mortimer Zuckerman himself appears to have awakened to some unpleasant realities. On August 6, 2014, without mentioning his own involvement in raising money to help the Palestinians continue to operate the greenhouses, he wrote:

> Let us remember that Israel withdrew all of its citizens, uprooted its settlements, and completely disengaged from Gaza in 2005. It wanted this new Palestinian state to succeed. To help it economically, the Israelis left behind 3,000 working greenhouses. They also disassembled four smaller settlements in the northern West Bank—a sign that they wanted to live peacefully, side by side with Gaza. And how did the Palestinians respond? They demolished the greenhouses, elected Hamas, and instead of building a state, says Charles Krauthammer in the National Review Online, spent most of the last decade turning Gaza into a massive military base brimming with weapons to make endless war on Israel.[41]

The Death of the "Peace Process"

On January 25, 2006, Palestinians in the West Bank and Gaza went to the polls to elect members of the Palestinian Authority's legislature. The result was an overwhelming victory for Hamas, which won seventy-six of the 132 seats in a decisive repudiation of Mahmoud Abbas's negotiations with Israel, and of the very premise that negotiations with Israel were worth pursuing.

In Israel, interim Prime Minister Ehud Olmert held a three-hour emergency meeting to discuss the implications of the Hamas victory; his office issued a statement: "Israel will not conduct any negotiation with a Palestinian government, if it includes any (members of) an armed terror organisation that calls for Israel's destruction."[42] As Abbas named Hamas's Ismail Haniyeh Prime Minister of the Palestinian Authority, The Quartet and Israel initiated a boycott of the Palestinian government until it honored the existing agreements that had been made during the "peace process," including recognizing Israel's right to exist and ending jihad terrorism.

Hamas refused. On June 6, 2006, however, Haniyeh appealed directly to George W. Bush, writing: "We are an elected government which came through a democratic process.... We are so concerned about stability and security in the area that we don't mind having a Palestinian state in the 1967 borders and offering a truce for many years.... We are not warmongers, we are peace makers and we call on the American government to have direct negotiations with the elected government."[43]

Bush didn't answer, which proved to be wise when Hamas fired multiple rockets into Israel from Gaza the month after Haniyeh told Bush, "[W]e are peace makers." If Haniyeh's letter had been closely analyzed at the White House, it might have been noticed that Haniyeh was not offering even a semblance of a permanent peace, but only "a truce for many years." It is extremely unlikely that anyone in the Bush White House knew anything about Islam; if anyone did, however, he or she might have realized that Haniyeh's offer of a truce was an admission of weakness. Islamic law stipulates, here again based on the example of Muhammad's Treaty of Hudaybiyya, that truces can be made with non-Muslims for a period of ten years (although they can be extended if necessary) if the Muslim forces are weak and need time to gather strength.[44]

As weak as Hamas may have been, if Israel moved at that time to try to destroy it utterly, Israel would have become even more isolated worldwide. Although the "peace process" had never been anything but a resounding failure, the prevailing opinion among the intelligentsia in the West and the world over was that Israel needed to make more concessions to the Palestinians so as to bring about a lasting peace.

At this point, however, there was a stalemate. The Palestinian coalition government broke down in 2007; since then, Hamas has been in control of Gaza and the Palestinian Authority of the West Bank. Nonetheless, the "peace process" sputtered on. PLO chief negotiator Saeb Erekat revealed in December 2018 that ten years previously, Olmert had offered the Palestinians more than what they were demanding for a Palestinian state, including part of Jerusalem as well as the West Bank and Gaza—an offer even more generous than Ehud Barak's had been—and still Mahmoud Abbas rejected the offer. Recalled Erekat:

> I heard [former Israeli Prime Minister] Olmert say that he offered [Abbas] 100% of the West Bank territory. This is true. I'll testify to this. He [Olmert] presented a map [to Abbas], and said: "I want [Israel] to take 6.5% of the West Bank and I'll give [the PA] 6.5% of the 1948 territory (i.e., land in Israel) in return." [Olmert] said to Abbas: "The area of the West Bank and the Gaza Strip on the eve of June 4, 1967, was 6,235 sq. km. Erekat says (i.e., I, Erekat, said to Abbas): 'There are 50 sq. km. of no man's land in Jerusalem and Latrun.' We'll split them between us, so the territory will be 6,260 sq. km." [I said to Abbas:] Olmert wants to give you 20 sq. km. more, so that you could say [to Palestinians]: "I got more than the 1967 territories." Regarding Jerusalem, [Olmert said:] "What's Arab is Arab, and what's Jewish is Jewish, and we'll keep it an open city." Regarding the refugees, [Olmert] offered him [Abbas] 150,000 refugees… [Olmert] said: "The refugees' right to return to the State of Palestine is your law. But regarding Israel, we will accept 150,000 refugees over 10 years. 15,000 [per year] over 10 years.[45]

This was a remarkably generous offer, but it still contained that one element that no Palestinian Muslim leader could ever accept:

that the newly created Palestinian state would recognize the State of Israel as Jewish state, and stop all efforts to weaken and destroy it. The jihad imperative overruled all genuine aspirations for a Palestinian state, and Olmert's offer came to nothing.

Palestinian jihad terrorism against Israel fell off sharply with the construction in the first decade of the twenty-first century of a security fence cutting through the West Bank, but attacks still continued at a less frequent rate. The jihadist goal of destroying Israel utterly was still very much in play. Continuing rocket attacks from Gaza led Israeli forces to enter the Gaza Strip on December 27, 2008; Israel ended its operations on January 18, 2009, amid a chorus of international condemnation.

And with a new president in the White House, that condemnation would only get worse.

Barack Hussein Obama versus Israel

Four days later, two days after he had been inaugurated President of the United States on January 20, 2009, Barack Obama reiterated the Road Map to Peace's talking points: "To be a genuine party to peace, The Quartet has made it clear that Hamas must meet clear conditions: recognize Israel's right to exist; renounce violence; and abide by past agreements. Going forward, the outline for a durable ceasefire is clear: Hamas must end its rocket fire; Israel will complete the withdrawal of its forces from Gaza; the United States and our partners will support a credible anti-smuggling and interdiction regime, so that Hamas cannot rearm."[46]

Obama gave a hint of where his sympathies lay when he added: "Just as the terror of rocket fire aimed at innocent Israelis is intolerable, so, too, is a future without hope for the Palestinians. Our hearts go out to Palestinian civilians who are in need of immediate food, clean water, and basic medical care."[47] About the Israeli civilians who had to live with the daily fear of Hamas rockets, Obama had nothing to say.

This wasn't inadvertent. During his entire political career, Obama had had close associations with foes of Israel and outright anti-Semites, and they were well represented in his administration. His national security adviser, General Jim Jones, once began a speech with an anti-Semitic joke about greedy Jews; Obama's closest adviser, Valerie Jarrett, spoke at conference of the Islamic Society of North America that featured discussions of how Jews "have control of the world" and the Holocaust is the Jews' punishment for being "serially disobedient to Allah."[48] She did not make any reference to the conference's anti-Semitism; nor did Obama. Obama appointed Chuck Hagel secretary of defense—a man who spoke of a "worldwide Jewish conspiracy" and claimed that "the Jewish lobby intimidates a lot of people up here."[49]

He gave the Presidential Medal of Freedom to South African bishop Desmond Tutu, who once claimed: "People are scared in this country [the U.S.], to say wrong is wrong because the Jewish lobby is powerful" and "[T]he Jews thought they had a monopoly on God," and he also gave the medal to Irish politician Mary Robinson, who once chaired the World Conference against Racism, Racial Discrimination, Xenophobia and Related Intolerance, which was so viciously anti-Israel that the U.S. secretary of state at the time, Colin Powell, walked out.[50]

"The Situation for the Palestinian People Is Intolerable"

On May 7, 2009, the Palestinian Authority's ambassador to Lebanon, Abbas Zaki, said in a television interview that he favored the two-state solution. He warned against concluding a temporary truce (*hudna*) with Israel, because that would enable Israel to "become a fact on the ground, and we will end up as small enclaves, and should be driven out with time."[51]

Zaki presented the two-state solution as the alternative to this, as it would lead not to Israel's being "a fact on the ground" but to its collapse:

> *It is high time that we found a final, comprehensive solution.... With the two-state solution, in my opinion, Israel will collapse,*

because if they get out of Jerusalem, what will become of all the talk about the Promised Land and the Chosen People? What will become of all the sacrifices they made—just to be told to leave? They consider Jerusalem to have a spiritual status. The Jews consider Judea and Samaria to be their historic dream. If the Jews leave those places, the Zionist idea will begin to collapse. It will regress of its own accord. Then we will move forward.[52]

Less than a month later, on June 4, 2009, Obama gave a major policy speech in Cairo in which he reaffirmed U.S. support for that two-state solution. He once again called on both the Israelis and the Palestinians to abide by the provisions of the Road Map, and again revealed his decided preference for the Palestinians, speaking of the creation of the State of Israel as a reaction to the Holocaust, with no mention of the ancient and continuous Jewish presence in the land. Then he spoke in lurid terms about the plight of Palestinians:

On the other hand, it is also undeniable that the Palestinian people—Muslims and Christians—have suffered in pursuit of a homeland. For more than sixty years they have endured the pain of dislocation. Many wait in refugee camps in the West Bank, Gaza, and neighboring lands for a life of peace and security that they have never been able to lead. They endure the daily humiliations—large and small—that come with occupation. So let there be no doubt: the situation for the Palestinian people is intolerable. America will not turn our backs on the legitimate Palestinian aspiration for dignity, opportunity, and a state of their own.[53]

A state of their own: just what Abbas Zaki wanted.

Even that wasn't all. Obama also likened the Palestinians' situation to that of black Americans during the slavery and Jim Crow eras:

Palestinians must abandon violence. Resistance through violence and killing is wrong and does not succeed. For centuries, black people in America suffered the lash of the whip as slaves and the humiliation of segregation. But it was not violence that won full and equal rights. It was a peaceful and determined insistence upon the ideals at the center of America's founding. This same story can be told by people from South Africa to South Asia; from Eastern Europe to Indonesia. It's a story with a simple truth: that violence is a dead end. It is a sign of neither courage nor power to shoot rockets at sleeping children, or to blow up old women on a bus. That is not how moral authority is claimed; that is how it is surrendered.[54]

Equating Israeli self-defense measures with slavery and racism was a revealing indication of how little Obama thought of Israel. He thought even less of Israeli Prime Minister Benjamin Netanyahu. In November 2011 at the G20 summit, French President Nicolas Sarkozy told Obama: "I cannot bear Netanyahu, he's a liar."[55] Obama was sympathetic, responding: "You're fed up with him, but I have to deal with him even more often than you."[56]

On March 21, 2013, when Obama spoke in Jerusalem, he claimed that Israel was not prosecuting those who committed crimes against Palestinians, and portrayed Israel's self-defense measures as gratuitous oppression of the Palestinian people. Nonetheless, the *New York Times* transcript makes it clear that his speech was enthusiastically received:

It is not fair that a Palestinian child cannot grow up in a state of their own—(cheers, applause)—living their entire lives with the presence of a foreign army that controls the movements, not just of those young people but their parents, their grandparents, every single day. It's not just when settler violence against Palestinians goes unpunished. (Applause.) It's not right to prevent Palestinians from farming their lands or restricting a student's ability to move around the West Bank—(applause)—or displace Palestinian families from their homes. Neither occupation nor expulsion is the answer. (Cheers, applause.) Just as Israelis built a state in their homeland, Palestinians have a right to be a free people in their own land. (Applause.)[57]

Obama suggested that Israelis' views of the Palestinians were based not on the grim reality of jihad terror but on prejudice and ignorance:

But I—I'm going off script here for a second, but before I—before I came here, I—I met with a—a group of young Palestinians from the age of 15 to 22. And talking to them, they weren't that different from my daughters. They weren't that different from your daughters or sons.

I honestly believe that if—if any Israeli parent sat down with those kids, they'd say, I want these kids to succeed. (Applause.) I want them to prosper. I want them to have opportunities just like my kids do. (Applause.) I believe that's what Israeli parents would want for these kids if they had a chance to listen to them and talk to them. (Cheers, applause.) I believe that. (Cheers, applause.)[58]

Obama pressed Israel to enter into another round of the "peace process":

Now, Israel cannot be expected to negotiate with anyone who's dedicated to its destruction. (Applause.) But while I know you have had differences with the Palestinian Authority, I genuinely believe that you do have a true partner in President Abbas and Prime Minister Fayyad. (Applause.) I believe that. And they have a track record to prove it. Over the last few years, they have built institutions and maintained security on the West Bank in ways that few could have imagined just a few years ago. So many Palestinians, including young people, have rejected violence as a means of achieving their aspirations.[59]

Israeli-Palestinian talks did continue, but without much in the way of concrete results, and less than a month after Obama's speech, Mahmoud Abbas showed how much of a partner for peace he really was. At a meeting of the PLO Executive Committee that was carried on official Palestinian Authority television, he called jihad terrorists in Israeli prisons heroes: "We will continue the fight for [the prisoners' issue] until all these heroes, the prisoners of freedom, are freed. In a few days there will be a rally for brother Marwan Barghouti, who is a brother, prisoner and commander. We must mark the day of his [arrest] and salute him in his prison eleven years after he was kidnapped. Likewise, we cannot forget brother Ahmad Sa'adat and the rest of the leader prisoners, such as the MPs and the veteran [prisoners]."[60] Marwan Barghouti was in prison for his involvement in jihad terror attacks that had targeted Israeli civilians. Ahmad Sa'adat was the head of another terror group, the Popular Front for the Liberation of Palestine.

This was not some aberration; it was and remains Abbas's consistent stance. On May 2, 2013, Sultan Abu Al-Einein, an adviser to Abbas, praised a jihadi who had murdered an Israeli civilian. Learning of this, five members of the U.S. House of Representatives wrote to Abbas: "President Abbas, allowing this type of incitement and hatemongering to take place within your ranks is intolerable if you are truly dedicated to non-violence. We ask that you publically and officially denounce and condemn Mr. Al-Einein's remarks at once and remove him from his position in your government. We also request that Fatah immediately remove its Facebook page glorifying this murder."[61]

Al-Einein was neither fired nor repudiated. According to Fatah's Lebanese branch, "President Abbas resisted pressures put on him and spoke angrily in the wake of American intervention in internal Palestinian matters."[62] Adel Abd Al-Rahman, a columnist for the official PA daily *Al-Hayat Al-Jadida*, in a June 17, 2013, column thundered:

> *The American government's request that the Palestinian leadership 'dismiss' brother fighter Sultan Abu Al-Einein from Fatah's Central Committee is nothing more than the continuation of that same domineering conduct that is completely at odds with the language of political and diplomatic etiquette. This interferes in Palestinian internal, political and partisan affairs, and disregards all values of diplomacy...*

What Al-Einein did doesn't matter. The American government is not allowed to interfere in internal Palestinian affairs while the Palestinian leadership labors day and night for peace....

Al-Einein had praised a jihad murderer, and Adel Abd Al-Rahman was claiming that calling for him to be fired interfered with the Palestinian work for peace.

Yes, we want the support of the USA and the world's peace forces, including Israeli peace forces– but this doesn't mean that we will turn a blind eye to American or Israeli humiliation or humiliation by any other party. The American logic, the cowboy logic devoid of political and diplomatic tact, is unacceptable.[63]

Abbas never changed his tune. After two jihad groups, the Mourabitoun and the Mourabitat, began violent riots on the Temple Mount in September 2015, he applauded: "We bless you; we bless the Mourabitoun and the Mourabitat. We welcome every drop of blood spilled in Jerusalem. This is pure blood, clean blood, blood on its way to Allah. With the help of Allah, every shaheed (martyr) will be in heaven, and every wounded will get his reward. All of their steps, we will not allow them. All these divisions, Al-Aqsa is ours, and the (Church of the) Holy Sepulcher is ours, everything is ours, all ours. They (the Jews) have no right to desecrate them with their filthy feet and we won't allow them to."[64]

So much for Barack Obama's "peace partner."

The relationship between the United States and Israel deteriorated more during Obama's presidency than at any other time since the State of Israel was founded. Obama pursued a disastrous deal with the Islamic Republic of Iran that after ten years would leave no barriers in the way of that rogue regime's development of nuclear weapons, heedless of the fact that Iranian leaders had repeatedly vowed the imminent destruction of Israel.[65] In one of many such statements, on July 23, 2014, Iran's Supreme Leader, Ayatollah Ali Khamenei, tweeted: "This barbaric, wolflike &

infanticidal regime of #Israel which spares no crime has no cure but to be annihilated."[66]

In an unsuccessful attempt to head off the deal, Israeli Prime Minister Benjamin Netanyahu addressed the U.S. Congress on March 3, 2015. It was not Obama but House speaker John Boehner and other congressional Republican Party leaders who had extended the invitation. Boehner did not notify Obama that he was inviting Netanyahu, explaining: "I wanted to make sure that there was no interference. There's no secret here in Washington about the animosity that this White House has for Prime Minister Netanyahu. I frankly didn't want that getting in the way, quashing what I thought was a real opportunity."[67]

Obama's final betrayal of Israel came less than a month before he left office, when he instructed his ambassador to the United Nations, Samantha Power, not to veto a resolution calling upon Israel to halt all settlement activity in East Jerusalem and the West Bank. In a speech to the UN explaining why, Power said: "The settlement problem has gotten so much worse that it is now putting at risk the very viability of that two-state solution."[68]

Power said that the U.S. would have vetoed the resolution had it not also called upon the Palestinians to renounce terrorism, and she addressed Palestinian leaders as if they really did want to make peace with Israel, imploring them to recognize "the obvious: that in addition to taking innocent lives—the incitement to violence, the glorification of terrorists, and the growth of violent extremism erodes prospects for peace, as this resolution makes crystal clear."[69]

Power reiterated her administration's support for the idea that Israel and a new state of Palestine could live as neighbors in peace:

Some may cast the U.S. vote as a sign that we have finally given up on a two-state solution. Nothing could be further from the truth. None of us can give up on a two-state solution. We continue to believe that that solution is the only viable path to provide peace and security for the state of Israel, and freedom and dignity for the

Palestinian people. And we continue to believe that the parties can still pursue this path, if both sides are honest about the choices, and have the courage to take steps that will be politically difficult. While we can encourage them, it is ultimately up to the parties to choose this path, as it always has been. We sincerely hope that they will begin making these choices before it is too late.[70]

How a Palestinian state could mean peace and security for Israel in light of the jihad ideology so fervently held by Hamas, Hizballah, Islamic Jihad, and others arrayed against Israel, Power did not explain. But that ideology was the primary obstacle to the "peace process" and the destroyer of any and all negotiated agreements: it made it impossible for Palestinian Arab leaders to accept a Jewish state in any form, and made it certain that a Palestinian state would be only a new jihad base for strikes against a diminished Israel. What Power called "the only viable path to provide peace and security for the state of Israel" would actually be a serious threat to its existence.

Of course, Power wasn't saying anything new. Numerous other politicians from all points on the political spectrum had affirmed that the two-state solution was the only viable path to peace. They never seemed to reflect upon why it had never worked, and while they pressed Israel to stop constructing settlements and the Palestinians to stop terror attacks, they never seemed to ask themselves why the Palestinians never actually did stop engaging in terrorism, or to consider that to continue sending massive amounts of aid to the Palestinians while the Palestinian media routinely incited hatred and violence against Israel was only encouraging terrorism, and not giving the Palestinians any incentive to do anything to try to end it.

The situation was at an impasse. At the end of the Obama administration, the purveyors of the "peace process" were out of ideas, and were reduced to offering the same failed "solutions" again and again.

Until, that is, Donald Trump was elected President of the United States.

This Year in Jerusalem

As president, Donald Trump departed from what had been standard "peace process" procedure since the British incited riots against Jews in Palestine in 1920: demand substantive concessions from the Israelis and promises from the Palestinian Arabs, and continue to do so even as Palestinians flout all agreements and promises they make, never holding them accountable for their actions or attaching any consequences to them.

After nearly a century of this, Trump began to reward the Israelis for their commitment to peace and penalize the Palestinians for their commitment to war. On December 6, 2017, Trump fulfilled a campaign promise and shocked the world by recognizing Jerusalem as Israel's capital, and announcing that the U.S. embassy would move there. "When I came into office," Trump said, "I promised to look at the world's challenges with open eyes and very fresh thinking. We cannot solve our problems by making the same failed assumptions and repeating the same failed strategies of the past. Old challenges demand new approaches."[71] If that were true of anything, it was true of the "peace process."

Trump continued: "My announcement today marks the beginning of a new approach to conflict between Israel and the Palestinians."[72] He pointed out that in 1995, the U.S. Congress passed the Jerusalem Embassy Act, asking that the U.S. recognize Jerusalem as Israel's capital and move the embassy there. Bill Clinton, George W. Bush, and Barack Obama had all promised to do so but signed a waiver every year postponing the recognition and the move. This was a clear capitulation to jihad terror: Clinton, Bush, and Obama were allowing jihad terrorists' threats to dictate American policy.

"Presidents issued these waivers," Trump said, "under the belief that delaying the recognition of Jerusalem would advance the cause of peace."[73] However, "after more than two decades of waivers, we are no closer to a lasting peace agreement between Israel and the Palestinians. It would be folly to assume that repeating the exact same formula would now produce a different or better result. Therefore, I have determined that it is time to officially recognize Jerusalem as the capital of Israel."[74]

Trump also noted that denying Israel the right that every nation had, to determine its own capital, was a challenge to its very status as an independent nation: "Israel is a sovereign nation with the right like every other sovereign nation to determine its own capital. Acknowledging this as a fact is a necessary condition for achieving peace."[75]

Trump's approach wasn't entirely new: he emphasized that the move was "not intended, in any way, to reflect a departure from our strong commitment to facilitate a lasting peace agreement. We want an agreement that is a great deal for the Israelis and a great deal for the Palestinians. We are not taking a position of any final status issues, including the specific boundaries of the Israeli sovereignty in Jerusalem, or the resolution of contested borders. Those questions are up to the parties involved.... The United States would support a two-state solution if agreed to by both sides."[76]

Enraged, Mahmoud Abbas severed all diplomatic contact between the Palestinian Authority and the United States. But unlike his predecessors, Trump was not intimidated, and moved swiftly to make the embassy move a reality: the new U.S. embassy in Jerusalem opened on May 14, 2018, the seventieth anniversary of Israel's independence.

"They Don't Even Want to Negotiate"

Trump also moved decisively to do something no American president or anyone else outside of Israel in a position of power had ever done: hold the Palestinians accountable for their nonstop incitement and glorification of violence against Israel.

On January 2, 2018, Trump took to Twitter, tweeting: "we pay the Palestinians HUNDRED OF MILLIONS OF DOLLARS a year and get no appreciation or respect. They don't even want to negotiate a long overdue peace treaty with Israel. We have taken

Jerusalem, the toughest part of the negotiation, off the table, but Israel, for that, would have had to pay more. But with the Palestinians no longer willing to talk peace, why should we make any of these massive future payments to them?"[77]

The Trump administration followed through, announcing a cut in aid of $65 million to the UN agency devoted to the Palestinian refugees, the United Nations Relief and Works Agency (UNRWA), on January 16, 2018.[78] It cut another $45 million just days later, and ended all aid to UNRWA on August 31, 2018.[79]

This was long overdue. UNRWA had for a considerable period been not a humanitarian agency but an agent of the jihad. During Operation Protective Edge, another Israeli defensive action in Gaza in the summer of 2014, Hamas weapons stockpiles were three times found in UNRWA schools.[80] The United Nations, no friend of Israel, confirmed this in a 2015 report.[81]

During the same operation, UNRWA demonstrated its readiness to demonize Israel under false pretenses, charging that the Israel Defense Forces (IDF) had refused to allow it to evacuate civilians from a school where fifteen people had been killed. UNRWA issued a statement saying: "UNRWA had been attempting to negotiate with the [IDF] a pause in the fighting during which they would guarantee a safe corridor to relocate staff and any displaced persons who chose to evacuate to a more secure location. Approval for that never came to UNRWA."[82] UNRWA spokesman Chris Gunness tweeted: "Over the course of the day UNRWA tried 2 coodinate [sic] with the Israeli Army a window for civilians 2 leave & it was never granted."[83]

An IDF official, however, sharply contradicted UNRWA and Gunness: "For two days we were trying to move people out of that school in particular and the Beit Hanoun area in general. This morning we sought a cease-fire in the area and a humanitarian evacuation of civilians, but Hamas refused—because they wanted to keep civilians in the area to protect their fighters who were firing on the IDF."[84] The official called the charges from Gunness and UNRWA "a flat-out complete and total lie."[85]

For years, UNRWA schools have been using textbooks produced by the Palestinian Authority that encourage Palestinian students to hate Israel and that call for jihad against the Jewish state. Members of Hamas have taught in them; UNRWA head Peter Henson waved away concerns about this, saying: "There are Hamas members on the UNRWA payroll and I don't see that as a crime."[86] A key Hamas leader, Said Sayyam, who ruthlessly hunted down and killed Palestinians suspected of aiding Israel, was a science and math teacher in UNRWA schools from 1980 to 2003.[87]

Palestinian children in UNRWA summer camps in the summer of 2013 learned that "Jews are the wolf" and that the Palestinians would one day conquer Israel.[88] One camp speaker told children: "With God's help and our own strength we will wage war. And with education and Jihad we will return to our homes!"[89] A child at one camp exclaimed: "We are filled with rage."[90] Another said, "I will defeat the Jews. They are a gang of infidels and Christians. They don't like Allah and do not worship Allah. And they hate us."[91]

Amina Hinawi, director of a UNRWA camp in Gaza, explained: "We teach the children about the villages they came from.... [T]his way, every child will be motivated to return to their original village. UNRWA finances this summer camp. I'm very, very, very appreciative of UNRWA."[92]

In June 2016, a student at an UNRWA school said: "They teach us in school that Jews are fickle, bad people. I am ready to stab a Jew, and drive over them."[93] Another UNRWA school student added: "Stabbing and running over Jews brings dignity to the Palestinians. I'm going to run them over and stab them with knives."[94] A third declared: "With Allah's help, I will fight for ISIS, the Islamic State."[95]

David Bedein of the Center for Near East Policy Research charged in January 2019 that in UNRWA schools, "every child is indoctrinated that they should kill the Jews."[96]

UNRWA has also fabricated Israeli atrocities. In June 2017, it ran an appeal for donations featuring a photo of a little girl standing in the rubble of a bombed-out building. UNRWA's donation appeal gave what it claimed was the background of the photo: the girl had lived a life of hardship because of Israeli oppression:

Imagine being cut off from the world—for your whole life. That's reality for children like Aya. The blockade of Gaza began when she was a baby, the occupation in the West Bank before her parents were born. Now she is eleven, and the blockade goes on.

Aya's childhood memories are of conflict and hardship, walls she cannot escape, and the fear that the only home she knows, however tiny, could be gone when she returns from school.

This Ramadan, please help support children like Aya who have known nothing but conflict and hardship...[97]

There was just one detail that prevented this story from having its intended effect: it was entirely false. The photo actually had nothing to do with Israel at all; it was taken in Damascus, Syria, in 2014. What's more, UNRWA had used the identical photo in a 2015 publication touting its work in Syria, with the caption: "A young girl stands in the rubble of Qabr Essit, near Damascus. In 2014, UNRWA was able begin [sic] rebuilding facilities within the neighbourhood, including a school and community centre © 2014 UNRWA Photo by Taghrid Mohammad."[98]

Thus U.S. State Department spokesperson Heather Nauert was absolutely right when she called UNRWA "irredeemably flawed" in announcing that the U.S. was cutting off funding.[99] UNRWA wasn't conceivably a part of any "peace process"; it was a weapon in the jihad against Israel. But no president had done anything to call it to account—until Donald Trump.

On September 10, 2018, the Trump administration ordered the closing of the PLO's diplomatic office in Washington, D.C., because of the fact that the PLO "has not taken steps to advance the start of direct and meaningful negotiations with Israel."[100] Referring to Trump's undisclosed plan for peace between Israel and the Palestinians, the State Department issued a statement saying that "the PLO has condemned a U.S. peace plan they have not yet seen and refused to engage with the U.S. government with respect to peace efforts and otherwise." Trump's national security adviser, John Bolton, affirmed that "the United States supports a direct and robust peace process," while also reaffirming "Israel's right to self-defense."

The PLO's Saeb Erekat shot back: "These people have decided to stand on the wrong side of history by protecting war criminals and destroying the two-state solution." He said that Trump administration officials were not "part of the peace process" and would not even be permitted to "sit in the room" during any future negotiations.

The prospects of there even being any future negotiations looked dim. On October 29, 2018, the PLO revoked its recognition of Israel, which had always been hollow anyway, until the Israelis would agree to the establishment of a Palestinian state with borders of 1967 and East Jerusalem as its capital. It also revoked its acceptance of the Oslo Accords.[101]

That the Palestinian leadership was now demanding implementation of the two-state solution was further evidence that Palestinian leaders, as Abbas Zaki had made clear in 2009, now recognized the utility of establishing a Palestinian state as a step toward the ultimate destruction of Israel altogether. Even Hamas in May 2017 had released a new political program stating its readiness to accept a Palestinian state in the West Bank and Gaza. The leader of Hamas's political wing, Khaled Mashaal, made it clear that this did not mean recognition of Israel's right to exist as a Jewish state. He explained that "Hamas advocates the liberation of all of Palestine but is ready to support the state on 1967 borders without recognising Israel or ceding any rights."[102] A Palestinian state would simply be a base from which Palestinians would continue to try to destroy Israel.

Erekat's fury was understandable for another reason as well: for decades, Palestinian leadership had been allowed to get away with calling for jihad and inciting violence, while claiming to support a negotiated peace with Israel. Now, for the first time, an American president was making it clear that this would no longer be tolerated. On February 6, 2019, Jason Greenblatt, Trump's special representative for international negotiations, directed a series of tweets to Palestinian information minister Nabil Abu Rudeineh, whom he quoted as saying: "'The American support for settlements through silence is doomed to failure because there is no peace and stability without an agreement with the Palestinian people.... Well, Mr. Nabil, we agree on something—there is no peace without an agreement. We are working hard on that. You're doing nothing. You can't claim to want peace and also try to sabotage the potential for an agreement. It can't go both ways.... And the Palestinians deserve stability too. You're holding that back as well. Don't waste more time—do something meaningful for your people."[103]

There didn't appear to be any interest in doing that among Palestinian leadership. That same day, Abu Rudeinah declared that if the U.S. would throw its support behind a Palestinian state with pre-1967 borders and a capital in East Jerusalem, "we are ready to sit at the table and negotiate immediately." According to Bloomberg News, "such positions would mean Trump has in effect backtracked on his support for Israeli claims in Jerusalem, even if he doesn't say so outright, Abu Rudeineh said." It was inconceivable that Trump would backtrack on his statements about Jerusalem's being the capital of Israel and move the U.S. embassy back to Tel Aviv, but that was essentially what Abu Rudeineh was demanding: that Trump restore the status quo of previous presidencies and negotiate with the Israelis and Palestinians in the old manner, demanding concessions from Israel alone.

Greenblatt tweeted to Abu Rudeineh on February 1, 2019: "Mr. Abu Rudeineh: time to get serious. Either work on peace and/ or work on helping Palestinians. The old messages and methods don't work anymore- not with the US, and not with many other countries. It's only a matter of time until other countries say this out loud too."[104]

But Palestinian leadership was not listening, and neither were the people. A December 2018 poll showed that Hamas leader Ismail Haniyeh would defeat Abbas if an election were held for the

Palestinian Authority presidency.[105] Such an election was unlikely to happen; the "democracy" that George W. Bush had wanted to see established dispensed with such formalities after 2004.

"Palestinian Leadership Has Been Allowed to Live in a False Reality for Too Long"

For years, the Palestinian Authority has been rewarding terrorism with its infamous "Pay for Slay" program, paying the families of jihad terrorists who have been imprisoned or killed. This is a massive program: it paid jihad terrorists and their families over $347 million in 2017 alone.[106] Mahmoud Abbas has refused multiple demands from the Israeli government and others to end this program. In July 2018, the Knesset passed a bill directing that the amount of these payments be deducted from the Israeli taxpayer money that was collected for the Palestinians. (How many people who condemned Israel for its supposed oppression of the Palestinians were even aware that Israeli taxpayer money went to the Palestinian Authority?)

Abbas spokesman Nabil Abu Rudeineh called this bill a "declaration of war," and Abbas himself was defiant: "We will not accept a cut or cancellation of salaries to the families of martyrs and prisoners, as some are trying to bring about. We view the prisoners and the martyrs as planets and stars in the skies of the Palestinian struggle, and they have priority in everything."[107] They were, he said, "paving the way for the independence of Palestine."

On February 1, 2019, however, the U.S. Anti-Terrorism Clarification Act (ATCA) came into effect, allowing families of victims of terror attacks in foreign countries to sue foreign governments. The Palestinian Authority thereupon asked the U.S. government to end its funding of the Palestinian security services, which amounted to sixty million dollars annually, as continuing to take it would expose the Palestinian government to lawsuits under the new law.[108]

Palestinian leaders had been encouraging and rewarding terrorism for years, and world leaders would condemn Israel and pressure it to make more concessions to the Palestinians. There had never been any cost to the Palestinians for their jihad activity. Now there was.

The U.S. ambassador to the UN, Nikki Haley, told the Security Council on July 24, 2018: "Palestinian leadership has been allowed to live in a false reality for too long."[109]

Indeed, that had been a hallmark of the "peace process."

Trump's "Deal of the Century"

On June 22, 2019, the Trump administration nevertheless made yet another attempt to achieve peace between Israel and the Palestinians, unveiling the economic portion of its much-touted peace plan, popularly known as the "Deal of the Century."

The economic plan was essentially another exercise in showering money upon the Palestinians, hoping that this would finally induce them to lay down their arms and live in peace with the Israelis. The Trump plan offered over 50 billion dollars to the Palestinians who were living, not just in the West Bank and Gaza, but also to those in Egypt, Lebanon, and Jordan.[110] It was the largest aid package ever offered to a single recipient: in contrast, the Marshall Plan gave European nations $12 billion—$100 billion in 2018 dollars—divided among sixteen countries.[111]

The prospects for this deal were never good. On May 30, 2019, over three weeks before the economic plan was even released, Palestinian Islamic Jihad leader Ziad al-Nakhala declared: "The Palestinian people are ready for a prolonged confrontation with the Israeli occupation. Not everything that they hope for in the framework of the 'Deal of the Century' will be carried out. The 'Deal of the Century' was born dead and has no value."[112]

The deal was no more popular among the rulers of the Palestinian Authority. Mahmoud Abbas boycotted a conference in Manama, Bahrain on economic development for the Palestinians that was based on the deal. "We are certain," he said, "that the workshop in Manama will not be successful."[113] Abbas grew angrier the longer he spoke, finally thundering: "We will not be slaves or servants for

Greenblatt, Kushner, and Friedman"—that is, three Jews: Jason Greenblatt, Trump's son-in-law Jared Kushner, who was instrumental in formulating the deal, and the U.S. Ambassador to Israel, David M. Friedman.[114]

It was certain that whenever the political portion of the Deal of the Century was to be unveiled, it would be rejected with similar scorn and contempt. Although almost universally ignored, the jihad imperative continued to make it impossible for the Palestinians to accept any peace agreement that allowed for the indefinite existence of the Jewish state of Israel—no matter how advantageous to their people it might be.

CHAPTER NINE

The Palestinian Victimhood Machine

A growing number of people all around the world believe that Palestinian terrorism against Israel is actually justified, as the Israel government is a racist, repressive regime that is one of the world's worst abusers of human rights.

The United Nations aids and abets this impression by spending an astonishing amount of its time issuing condemnations of Israel, while turning a blind eye to actual and serious human rights abuses committed by other countries. In 2018 alone, the UN condemned Israel twenty-one times while not condemning Hamas even once.[1]

This has been a long-standing pattern. Even Barack Obama's UN ambassador, Samantha Power, as she was in the process of explaining in December 2016 why the U.S. was taking the unprecedented step of not blocking a UN resolution calling for a complete halt to Israeli settlement activity, noted the UN's vicious anti-Israel bias: "As long as Israel has been a member of this institution, Israel has been treated differently from other nations at the United Nations. And not only in decades past—such as in the infamous resolution that the General Assembly adopted in 1975, with the support of the majority of Member States, officially determining that, 'Zionism is a form of racism'—but also in 2016, this year. One need only look at the eighteen resolutions against Israel adopted during the UN General Assembly in September; or the twelve Israel-specific resolutions adopted this year in the Human Rights Council—more than those focused on Syria, North Korea, Iran, and South Sudan put together—to see that in 2016 Israel continues to be treated differently from other Member States."[2]

Many of these condemnations came in the wake of Israeli military actions, condemning the Jewish state for using excessive force in defending itself. The UN never acknowledged, however, that much of the evidence on which it had built its case against Israel was not even real.

Projection

A cornerstone of the Palestinian cause in the court of world opinion is projection and deception on a massive scale. Muhammad, the prophet of Islam, declared: "War is deceit."[3] He also elucidated the conditions under which deceit was permissible: "It is not lawful to lie except in three cases: Something the man tells his wife to please her, to lie during war, and to lie in order to bring peace between the people."[4]

This permission for deception, since it came from Muhammad, is normative for Islamic law. The renowned eleventh-century Muslim thinker al-Ghazali explained the purposes of deception: "Know that a lie is not haram [wrong] in itself, but only because [of] the evil conclusions to which it leads the hearer, making him believe something that is not really the case…. If a lie is the only way of obtaining a good result, it is permissible…. We must lie when truth leads to unpleasant results."[5]

Palestinian leaders have refined lying during war into a fine art. Palestinian leaders and spokesmen portray Israel as an outrageously repressive regime, routinely committing atrocities against the Palestinian people, who deserve aid from the international community as much as the Israelis warrant condemnation.

This initiative, too, has been wildly successful. The United Nations condemns Israel far more often than any other nation; many of these condemnations have been based on reports about Israeli atrocities that were entirely fabricated. World opinion has largely turned against Israel as well, as it has an international reputation today of being one of the world's most unjust and repressive regimes.

Palestinian leaders have claimed that Jewish religious imperatives move Israelis to repress them. Their own religion mandates warfare against and the subjugation of unbelievers, and makes it impossible for them ever to accept the Jewish state, but in a neat inversion of reality, they claim that actually Israel is pursuing a war against them based on religious dogma.

On October 14, 2018, Fatah Revolutionary Council member and TV host Muwaffaq Matar gave his column in the Palestinian daily *Al-Hayat Al-Jadida* the title "The settlers are sacrificing the Palestinians' blood as a sacrifice to Netanyahu."[6] He said that the Israelis in the disputed settlements were "criminals, mass murderers, obsessed with bloodshed, wild unbridled foreigners, but also directed—these are the settlers, the colonialists, the pawns of the racist regime in Tel Aviv."[7] Matar charged that the leaders of Israel's government and military were both "trying to inflict a heavy toll on the Palestinian citizens by means of groups of people devoid of the elements of human nature, who have no connection to the civilized societies other than [their] human form."[8]

Matar was just getting warmed up. "The occupiers and the settlers," he repeated, "are criminals." And worse than criminals: "They have gone beyond the natural bounds of wild animals, which kill only when they are hungry...while they [the occupiers and the settlers] kill only to satisfy their desires. According to their belief, by murdering Palestinians they are carrying out religious ceremonies, and through the sacrifices they are drawing nearer to their great God—Netanyahu."[9]

For a believer in a religion whose founding prophet taught that the end of days and the consummation of all things would not come until believers killed Jews to claim that the Jews themselves were "carrying out religious ceremonies" by "murdering Palestinians" took a breathtaking level of audacity, but many Palestinian leaders and spokesmen besides Matar had that in abundance.

They demonstrated this audacity in charging Israel with all manner of war crimes that it hasn't committed. The claim that the Israelis are perpetrating a new Holocaust against the Palestinians is often repeated on Palestinian TV. On March 25, 2004, it was even included on a show for children. A children's play included that claim that the Jews "are the ones who did the Holocaust, their knife cuts to the length and the width of our flesh…. They opened ovens for us, to bake human beings. They destroyed the villages and burnt the cities. And when an oven stops burning, they light a hundred [more] ovens. Their hands are covered with the blood of our children."[10]

On May 14, 2018, Fatah Revolutionary Council member Osama Al-Qawasmi marked the seventieth anniversary of Israel's proclamation of independence by claiming on official Palestinian Authority TV: "There is no regime in history—believe me, not Hitler, not the Nazis, not fascism—that has implemented what Israel is implementing against the Palestinians."[11]

The Nonmassacre at Deir Yassin

Arabs have been saying such things since before the State of Israel was even founded. On April 12, 1948, the *New York Times* reported: "Dr. Hussein Khalidi, secretary of the Palestine Arab Higher Committee, denounced the 'massacre' of 250 Arab men, women, and children by Irgun Zvai Leumi and the Stern Gang, Zionist terrorist groups, at Deir Yassin on Friday."[12] (The characterization of the Irgun organization and the Stern Gang as "Zionist terrorist groups" was tendentious; neither group deliberately targeted innocent civilians.) Making matters even worse, Arab spokesmen also claimed that Jews had committed mass rapes of Arab women in Deir Yassin.[13]

A member of the staff of the Palestine Broadcasting Service at the time, Hazem Nusseibeh, appeared in a 1998 BBC documentary about the Arab-Israeli conflict and explained how these claims had begun circulating: "I asked Dr. Khalidi how we should cover the story. He said, 'We must make the most of this. So he wrote a press release, stating that at Deir Yassin, children were murdered. Pregnant women were raped. All sorts of atrocities."[14] Arab radio stations broadcast these reports, ignoring eyewitness accounts stating that no such atrocities had been committed.

One of those eyewitnesses told the BBC, "We said there was no rape, but [Khalidi] said, 'We have to say this, so the Arab armies will come to liberate Palestine from the Jews.'"[15] Nusseibeh recalled that Khalidi said, "[W]e should give this the utmost propaganda possible because the Arab countries apparently are not interested in assisting us and we are facing a catastrophe…. So we are forced to give a picture—not what is actually happening—but we had to exaggerate."[16] The intention was to enflame the Arabs with a desire for revenge against the Jews who had committed these atrocities, such that Israel would be destroyed before it was able to declare itself a state, and Jewish immigration to Palestine would cease.

But the plan backfired. Nusseibeh lamented: "This was our biggest mistake. We did not realize how our people would react. As soon as they heard that women had been raped at Deir Yassin, Palestinians fled in terror. They ran away from all our villages."[17] Another Arab from Deir Yassin said bitterly: "Dr. Khalidi was the one who caused the catastrophe. Instead of working in our favor, the propaganda worked in favor of the Jews. Whole villages and towns fled because of what they heard had happened in Deir Yassin."[18] However, the fabrications did have their desired effect upon at least some of the Arabs: four days after the reports about Deir Yassin began to circulate, Arab forces ambushed a Jewish convoy bringing doctors, nurses, and medical supplies to Hadassah hospital on Mount Scopus, murdering seventy-seven Jewish civilians and injuring twenty-three more.[19]

The Irgun, which had warned the Arab civilians of Deir Yassin to evacuate before it entered the village, held a press conference at the time and stated that two hundred Arab civilians had been killed, mostly after pretending to surrender and then attacking the Jewish forces.[20] But there were some inexcusable acts. One Arab stated: "The Jews found out that Arab warriors had disguised themselves as women. The Jews searched the women too. One of the people being checked realized he had been caught, took out a pistol and shot the Jewish commander. His friends, crazed with anger, shot in all directions and killed the Arabs in the area."[21]

However, another Arab in Deir Yassin at the time later stated: "I believe that most of those who were killed were among the fighters and the women and children who helped the fighters."[22] A group of Palestinian researchers later set the number of civilians dead at 107. In reality, the total number of Arabs killed in Deir Yassin was 101; about twenty-five of those were active combatants, and most of the others were killed while attacking the Jewish forces.[23]

The Jewish Agency stated its "horror and disgust" at the fact that civilians had been killed at Deir Yassin, and sent a letter emphasizing this to King Abdullah of Transjordan, who was unmoved, stating that the Deir Yassin "massacre" made him decide to join the forces that were preparing to invade the Jewish state when it declared its independence.[24]

Nevertheless, in Palestinian victimhood propaganda the Deir Yassin civilian deaths have become a wanton massacre of blood-thirsty Jewish terrorists gleefully murdering Palestinian civilians. The legend has far outrun the facts. The internationally renowned Muslim cleric Sheikh Yusuf al-Qaradawi has repeatedly claimed that at Deir Yassin, "as a climax of cruelty certain Jewish terrorists laid wagers on the sex of the unborn babies of expectant mothers. The wretched women were cruelly disemboweled alive, their wombs drawn out and searched for the evidence which would determine the winner."[25] This was a falsehood that would have boggled the mind even of Dr. Hussein Khalidi.

This propaganda has become mainstream. On November 27, 2001, journalist Julie Flint made reference in the *Guardian* to Deir Yassin as "the Palestinian village where 254 villagers were massacred in April 1948, in the most spectacular single attack in the conquest of Palestine." Flint's phrase "the conquest of Palestine" was as tendentious as the *New York Times*' 1948 characterization of the Irgun and the Stern Gang as Zionist terrorist groups, conjuring up an image of a peaceful state of Palestine that was invaded and overrun by pitiless Jewish armies. But by 2001, this fiction was taken for granted as fact all over the world.

Fabricating Palestinian Victimhood

The use of Deir Yassin in Arab and Palestinian propaganda set a precedent and became a paradigm. If evidence for the horrific evil of the Israeli regime was lacking, it would simply have to be invented. On October 28, 2018, on the official Palestinian Authority TV program *Palestine This Morning*, a black-and-white image was shown of an appallingly large group of dead bodies lying in neat rows on the ground. The caption was "70 years since the occupation's massacre at the village of Al-Dawayima."[26]

It was shocking, but it was false. The photo actually dates from 1945 and shows Jewish victims in the Nazi concentration camp of Nordhausen. Even more audacious than taking a photo of Jewish victims of mass murder and claiming that it depicted Jews perpetrating mass murder is that the Palestinian media had used the same photo in April 2018, claiming that it depicted Arab victims of Jews not in al-Dawayima but in Deir Yassin.[27]

It was clear that Palestinian officials didn't think that their supporters would notice the deception, or would care if they did.

Abdullah Alsaafin, who describes himself on Twitter as a "journalist and media trainer," on August 9, 2018, tweeted a photo of a cute, smiling toddler with this explanation: "This baby, Bayan abu khamash, 2 years old, was killed last night along with her pregnant mother when an Israeli rocket hit their house in Gaza Strip town of Der elbalah."[28] The photo, however, was not of Bayan abu Khamash at all, but of an American girl named Elle Lively McBroom. Alsaafin, or his source, picked up the little girl's photo from Instagram, apparently at random, in order to present the world with another Israeli atrocity.[29] There is no certainty that Bayan abu Khamash was killed by Israelis, or killed at all, or even that she really ever existed.

Manufacturing Israeli Atrocities at the Gaza Border

The international media often has accepted Palestinian claims uncritically and spread them throughout the world. The Gaza border protests of summer 2018 offer a superabundance of examples of this. Reuters reported on June 1, 2018, that "Israeli forces killed a Palestinian nurse on Friday as she tried to help a wounded protester at the Gaza border, according to health officials and a witness, while Israel said militants had attacked its troops with gunfire and a grenade."[30] Razan al-Najar, just twenty-one years old, "was shot as she ran toward the fortified border fence, east of the south Gaza city of Khan Younis, in a bid to reach a casualty, a witness said."[31]

The shooting appeared to be a clear case of the Israel Defense Forces' deliberately targeting and murdering a civilian. Reuters continued: "Wearing a white uniform, 'she raised her hands high in a clear way, but Israeli soldiers fired and she was hit in the chest,' the witness, who requested anonymity, told Reuters."[32]

Dr. Iyad Yaghi, a senior health official in Gaza, urged the world to make Razan al-Najar a symbol of Israeli crimes: "It is the first time the Israeli side have killed a paramedic, she is a female. They are targeting more than 245 paramedics. We are asking here, protesting here, asking the international community to put more pressure on Israel. It is time not to keep silent."[33]

However, several days later a video interview of Razan al-Najar emerged in which she said: "I act as a human shield and rescuer for the injured on the front lines."[34] A 2015 report from the United Nations, which has been an inveterate enemy of Israel for years, criticized the Gaza jihad organization Islamic Resistance Movement (Hamas) for using civilians as human shields—that is, mounting attacks against Israel from densely populated civilian areas so that

Israel's retaliatory fire would kill civilians, whose deaths could then be exploited for propaganda purposes.

An Israeli investigation also found that Razan al-Najar had not been hit intentionally; running toward, rather than away from, gunfire was just the sort of thing a self-designated human shield would do, so as to divert gunfire away from those who were trying to breach Israel's security fence.[35] IDF spokesman Ofir Gendelman said: "Razan Najjar was not an angel, like they made her out to be. Hamas puts her in front of the cameras, and she boasts of serving as a human shield for those who exploit even medical personnel to serve Hamas's terrorist purposes."[36]

Razan al-Najar was not the only person Hamas has exploited. The jihad group also paid eight thousand shekels (approximately $2,200) to the family of an eight-month-old baby, Layla Al Ghandour, in return for their claim that the little girl had been killed by Israeli tear gas during the Gaza border riots of June 2018. This was, as far as Hamas was concerned, money well spent: the girl's death made international headlines and led to a chorus of new condemnations of Israel. Seham Al Ghandour, Layla's mother, played her part to the hilt, telling reporters: "I went looking for my daughter and they told me she was taken to the hospital. I went to the hospital and I knew she was dead."[37] Little Layla's aunt, Fatma Al Ghandour, pointed the finger: "They did not have mercy on a girl, they threw gas bombs at her, they killed her with tear gas. They did not have mercy on the children or anyone else. What is she guilty of to die like this?"[38] Euronews intoned solemnly: "Traditionally, May 15th is the day Palestinians mark the 'Nakba' or 'Catastrophe'. But this year, they have even more reasons to grieve."[39]

But in reality, Layla Al Ghandour suffered from a heart defect known as patent ductus arteriosus (PDA), more commonly known as a hole in the heart. That was what killed her, not the tear gas.[40]

Hamas was so anxious to have Palestinian civilian casualties that it could parade before the world in order to gain propaganda victories that in April 2018, as protests raged at the Gaza border, the terror group offered five hundred dollars to Palestinians for getting shot and wounded at the border, and three thousand dollars to the families of those who got themselves killed during the protests.[41] This was too much for Mahmoud al-Habbash, Mahmoud Abbas's adviser on Islamic affairs and supreme Sharia judge, who denounced Hamas on official Palestinian Authority TV: "The Palestinian people…doesn't care about those [Hamas] with 'the emotional stories of heroism,' those with the slogans of heroism—slogans that when you hear them, you think that the people saying them are inside the al-Aqsa Mosque after they liberated it. And afterwards you discover that they're only selling illusions, trading in suffering and blood, trading in victims, [saying]: 'You Palestinians, our people, go and die so that we'll go to the TV and media with strong declarations.' These [Hamas] acts of 'heroism' don't fool anyone anymore. The Palestinian people…sides with the PLO."[42]

Whether the Palestinian people really sided with the PLO over Hamas, and there was considerable evidence that they did not, the fact that Hamas was sending Palestinians to die in order to manipulate world opinion against Israel was certain.

Deception Works

The Israel Defense Forces in May 2018 released footage of Palestinian protesters at the Gaza border carrying a wounded man on a stretcher; at one point, the injured person falls off the stretcher and simply walks away, obviously unhurt. In another clip, rioters take children as young as five to the border, where they throw rocks at IDF personnel; clearly those who took them there were hoping they would be injured or killed, so that they could be exploited for propaganda purposes. The IDF commented: "Throughout Hamas's activity, fake injuries and the exploitation of women and children are rampant. This was all intended to disguise terror activity, including hurling explosives and grenades, attempted infiltrations, and burning Israeli land."[43]

On May 14, 2018, Islamic Jihad released photographs of three of its members who had been killed during the border protests; all three were trained, uniformed operatives, not innocent civilians by any stretch of the imagination.[44] The same day, Hamas released photos of ten others who had been killed; all were members of the jihad terror group's internal security apparatus.[45]

Two days later, Hamas operative Salah Bardawil admitted: "In the last rounds of confrontations, if 62 people were martyred, 50 of them were Hamas."[46]

Nonetheless, on June 13, 2018, the United Nations General Assembly voted 120–8, with forty-five abstentions, to condemn Israel for using excessive force against Palestinian civilians, and called for the creation of an "international protection mechanism" for the Palestinians.[47] The UN had not learned the lessons of its own report on Israel's 2014 incursion into Gaza. At the time, the UN harshly condemned Israel, accusing it of killing forty-four Palestinian children in schools.[48] On July 30, 2014, UN secretary-general Ban Ki-moon harshly denounced Israel for bombing a Gaza school:

Nothing is more shameful than attacking sleeping children. At least 16 civilians are dead and many more are injured. I want to make it clear that the precise location of this Jabalia Elementary Girls School had been communicated to the Israeli military authorities 17 times—as recently as last night, just a few hours before the attack. They were aware of the coordinates and exact locations where these people are being sheltered.... I condemn this attack in the strongest possible terms. It is outrageous. It is unjustifiable. And it demands accountability and justice.[49]

The UN Human Rights Council mandate that began the inquiry into what happened in Gaza singled out Israel for criticism eighteen times and did not criticize Hamas at all. Yet the report that the UN produced found that Hamas was using children as human shields, placing them in harm's way so as to exploit their injury or death for propaganda purposes. And it also found that while Israel did indeed hit three schools—Hamas was stockpiling weapons in them—all three were empty when the Israeli bombs struck. That was not, however, for want of trying on Hamas's part: the UN report found that Hamas operatives helpfully unlocked the gate of one of the schools in the hope that children would be playing in the schoolyard when the Israeli bombs hit.[50]

The UN's 2018 condemnation of Israel for its actions during the Gaza border protests showed why the Palestinians engaged in such thoroughgoing, consistent, and cynical deception: it worked. By portraying Israel as an oppressor and the IDF as an amoral, savage war machine, they had managed to turn world opinion sharply against Israel and make Israel the UN's number-one target for condemnation. They forced the Israelis to go on the defensive and made it appear to be only a matter of simple justice that they make concession after concession to the Palestinians they had so cruelly victimized.

The manufacture of Israeli atrocities was, in sum, a spectacularly successful tactic in the ongoing jihad against Israel. The non-massacre at Deir Yassin led to Transjordan's joining the 1948 war against Israel, and has remained a centerpiece of the Palestinian case against Israel. The non-killing of Muhamed al-Durah helped touch off and sustain the Second Intifada. False accounts of Israeli atrocities fuel Palestinian rage against Israel and keep the fires of jihad burning.

CHAPTER TEN

What Is to Be Done?

The Elusive Solution

There have been innumerable "solutions" to the Israeli-Palestinian conflict, and none of them have actually solved anything. Yet it has never occurred to any of the American presidents who have tried to win a Nobel by being the man who finally brought peace to the Middle East, or to any of the Prime Ministers of Israel who, willingly or unwillingly, made massive concessions to the Palestinians in the hope of finally achieving peace, or to any of the professional diplomats and foreign service "experts" who have expended massive amounts of time trying to hit on the solution that would actually satisfy everyone, that perhaps there is a fatal flaw in the "peace process" itself, such that a peaceful negotiated settlement will never, ever be achieved.

Yet that flaw does exist. It is called jihad.

The Islamic doctrines of jihad, along with the supremacist and anti-Semitic passages of the Qur'an and Sunnah, have been responsible for the entire problem from the beginning up to now. They engendered the hostility that Arabs had for the Zionist settlers in Palestine, even as those Arabs moved close to the new Jewish arrivals in order to benefit from the economic opportunities they offered. They led to the failure of every negotiated peace settlement, because each was predicated upon the Arabs' accepting the existence of a Jewish state in Palestine, no matter how small, and such a state was plainly un-Islamic, a violation of the Qur'anic command to "drive them out from where they drove you out." They have led to the ferocious demonization of the Jewish state among young Palestinians, ensuring that the conflict will continue for decades to come no matter what agreements are made.

So what is the solution?

The reality is that there is no solution, at least not one that will bring about genuine amity and a situation in which Israelis and Palestinians live peacefully as neighbors.

That is not something that people today, particularly Americans, want to hear. There is a prevailing assumption that if we just sit down and talk with one another, we will ultimately be able to find common ground and work out all our differences.

Well, the Israelis and the Muslim Arabs have done this again and again and again for more than four decades now, and the conflict still rages. Borders have been adjusted, troops have been withdrawn, settlements have been dismantled, and yet the Palestinian media still daily seethes with rage and hate against Israel, and calls for its destruction. For talks to succeed, both sides have to be willing to make compromises and abide by agreements; the Palestinians have repeatedly shown that they are willing to do neither. They clearly see negotiations with Israel as a means to gain concessions that are steps on the way to the ultimate collapse of the Jewish state.

Going forward, therefore, there should be no negotiations at all, or if there are, they must be conducted on a more realistic basis.

Negotiate on the Basis of Reality, Not Fantasy

If open-eyed and courageous leaders were in office in Jerusalem and Washington, they would make any further negotiations with the Palestinians contingent upon the renunciation of jihad terrorism in word and in deed. That is, Palestinian leaders must arrest and prosecute the leaders of Hamas and Islamic Jihad and other terror groups, and move energetically to end all terror activities against Israel. Programs must be instituted in mosques and Islamic schools in Israel, the West Bank, and Gaza, teaching young Muslims that the doctrine of jihad and the idea that no land can be ruled by non-Muslims after it has been ruled by Muslims are obsolete and must be rejected now and for all time. This cannot be a matter to which the Palestinians pay lip service while continuing jihad activities; jihad terror must be fought in word and in deed, in a manner that would be transparent on inspection.

Previous negotiated settlements have included the requirement that Palestinians renounce terrorism, and they did so on paper but never made even a token effort to do so in reality. Any future negotiations should not even begin until this has been done and the Palestinians can show that it has been done to the satisfaction of all parties.

Is that likely ever to happen? No. But future participants in the "peace process" will be foolish, and will be played for fools, if they continue to negotiate with the Palestinians while the Palestinians continue to incite hatred and violence against Israel.

Political Settlements

Prime ministers, presidents, diplomats, and other negotiators should also realize that the two-state solution and any other solution that will ever be devised will never blunt the force of the jihad against Israel, or take away the impetus for that jihad. In light of that, it doesn't really matter which one is ultimately implemented; none will solve the problem.

The Two-State Solution

The Israeli withdrawal from Gaza in 2005 gave the world an intimation of what a Palestinian state would be like. Mortimer Zuckerman and the others who raised money for greenhouse equipment for the

Palestinians assumed that once the Israelis were gone and the "occupation" was over, the Palestinians would lay down their weapons and resume normal life. Many likewise continue to hope that if a Palestinian state is finally established, Palestinians will end their jihad against Israel and the two states will indeed live side by side in peace.

But the "river to the sea" chant that has become so popular among leftists in the United States is a maximalist imperative that leaves no room for any Jewish state at all. The State of Palestine would, like unoccupied Gaza, become a new base for jihad attacks against a diminished Israel. It would inevitably be a rogue state, dedicated only to the destruction and conquest of its Jewish neighbor.

The One-State Solution

Some say that in light of these realities, and in light of the fact that Israel has a perfectly reasonable claim to sovereignty over the West Bank and Gaza, by dint of international agreements and the right of conquest, it should simply annex those territories and make the Arabs living in them citizens of Israel. Israel can simply enforce its laws impartially upon all citizens, prosecuting terror activity as it does now. It has even been argued that many Palestinians would welcome becoming citizens of Israel, as they are tired of their society that idolizes rage and hate, and are ready to live in peace.

Particularly maddening to many Palestinians is the vast corruption of their leaders. Mahmoud Abbas and his two sons control a business empire worth four hundred million dollars. Two of the Hamas leaders have done even better. Dr. Musa Abu Marzook, the number-two man in Hamas, has a net worth of two to three billion dollars. The leader of Hamas's political wing, Khaled Mashaal, is also a billionaire. Dr. Moshe Elad, a colonel in the Israeli army and a lecturer in the Middle East Department at Western Galilee Academic College, says: "Estimates around the world are that Mashaal is currently worth $2.6 billion, but the numbers mentioned by the Arab commentators (based on their many sources) are much higher, varying from two to five billion dollars invested in Egyptian and

Persian Gulf banks, and some in real estate projects in the Persian Gulf countries."[1] Hamas Prime Minister Ismail Haniyeh has an estimated four million dollars.

There are many others who have accumulated millions, both in Hamas and in the Palestine Authority. Their fortunes have largely been skimmed from the aid money that the United States, the European Union, and others have lavished upon the Palestinians. Palestinians who are less wealthy can see what is happening, and would prefer being citizens of Israel over continuing to live at the mercy of this corrupt band of kleptocrats.

Others, however, will never abandon the jihad. Thus a unitary state would be racked with unrest and violence against Jewish Israelis. It would also have a massive Muslim Arab population that could ultimately overwhelm the Jewish population of Israel and turn it into the twenty-third Arab state.

On the Palestinian side, the one-state solution refers to Palestinian "refugees" flooding into Israel and becoming citizens of a unitary state, which would, by the sheer force of numbers of these "refugees," quickly lose its character as a Jewish state and become part of the Arab Muslim conglomerate of states. The Jews would be massacred, expelled, or subjugated.

So What Is to Be Done?

There is no solution that will establish a permanent peace, but the problem can be managed.

Islamic jihadis respect nothing about those whom they regard as infidels except strength; indeed, Islamic law mandates that Muslims must not wage jihad when the enemy is more than twice as strong as they are and they have no chance of victory.

The key to Israel's survival, therefore, is not negotiations or more concessions of land for a chimerical peace, but strength: military, cultural, and societal strength. If a Palestinian state is established, Israel should not only recognize that it will be its inveterate enemy from the first moment of its existence and plan accordingly, but it should also constantly shed as bright a light as it possibly can upon the Palestinian state's jihadist activities, challenging the UN and the shapers of international opinion on their hypocrisy and the blind eye they turn to those activities. It should not pretend that the establishment of this state has solved or will solve anything.

If, on the other hand, Israel instead assumes full political control over what are at present considered to be the Palestinian territories, which would require a sea change in international politics ever to be even seriously considered, it should recognize that many, if not most, of the new Israeli Arabs would never accept its sovereignty and would constantly try to undermine the Jewish state. It should retreat from its acceptance of the "Palestinian" myth and remind the world as often as it possibly can that there is no ethnic, cultural, religious, or linguistic difference between the Palestinians, the Syrians, the Jordanians, and the Lebanese. It should challenge Syria, Lebanon, and the other Arab states on why they refuse to grant Palestinians citizenship. And it should state clearly and unapologetically its right to what are now known as the Palestinian territories. But as it does all this, it must be ready to become even more of an international pariah than it already is, for Palestinian propaganda seems constantly to outdo itself in being as mendacious as it is shrill and enraged.

These are grim scenarios. Many will prefer to be more optimistic and to press for a new round of negotiations that will surely, this time, finally hit on the solution that will bring peace. And so they will enter into those negotiations, and the Israelis will make still more concessions to the Palestinians, and the Palestinians will give nothing of substance in return, and what will have been gained? What has Israel gained by ignoring the reality of the jihad for over four decades and pretending that the Palestinians were good-faith peace partners?

It is time for a new approach. The response of Israel, and of the free world in general, should not be fear or hatred, but a sober realism and a determination to remain resolute against the jihad, to defend Israel as a legitimate state and a free society, and to stand firm for humane values and the principles of human rights.

The 1,400-year history of jihad is full of infidels deluded by wishful thinking or debilitated by cowardice, and the history of the Israel-Palestinian "peace process" is full of examples of both. These fantasies have been fatal for all too many people.

It is time for Western politicians to stop whistling in the dark.

The people of Israel have endured enough. The Palestinian Arabs, in thrall to the dead-end ideology of jihad, have endured enough. All people of goodwill deserve better.

Endnotes

Chapter One

1 Isaac Stanley-Becker, "CNN fired him for speech some deemed anti-Semitic. But his university says the Constitution protects him." *Washington Post*, December 12, 2018.

2 Pamela Geller, "Brown University Celebrates 'Palestinians' on 'Indigenous Peoples' Day,'" *Breitbart*, October 8, 2018.

3 Ibid.

4 Hatem Bazian, "The Indigenous Palestinians," *Harvard International Review*, March 23, 2014.

5 World Directory of Minorities and Indigenous Peoples—Palestine," UN Refugee Agency (UNHCR), August 2009. https://www.refworld.org/docid /4954ce4d23.html

6 Itamar Marcus, "Abbas falsely claims 6,000-year-old Palestinian nation," Palestinian Media Watch, June 6, 2016.

7 Matthew Gindin, "Are Both Jews and Palestinians Indigenous To Israel?," Forward, May 24, 2017.

8 Caroline Glick, "Yes, Palestinians Are an Invented People," Real Clear World, December 13, 2011.

9 Ibid.

10 Samuel Katz, *Battleground: Facts and Fantasy in Palestine*, Taylor Productions, revised edition 2002, p. 89.

11 Ibid., p. 97.

12 Carole Hillenbrand, *The Crusades: Islamic Perspectives,* Routledge, 2000, pp. 64-65.

13 Ibid.

14 Richard Gottheil, Max Schloessinger, and Isaac Broydé, "Judah Ha-Levi (Arabic, Abu al-Hasan al-Lawi)," *Jewish Encyclopedia*, 1906. http://www.jewish encyclopedia.com/articles/9005-judah-ha-levi#2223

15 Katz, p. 92.

16 Ibid.

17 Ibid., p. 94.

18   Ibid., pp. 94–5.

19   Ibid., p. 95.

20   Ibid.

21   Eli E. Hertz, "Palestinians 'Peoplehood' Based on a Big Lie," Myths and Facts, December 4, 2018; Katz, p. 96.

22   Katz, pp. 100–101.

23   William F. Lynch, *Narrative of the United States' Expedition to the River Jordan and the Dead Sea*, Lea and Blanchard, 1850, p. 89.

24   Ibid., p. 92.

25   Ibid., p. 93.

26   Ibid., p. 280.

27   Joan Peters, *From Time Immemorial: The Origins of the Arab-Jewish Conflict Over Palestine*, JKAP Publications, 1984, p. 157.

28   Ibid., p. 158.

29   Ibid.

30   Ibid.

31   Ibid.

32   Ibid.

33   Ibid.

34   Ibid.

35   Alexander William Crawford Lindsay, Lord Lindsay, *Letters on Egypt, Edom, and the Holy Land*, Henry G. Bohn, fifth edition, 1858, p. 251.

36   Peters, p. 159.

37   Ibid.

38   Lynch, p. 298.

39   Henry Burgess Whitaker Churton, *Thoughts on the Land of the Morning: A Record of Two Visits to Palestine*, T. Hatchard, 1852, pp. 186–187.

40   Arthur G. H. Hollingsworth, *Remarks on the present condition and future prospects of the Jews in Palestine*, Seeleys, second edition 1853, p. 4.

41   Ibid.

42   Ibid.

43   Ibid., p. 5.

44   Ibid., pp. 6–7.

45   Peters, p. 159.

46   Ibid., p. 159.

47   Mark Twain, *The Innocents Abroad*, American Publishing Company, 1869, ch. LVI. https://www.gutenberg.org/files/3176/3176-h/3176-h.htm

48   Ibid., ch. XLVI.

49   Ibid., ch. XLVIII.

50   Katz, p. 107.

51   Alan Dershowitz, *The Case for Israel*, John Wiley & Sons, Inc., 2003, p. 27.

52   Lindsay, p. xi.

53   Lindsay, p. 251.

54 Nahum Sokolow, *History of Zionism 1600-1918*, vol. I. Longmans, Green, and Co., 1919, p. 123.

55 Ibid.

56 Ibid.

57 Anthony Ashley Cooper, 7th Earl of Shaftesbury, "ART. VII.-Letters on Egypt, Edom, and the Holy Land. By Lord Lindsay.—London, 2 vols. 8vo., 1838." *The London Quarterly Review*, Vol. LXIII. January-April 1839. P. 105.

58 Nur Masalha, *The Zionist Bible Biblical Precedent, Colonialism and the Erasure of Memory*, Routledge, 2013, p. 83.

59 Benjamin Netanyahu, *A Durable Peace, Israel and its Place Among the Nations*, Warner Books, 1993, p. 27.

60 Ibid., p. 28.

61 Paul Richard Wilkinson, *For Zion's Sake: Christian Zionism and the Role of John Nelson Darby*, Wipf and Stock Publishers, 2008, p. 208.

62 Sir William Arthur White, letter to Robert Gascoyne-Cecil, Marquess of Salisbury, November 19, 1891.

63 Jonathan Adelman, *The Rise of Israel: A History of a Revolutionary State*, Taylor & Francis, 2008, p. 58.

64 Katz, pp. 122–124.

65 Peters, p. 147.

66 W. M. Christie, "Arabs and Jews in Palestine," *Journal of the Transactions of The Victoria Institute*, vol. LXII, Victoria Institute, 1930, p. 98.

67 Ibid.

68 Ibid., p. 97.

69 Ibid.

70 Ibid.

71 Ibid.

72 Ibid.

73 Ibid., p. 98.

74 William B. Ziff, *The Rape of Palestine*, Longmans, Green, and Co., 1938, p. 385.

75 Daniel Grynglas, "Debunking the claim that 'Palestinians' are the indigenous people of Israel," *Jerusalem Post*, May 12, 2015.

76 Hertz, Myths and Facts.

77 Theodor Herzl, *The Jewish State*, Scopus Publishing Company, 1943. http://www.gutenberg.org/files/25282/25282-h/25282-h.htm

78 Ibid.

79 "The First Aliyah," JewishHistory.org. https://www.jewishhistory.org/the-first-aliyah/

80 Peters, p. 252.

81 Ziff, p. 50.

82 Ibid.

83 Howard M. Sachar, *A History of Israel From the Rise of Zionism to Our Time*, Alfred A. Knopf, second edition, 2001, p. 200.

84 League of Nations Mandates Palestine Report of the Royal Palestine Commission, presented by the Secretary of State for the Colonies to the United Kingdom Parliament by Command of His Britannic Majesty, July 1937. https://www.jewishvirtuallibrary.org/text-of-the-peel-commission-report

85 Ibid.

86 Lord Balfour to Lord Rothschild, November 2, 1917.

87 Katz, pp. 65–66.

88 Ibid., p. 66.

89 Ibid., pp. 65–66.

90 Ibid., p. 49.

91 Ibid.

92 Ibid., p. 50.

93 Ibid., p. 51.

94 "The 'Mandate' Defined Where Jews Are and Are Not Permitted to Settle," League of Nations Mandate for Palestine, http://www.mandateforpalestine.org /10-permissions.html.

95 Ibid.

96 Ronn Torossian, "If the West Bank is 'Occupied,' Who Are the Occupiers?," Algemeiner, July 16, 2012.

97 Zena Tahhan, "Israel's settlements: 50 years of land theft explained," Al Jazeera, November 21, 2017.

98 John Hope Simpson, *Palestine: Report on Immigration, Land Settlement and Development*, His Majesty's Stationery Office, 1930.

99 "Immigration to Israel: The First Aliyah (1882-1903)," Jewish Virtual Library, https://www.jewishvirtuallibrary.org/the-first-aliyah-1882-1903.

100 "Immigration to Israel: The Second Aliyah (1904-1914)," Jewish Virtual Library, https://www.jewishvirtuallibrary.org/the-second-aliyah-1904-1914; "Immigration to Israel: The Third Aliyah (1919-1923)," Jewish Virtual Library, https://www.jewishvirtuallibrary.org/the-third-aliyah-1919-1923.

101 "Immigration to Israel: The Fourth Aliyah (1924-1929)," Jewish Virtual Library, https://www.jewishvirtuallibrary.org/the-fourth-aliyah-1924-1929; "Immigration to Israel: The Fifth Aliyah (1929-1939)," Jewish Virtual Library, https://www.jewishvirtuallibrary.org/the-fifth-aliyah-1929-1939.

102 Benny Morris, *1948: The First Arab-Israeli War*, Yale University Press, 2008, p. 15.

103 Jacqueline Shields, "Pre-State Israel: Arab Riots of the 1920's," Jewish Virtual Library, https://www.jewishvirtuallibrary.org/arab-riots-of-the-1920-s.

104 Ibid.

105 Ibid.

106 Katz, p. 64.

107 Ibid.

108 Edy Cohen, "How the Mufti of Jerusalem Created the Permanent Problem of Palestinian Violence," The Tower, November 2015, http://www.thetower.org/article/how-the-mufti-of-jerusalem-created-the-permanent-problem-of-palestinian-violence/.

109 Ibid.

110 Walter Sidney Shaw, *Report of the Commission on the Palestine disturbances of August, 1929*, His Majesty's Stationery Office, 1930.

111 Ibid.

112 Ibid.

113 Ibid.

114 Ibid.

115 Ibid.

116 Simpson, *Palestine*.

117 Joseph M. Hochstein and Ami Isseroff, "Orde Charles Wingate: 'Hayedid,'" Zionism-Israel.com, http://www.zionism-israel.com/bio/Charles_Orde_Wingate.htm.

118 Ibid.

119 Ibid.

120 Ibid.

121 Ibid.

122 League of Nations Mandates Palestine Report of the Royal Palestine Commission. https://www.jewishvirtuallibrary.org/text-of-the-peel-commission-report

123 Ibid.

Chapter Two

1 "The First Aliyah," JewishHistory.org. https://www.jewishhistory.org/the-first-aliyah/

2 Sayyid Abul A'la Maududi [here, Mawdudi], *Towards Understanding the Qur'an*, Zafar Ishaq Ansari, translator, The Islamic Foundation, revised edition 1999. Vol. 3, p. 202.

3 Ibid.

4 Imam Muslim, *Sahih Muslim*, translated by Abdul Hamid Siddiqi, Kitab Bhavan, revised edition 2000, 2997.

5 Muhammed Ibn Ismaiel Al-Bukhari, *Sahih al-Bukhari: The Translation of the Meanings*, translated by Muhammad M. Khan, Darussalam, 1997, vol. 8, book 86, no. 437.

6 Jami at-Tirmidhi, vol. 5, book 44, no. 3954. Sunnah.com. https://sunnah.com/urn/639380

7 Muslim, 6985.

8 Itamar Marcus and Nan Jacques Zilberdik, "Hamas: Killing Jews is worship of Allah," Palestinian Media Watch, November 27, 2012.

9 Itamar Marcus and Nan Jacques Zilberdik, "PA Mufti: Muslims' destiny is to kill Jews," *Palestinian Media Watch*, January 15, 2012.

10 Itamar Marcus and Nan Jacques Zilberdik, "Abbas' advisor: Islam's religious war to destroy Israel has started," *Palestinian Media Watch*, October 10, 2018.

11 Ibid.

12 Ibid.

13 "Qatari Cleric Sheik Muhammad Al-Muraikhi: The Jews Are Our Enemies Because They Are Infidels, Not Because They Occupied Palestine," MEMRI, January 9, 2009.

14 "Egyptian Cleric Muhammad Hussein Ya'qoub: The Jews Are the Enemies of Muslims Regardless of the Occupation of Palestine," MEMRI, January 17, 2009.

15 Ibid.

16 "Egyptian Cleric Said Al-Afani: Jews Are the Offspring of Snakes and Vipers and Were Behind All Wars," MEMRI, January 17, 2009.

17 Ibid.

18 "Egyptian Clerics Encourage Martyrdom in Gaza: 'We Must Love Death'; 'There Are Black-Eyed Virgins Ready For You'; 'We Must Teach Our Children to… Hate the Jews,'" MEMRI, February 3, 2009.

19 "On Al-Aqsa TV, Hamas Deputy Minister of Religious Endowments Calls for Jews to be Annihilated, Saying They Are Bacteria, Not Human Beings; Following President Obama's Election, Said in Friday Sermon: We Must 'First Check if His Heart is Black or White,'" MEMRI, March 15, 2010.

20 Itamar Marcus and Nan Jacques Zilberdik, "Jews 'dance and live on the body parts of others' and are behind 'global corruption,' says PA Islamic Judge on PA TV," Palestinian Media Watch, October 17, 2018.

21 "Florida Friday Sermon - Imam Hasan Sabri: Palestine In Its Entirety Should Be Liberated, Even If This Leads to the Martyrdom of Tens of Millions of Muslims," MEMRI, October 12, 2018.

22 Ibid.

23 Ibid.

24 "Gaza Imam Musa Abu Jleidan Calls the Jews Treacherous Cheaters, Claims Israeli National Anthem Says: 'We Will Go Where Allah Wants When We See Our Enemies' Severed Heads,'" MEMRI, November 23, 2018.

25 "Egyptian Cleric Sheik Masoud Anwar: The Worst Enemies of the Muslims - after Satan - Are the Jews," MEMRI, January 9, 2009.

26 "Imam at NJ Islamic Center Workshop: Palestinian Cause Is 'Islamic' but Must Be Marketed as 'Humanitarian' to Garner Everybody's Support; Speakers Praise BDS, Say Israel Likely to Cease Existing within 50 Years," MEMRI, November 17, 2018.

27 "Leader of Jordanian Muslim Brotherhood Hammam Saeed: Peace Negotiations Are Heresy," Middle East Media Research Institute, n.d.

28 "Jordanian newspaper: 'Let's kill the Jews everywhere,'" Elder of Ziyon, June 16, 2013.

29 Marcus and Zilberdik, "Islam's religious war."

30 "Gaza Imam Ahmad Okasha: Jihad in Palestine—the Most Obvious Jihad on the Face of the Earth," MEMRI, November 5, 2018.

31 Ibid.

32 Itamar Marcus and Barbara Crook, "Hamas Spokesman: Genocide of Jews remains Hamas goal," Palestinian Media Watch, April 12, 2007.

33 Benjamin Weinthal, "Switzerland bans cleric for anti-Semitic rhetoric," *Jerusalem Post*, May 28, 2013.

34 Marcus and Zilberdik, "Muslims' destiny."

35 "Mauritanian Cleric Ould Al-Dadou Al-Shanqiti: On Judgment Day, the Muslims Will Kill the Jews, the 'Brothers of Apes and Pigs,'" MEMRI, July 28, 2018.

36 "Montreal police issue arrest warrant for imam who called for Jews to be killed in sermon," CBC News, July 17, 2017.

37 "French watchdog accuses Muslim leader of inciting hatred of Jews," Jewish Telegraph Agency, July 6, 2018.

38 Ibid.

39 Benjamin Kerstein, "Danish Imam Defends Himself Against Hate Speech Charges by Calling for Jihad Against Israel," Algemeiner, August 6, 2018.

40 Ibid.

41 Ibid.

42 Ibid.

43 Ibid.

44 "Jordanian Friday Sermon by Imam Ahmad Al-Rawashdeh: Allah Gathered the Jews in Palestine So That It Would Be Possible to Annihilate Them; Benjamin Franklin Called to Banish the Jews from America," MEMRI, December 13, 2017.

45 "Hamas Cleric Wael Al-Zarad Calls for the Annihilation of Jews and States: If Each Arab Spat on the Jews, They Would Drown in Arab Spit," MEMRI, February 28, 2008.

46 Simon Rocker, "What the Qur'an says about the land of Israel," *The Jewish Chronicle*, March 19, 2009.

47 Ibn Kathir, *Tafsir Ibn Kathir* (Abridged), volume 3, Darussalam, 2000, p. 142.

48 Ibid., pp. 142–3.

49 Ibn Ishaq, *The Life of Muhammad: A Translation of Ibn Ishaq's Sirat Rasul Allah*, translated by Alfred Guillaume, Oxford University Press, 1955, p. 182.

50 Bukhari, vol. 5, book 63, no. 3887.

51 Muslim, 309.

52 Ibn Ishaq, p. 182.

53 Bukhari, vol. 5, book 63, no. 3887.

54 Ibn Ishaq, p. 183.

55 Jeffrey Herf, "Haj Amin al-Husseini, the Nazis and the Holocaust: The Origins, Nature and Aftereffects of Collaboration," Jerusalem Center for Public

Affairs, January 5, 2016, http://jcpa.org/article/haj-amin-al-husseini-the-nazis-and-the-holocaust-the-origins-nature-and-aftereffects-of-collaboration/.
56 Joseph Lelyveld, *His Final Battle: The Last Months of Franklin Roosevelt*, Knopf Doubleday Publishing Group, 2017, p. 79.
57 Morris, p. 3.

Chapter Three

1 Max Fisher, "The Two-State Solution: What It Is and Why It Hasn't Happened," *New York Times*, December 29, 2016.
2 "Negotiated two-State solution still 'the only option' for Palestine: Guterres," UN News, November 28, 2018.
3 Steve Holland and Yara Bayoumy, "Trump says he wants two-state solution for Middle East conflict," Reuters, September 26, 2018.
4 Jacqueline Shields, "Pre-State Israel: Arab Riots of the 1920's," Jewish Virtual Library, https://www.jewishvirtuallibrary.org/arab-riots-of-the-1920-s.
5 Sachar, p. 195.
6 Ibid., p. 210.
7 Ibid., p. 211.
8 Ibid., p. 203.
9 Ibid.
10 League of Nations Mandates Palestine Report of the Royal Palestine Commission.
11 Ibid.
12 Ibid.
13 *Palestine: Statement by His Majesty's Government in the United Kingdom*, His Majesty's Stationery Office, 1938, 4.
14 Sachar, p. 220.
15 Shabtai Teveth, *Ben-Gurion: The Burning Ground 1886-1948*, Houghton Mifflin, 1987, p. 696.
16 John Marlowe, *Rebellion in Palestine*, Cresset Press, 1946, p. 215.
17 Teveth, p. 700.
18 "British White Paper of 1939," The Avalon Project: Documents in Law, History and Diplomacy, Yale Law School, https://web.archive.org/web/20160420184256/http://avalon.law.yale.edu:80/20th_century/brwh1939.asp.
19 Martin Gilbert, *Israel: A History*, Harper Perennial, 1998, pp. 89–90.
20 "British White Paper of 1939."
21 Ibid.
22 Ibid.
23 Ibid.
24 Ibid.
25 Gilbert, p. 90.

26 Morris, p. 20.
27 Sachar, p. 221.
28 Ibid., p. 219.
29 Gilbert, p. 100.
30 Ibid., p. 101.
31 Sachar, p. 228.
32 Morris, p. 22.
33 Ibid., p. 24.
34 Ibid.
35 Sachar, pp. 255–256.
36 Ibid., p. 256.
37 "The Anglo-American Committee of Inquiry: Recommendations and Comments (May 1, 1946)," *The Israel-Arab Reader: A Documentary History of the Middle East Conflict*, Walter Laqueur and Barry Rubin, editors, Penguin Books, sixth revised edition, 2001, p. 63.
38 Ibid.
39 Ibid., pp. 63–64.
40 Ibid., p. 64.
41 Robert P. Barnidge, Jr., *Self-Determination, Statehood, and the Law of Negotiation: The Case of Palestine*, Bloomsbury Publishing, 2016, p. 197.
42 Ibid., pp. 197–198.
43 Morris, p. 34.
44 Morris, pp. 34–35; 424 n. 78.
45 Morris, p. 37.
46 "UN Special Committee on Palestine: Summary Report (August 31, 1947)," *The Israel-Arab Reader: A Documentary History of the Middle East Conflict*, Laqueur and Rubin, p. 67.
47 Ibid., p. 67.
48 Sachar, p. 284.
49 "UN Special Committee on Palestine: Summary Report (August 31, 1947)," Laqueur and Rubin, p. 68.
50 Sachar, p. 290.
51 Ibid., p. 305.
52 Ibid., pp. 297–298.
53 Morris, p. 70.
54 Sachar, p. 298.
55 "State of Israel: Proclamation of Independence (May 14, 1948)," Laqueur and Rubin, p. 82.
56 Ibid., p. 81.
57 Ibid.
58 Ibid., p. 83.
59 Ibid.
60 Ibid.

61 Morris, p. 16.
62 Ibid., p. 395.
63 Ibid., p. 393.
64 Ibid.
65 Ibid., p. 182.
66 Ibid., p. 394.
67 Ibid., p. 395.
68 Ahmed ibn Naqib al-Misri, *Reliance of the Traveller ('Umdat al-Salik): A Classic Manual of Islamic Sacred Law*, translated by Nuh Ha Mim Keller (Amana Publications, 1999), p. xx; sections o9.1, o9.3.
69 Morris, p. 209.
70 Ibid., p. 232.
71 Ibid.
72 Ibid.
73 Ibid., p. 67.
74 Katz, p. 14.
75 Ibid., p. 15.
76 Joseph Farah, "The World's Collective Amnesia," World Net Daily, September 19, 2002.
77 Katz, p. 15.
78 Farah, "The World's Collective Amnesia."
79 Ibid.
80 Katz, pp. 14–15.
81 Ibid., p. 17.
82 Farah, "The World's Collective Amnesia."
83 Katz, p. 15.
84 Ibid., p. 16.
85 Ibid., p. 17.

Chapter Four

1 Daniel Pipes, "The Year the Arabs Discovered Palestine," *Middle East Review*, Summer 1989.
2 Ibid.
3 Ibid.
4 Ibid.
5 Ibid.
6 Ibid.
7 Jean Patrick Grumberg, "When Was the 'Palestinian People' Created? Google Has the Answer." Gatestone Institute, November 20, 2017.
8 "Palestinians: The Invented People," News and Views for Jews Down Under, August 17, 2014. https://jewsdownunder.com/2014/08/17/palestinians-the-invented-people/

9   Grumberg, "When Was the 'Palestinian People' Created?"

10   "Palestinians: The Invented People."

11   Ibid.

12   "Palestine Liberation Organization: Draft Constitution (1963)," *The Israel-Arab Reader: A Documentary History of the Middle East Conflict*, Laqueur and Rubin, p. 93.

13   Ibid.

14   Ibid.

15   Jamie Glazov, "From Russia With Terror," FrontPageMagazine.com, March 31, 2004.

16   Grumberg, "When Was the 'Palestinian People' Created?"

17   Ion Mihai Pacepa, "The KGB's Man," *The Wall Street Journal*, September 22, 2003.

18   "Rewriting history: Jesus misrepresented as 'Muslim Palestinian,'" Palestinian Media Watch, n.d. http://palwatch.org/main.aspx?fi=505

19   Ibid.

20   Ibid.

21   Ibid.

22   Ibid.

23   Ibid.

24   Ibid.

25   Ibid.

26   Ibid.

27   Ibid.

28   Ibid.

29   Ibid.

30   Golda Meir, "Who Can Blame Israel?," *Sunday Times*, June 15, 1969.

31   Ibid.

32   "Palestinians: The Invented People."

33   Ibid.

34   James Dorsey, "Wij zijn alleen Palestijn om politieke redden," Trouw, March 31, 1977. https://brabosh.com/2016/02/18/pqpct-bbo/

35   "Palestinians: The Invented People."

36   Ibid.

37   Ibid.

38   "Palestinian Social Customs and Traditions," Institute for Middle East Understanding, June 26, 2006. https://imeu.org/article/social-customs-and-traditions

39   "The Culture of Palestine," The Excellence Center in Palestine, n.d., http://excellencenter.org/the-culture-of-palestine/

40   "Palestinians are an invented people, says Newt Gingrich," Associated Press, December 9, 2011.

41   Ibid.

42   Glick, "Yes, Palestinians Are an Invented People."

43 "Palestinians tell Gingrich to learn history after 'invented people' claim," *The Guardian*, December 10, 2011.

44 Ibid.

45 Ibid.

46 Glick, "Yes, Palestinians Are an Invented People."

47 Ibid.

Chapter Five

1 Sachar, p. 455.

2 "UN Security Council Resolutions: Resolution 95 (September 1, 1951)," Jewish Virtual Library. https://www.jewishvirtuallibrary.org/un-security-council-reso lution-95-september-1951

3 Kameel B. Nasr, *Arab and Israeli Terrorism: The Causes and Effects of Political Violence, 1936-1993*, McFarland, 1996, p. 40.

4 Sachar, p. 513.

5 Ibid., p. 503.

6 Ibid., p. 506.

7 Ibid., p. 508.

8 Ibid.

9 Katz, p. 185.

10 Netanel Lorch, *One Long War: Arab Versus Jew Since 1920*, Keter, 1976, p. 104.

11 Ibid., p. 109.

12 Ibid., p. 108.

13 Isi Leibler, *The Case For Israel*, Globe Press, 1972, pp. 59-60.

14 Ibid., p. 60.

15 Sachar, p. 633.

16 Ibid.

17 Ibid., pp. 633–634.

18 Ibid., pp. 673.

19 "Israel-Arab Peace Process: The Khartoum Resolutions (September 1, 1967)," Jewish Virtual Library, https://www.jewishvirtuallibrary.org/the-khartoum -resolutions.

20 Lawrence Wright, *Thirteen Days in September: The Dramatic Story of the Struggle for Peace*, Vintage Books, 2014, p. 260.

21 "UNSC Resolutions on Israel: Resolution 242 (November 22, 1967)," Jewish Virtual Library, https://www.jewishvirtuallibrary.org/un-security-council-reso lution-242.

22 William B. Quandt, *Peace Process: American Diplomacy and the Arab-Israeli Conflict Since 1967*, Brookings Institution Press, 2001, p. 46.

23 "Resolution 242: The Drafters Clarify Its Meaning," The Six-Day War, CAMERA (Committee for Accuracy in Middle East Reporting in America), n.d. http://www.sixdaywar.org/content/242drafters.asp

24 Ibid.
25 Ibid.
26 Ibid.
27 Quandt, p. 124.
28 "UNSC Resolutions on Israel: Resolution 338 (October 22, 1973)," Jewish Virtual Library. https://www.jewishvirtuallibrary.org/un-security-council-reso lution-338.
29 "Israel-Arab Peace Process: The Khartoum Resolutions (September 1, 1967)," Jewish Virtual Library, https://www.jewishvirtuallibrary.org/the-khartoum -resolutions.
30 Anatoly S. Chernyaev, *The Diary of Anatoly S. Chernyaev 1973*, translated by Anna Melyakova, edited by Svetlana Savranskaya, National Security Archive, 2013, p. 7.
31 Wright, p. 17.
32 Ibid.
33 Ibid., p. 86.
34 Chernyaev, p. 69.
35 Ibid.
36 Ibid.
37 Ibid.
38 Sachar, p. 673.
39 Quandt, p. 465, n. 23.
40 "Egypt-Israel Relations: Interim Peace Agreement (Sinai II) (September 1, 1975)," Jewish Virtual Library, https://www.jewishvirtuallibrary.org/egypt-israel-interim -peace-agreement-sinai-ii-september-1975.
41 Wright, p. 26.
42 Ibid., p. 27.
43 Ibid., p. 33.
44 "Egypt-Israel Relations: Address by Egyptian President Anwar Sadat to the Knesset (November 20, 1977)," Jewish Virtual Library, https://www.jewishvir-tuallibrary.org/address-by-egyptian-president-anwar-sadat-to-the-knesset.
45 Ibid.
46 Ibid.
47 Ibid.
48 Ibid.
49 Ibid.
50 Jeff Abramowitz, "With historic 1977 visit, Egypt's Sadat turned Israel's reality on its head," i24 News, November 19, 2017.
51 Wright, p. 49.
52 Ibid.
53 Zbigniew Brzezinski, *Power and Principle: Memoirs of the National Security Adviser 1977-1981*, Farrar Straus Giroux, 1983, p. 284.
54 Wright, p. 49.

Chapter Six

1   Wright, p. 52.
2   Ibid., p. 68.
3   Jimmy Carter, *Keeping Faith: Memoirs of a President*, Bantam Books, 1982, p. 269.
4   Brzezinski, p. 284.
5   Ibid.
6   Ibid.
7   "Camp David Negotiations: Draft Framework for the Comprehensive Peace Settlement of the Middle East Problem (September 1978)," Jewish Virtual Library. https://www.jewishvirtuallibrary.org/draft-framework-for-the-comprehensive-peace
8   Ibid.
9   Ibid.
10 Ibid.
11 Mohamed Ibrahim Kamel, *The Camp David Accords: A testimony by Sadat's Foreign Minister*, KPI, 1986, p. 298.
12 Ibid.
13 Ibid.
14 Wright, pp. 42–43.
15 Ibid., p. 81.
16 Ibid.
17 Ibid.
18 Kamel, p. 306.
19 Carter, p. 345.
20 Kamel, p. 307.
21 Ibid., pp. 307–308.
22 Ibid., p. 321.
23 Ibid.
24 Ibid.
25 Ibid.
26 Ibid.
27 Carter, p. 347.
28 Ibid.
29 Ibid., pp. 347–348.
30 Ibid., p. 348.
31 Wright, p. 114.
32 Carter, p. 349.
33 Wright, p. 115.
34 Ibid.
35 "Camp David Negotiations: Draft Framework."
36 Wright, p. 115.

37   Ibid., p. 116.

38   Ibid.

39   Ibid.

40   Ibid.

41   Ibid., p. 126.

42   Ibid.

43   Ibid., p. 130.

44   Ibid.

45   Ibid.; Brzezinski, p. 257.

46   Wright, p. 130.

47   Ibid.

48   Ibid., p. 149.

49   Ibid., p. 151.

50   Carter, p. 374.

51   Brzezinski, p. 260.

52   Kamel, p. 332.

53   Ibid.

54   Ibid.

55   Ibid.

56   Ibid., p. 331.

57   Wright, p. 226.

58   Ibid., p. 229.

59   Ibid., p. 270.

60   "Camp David Negotiations: Framework for Peace in the Middle East (Camp David Accords) (September 17, 1978)," Jewish Virtual Library. https://www.jewish virtuallibrary.org/framework-for-peace-in-the-middle-east-camp-david-accords

61   Ibid.

62   Ibid.

63   Ibid.

64   "Speeches by Jimmy Carter, Menachem Begin, Anwar Sadat at the White House After the Signing of the Camp David Accords," Haaretz, May 13, 2002.

65   Ibid.

66   Ibid.

67   Ibid.

68   Ibid.

69   Ibid.

70   *Peace in the Making: The Menachem Begin-Anwar el-Sadat Personal Correspondence*, edited by Harry Hurwitz and Israel Medad, Gefen Publishing House, 2011, p. 155.

71   "Speeches by Jimmy Carter, Menachem Begin, Anwar Sadat."

72   Ibid.

73   Ibid.

74   Ibid.

75 Stephen Ulph, "The Islambouli Enigma," The Jamestown Foundation, Global Terrorism Analysis, vol. 1, no. 3, September 3, 2004. https://web.archive.org/web/20060719010502/http://www.jamestown.org/terrorism/news/article.php?issue_id=3059

76 Brzezinski, p. 285.

77 Ibid.

78 Ibid.

79 Ibid., p. 284.

80 Barnidge, p. 60.

81 Ibid., pp. 61–62.

82 Ibid., p. 62.

83 Ibid.

84 Ibid., pp. 62–63.

85 Ibid., p. 62.

86 Ibid., p. 198, note 104.

87 Dennis Hevesi, "Shmuel Katz, an Opponent of Begin's Peace Effort, Dies at 93," *New York Times*, May 14, 2008.

88 Quandt, p. 216.

89 Wright, p. 364.

Chapter Seven

1 "Camp David Negotiations: Framework for Peace in the Middle East."

2 Barnidge, p. 63.

3 "The Palestinian National Charter: Resolutions of the Palestine National Council July 1–17, 1968," The Avalon Project: Documents in Law, History, and Diplomacy. http://avalon.law.yale.edu/20th_century/plocov.asp

4 Ibid.

5 Ibid.

6 "The Charter of Allah: The Platform of the Islamic Resistance movement (Hamas)," translated and annotated by Raphael Israeli, The International Policy Institute for Counter-Terrorism, April 5, 1998. https://www.ict.org.il/Article/299/The%20Charter%20of%20Allah%20%20The%20Platform%20of%20the%20Islamic%20Resistance%20Movement%20(Hamas)#gsc.tab=0.

7 Ibid.

8 Ibid.

9 Ibid.

10 Ibid.

11 Ibid.

12 Ibid.

13 Ibid.

14 Ibid.

15 Barnidge, p. 62.

16   "10 Point Program of the PLO (1974): Political Program Adopted at the 12th Session of the Palestine National Council, Cairo, 8 June 1974," Permanent Observer Mission of Palestine to the United Nations. https://web.archive.org/web/20110805192136/http://www.un.int/wcm/content/site/palestine/cache/offonce/pid/12354;jsessionid=ED2AC7E70A82F5C-7CCB42BC6357FCDEC

17   Palestine National Council, "Political Communiqué," official translation, Arab Gateway, November 15, 1988. https://web.archive.org/web/20010420191313/http://www.al-bab.com/arab/docs/pal/pal4.htm

18   "Palestinian Declaration of Independence, November 15, 1988," MidEast Web. http://www.mideastweb.org/plc1988.htm

19   Steve Lohr, "Arafat Says P.L.O. Accepted Israel," *New York Times*, December 8, 1988.

20   Ibid.

21   "Yasser Arafat: Speech to the U.N. General Assembly Renouncing Terror (December 13, 1988)," Jewish Virtual Library. https://www.jewishvirtuallibrary.org/arafat-speech-to-u-n-general-assembly-renouncing-terror

22   Barnidge, p. 63.

23   Lohr, "Arafat Says P.L.O. Accepted Israel."

24   Mark Tessler, *A History of the Israeli-Palestinian Conflict*, Indiana University Press, second edition, 2009, p. 726.

25   Quandt, p. 297.

26   Tessler, p. 728.

27   David Makovsky, *Making Peace with the PLO: The Rabin Government's Road to the Oslo Accord*, Westview Press, 1996, p. 111.

28   Gilbert, p. 552.

29   Makovsky, p. 112.

30   Gilbert, p. 552.

31   Makovsky, p. 113.

32   Ibid., p. 112.

33   Ibid.

34   Ibid., p. 110.

35   "Israel-Palestinian Peace Process: Declaration of Principles On Interim Self-Government Arrangements ('Oslo Accords') (September 13, 1993)," Jewish Virtual Library. https://www.jewishvirtuallibrary.org/declaration-of-principles

36   Ibid.

37   "Israel-Palestinian Peace Process: Letters of Mutual Recognition (September 9, 1993)," Jewish Virtual Library, https://www.jewishvirtuallibrary.org/israel-palestinian-letters-of-mutual-recognition-september-1993.

38   Efraim Karsh, "Why the Oslo Process Doomed Peace," Middle East Quarterly, Fall 2016.

39   Elaine Sciolino, "Mideast Accord: The Ceremony; Old Enemies Arafat and Rabin to Meet," *New York Times*, September 12, 1993.

40 Thomas L. Friedman, "Rabin and Arafat Seal Their Accord as Clinton Applauds 'Brave Gamble,'" *New York Times*, September 13, 1993.

41 Ibid.

42 Ibid.

43 Ibid.

44 Sciolino, "Mideast Accord: The Ceremony."

45 Friedman, "Rabin and Arafat Seal Their Accord."

46 Barnidge, p. 66.

47 Meir Hatina. "Hamas and the Oslo accords: Religious dogma in a changing political reality," *Mediterranean Politics*, 4:3, 1999, p. 48.

48 Pacepa, "The KGB's Man."

49 Radio Monte Carlo, September 1, 1993, in "Incitement to Violence Against Israel by Leadership of Palestinian Authority," Israel Ministry of Foreign Affairs, November 27, 1996. https://mfa.gov.il/mfa/foreignpolicy/peace/mfadocuments/pages/incitement%20to%20violence%20against%20israel%20by%20leadershi.aspx

50 "Arafat compares Oslo Accords to Muhammad's Hudaybiyyah peace treaty, which led to defeat of the peace partners," Palestinian Media Watch, May 10, 1994.

51 Voice of Palestine, April 16, 1995 cited in FBIS, April 18, 1995, in "Incitement to Violence Against Israel by Leadership of Palestinian Authority."

52 Ibn Ishaq, p. 504.

53 Ibid.

54 Ibid.

55 Ibid.

56 Ibid.

57 Ibid., p. 509.

58 Yahiya Emerick, *The Life and Work of Muhammad*, Alpha Books, 2002, p. 239.

59 Ibid., p. 240.

60 "Senior Palestinian Journalist: Arafat Told Me He Went Along With Oslo Accords Because It Would Make 'The Jews… Leave Palestine Like Rats Abandoning A Sinking Ship,'" MEMRI, September 18, 2018.

61 Ibid.

62 Ibid.

63 Ibid.

64 Gilbert, p. 567.

65 Tessler, p. 776.

66 Beverely Milton-Edwards, *Islamic Politics in Palestine*, Tauris Academic Studies, 1996, p. 166.

67 Pacepa, "The KGB's Man."

68 Ha'aretz, October 5, 1994, in "Incitement to Violence Against Israel by Leadership of Palestinian Authority."

69 Joel Greenberg, "Arafat Accuses Israel of Killing a Palestinian Bomb Maker," *New York Times*, January 8, 1996.

70 Yediot Ahronot, May 27, 1994, in "Incitement to Violence Against Israel by Leadership of Palestinian Authority."

71 Jordanian TV, September 13, 1993, in "Incitement to Violence Against Israel by Leadership of Palestinian Authority."

72 Voice of Israel, October 21, 1996, in "Incitement to Violence Against Israel by Leadership of Palestinian Authority."

73 Ma'ariv, November 24, 1993, in "Incitement to Violence Against Israel by Leadership of Palestinian Authority."

74 Voice of Palestine, March 31, 1995, in "Incitement to Violence Against Israel by Leadership of Palestinian Authority."

75 Associated Press, January 7, 1994, in "Incitement to Violence Against Israel by Leadership of Palestinian Authority."

76 Israel Radio, May 17, 1994; *Jerusalem Post*, May 18, 1994, in "Incitement to Violence Against Israel by Leadership of Palestinian Authority."

77 Ha'aretz, November 22, 1994, in "Incitement to Violence Against Israel by Leadership of Palestinian Authority."

78 "Yasser Arafat Nobel Lecture," translated by D. Karara, The Nobel Prize, December 10, 1994. https://www.nobelprize.org/prizes/peace/1994/arafat/lecture/

79 Voice of Palestine, December 15, 1994, in "Incitement to Violence Against Israel by Leadership of Palestinian Authority."

80 Voice of Palestine, February 14, 1995, in "Incitement to Violence Against Israel by Leadership of Palestinian Authority."

81 Ma'ariv, October 4, 1996, in "Incitement to Violence Against Israel by Leadership of Palestinian Authority."

82 *Jerusalem Post*, August 3, 1995, in "Incitement to Violence Against Israel by Leadership of Palestinian Authority."

83 Israel Channel Two Television, September 19, 1995, in "Incitement to Violence Against Israel by Leadership of Palestinian Authority."

84 Gilbert, p. 584.

85 Alan Makovsky, "Arab Reaction to Rabin's Assassination," Washington Institute for Near East Policy, November 7, 1995.

86 Ha'aretz, September 6, 1995; *Jerusalem Post*, September 7, 1995, in "Incitement to Violence Against Israel by Leadership of Palestinian Authority."

87 Israel Radio, June 7, 1996, in "Incitement to Violence Against Israel by Leadership of Palestinian Authority."

88 Yediot Ahronot, October 23, 1996, in "Incitement to Violence Against Israel by Leadership of Palestinian Authority."

89 Voice of Palestine, November 11, 1995, in "Incitement to Violence Against Israel by Leadership of Palestinian Authority."

90 "Letter From President Yasser Arafat to President Clinton," January 13, 1998. https://israelipalestinian.procon.org/sourcefiles/ispaldoc1998.pdf

91 Bukhari, vol. 4, book 56, no. 3030.

92 Karsh, "Why the Oslo Process Doomed Peace."

93 Lucinda Franks, "The Warrior's Peace," *New York*, January 4, 1999.

94 Ibid.

95 Ibid.

96 Ibid.

97 "Palestine refugees," United Nations Relief and Works Agency for Palestine Refugees in the Near East (UNRWA). https://www.unrwa.org/palestine-refugees

98 Ibid.

99 Jeremy Pressman, "Visions in Collision: What Happened at Camp David and Taba?," International Security, vol. 28, no. 2, Fall 2003, p. 8.

100 Ehud Barak, "Israel Needs a True Partner for Peace," *New York Times*, July 30, 2001.

101 Ibid.

102 Joel Greenberg, "Sharon Touches a Nerve, and Jerusalem Explodes," *New York Times*, September 29, 2000.

103 Ibid.

104 Ibid.

105 Ibid.

106 Ibid.

107 Ibid.

108 "Interview with Acting FM Ben-Ami on *NewsHour* with Jim Lehrer- PBS TV-1-Nov-2000," Israeli Ministry of Foreign Affairs, November 1, 2000. https://mfa.gov.il/mfa/pressroom/2000/pages/interview%20with%20acting%20fm%20ben-ami%20on%20newshour%20with.aspx

109 Ibid.

110 Ibid.

111 "Al Durah FAQ," The Second Draft. http://www.seconddraft.org/index.php?option=com_content&view=article&id=72&Itemid=83

112 Gilbert, p. 622.

113 Tessler, p. 817.

114 "Barak to Bush: Sharon is not bound by negotiating ideas," Israeli Ministry of Foreign Affairs, February 8, 2001. https://web.archive.org/web/2005040 6204002/http://www.mfa.gov.il/MFA/MFAArchive/2000_2009 /2001/2/Barak%20to%20Bush-%20Sharon%20is%20not%20bound %20by%20negotiating

115 Ibid.

116 Gilbert, p. 624.

117 Tessler, p. 821.

118 Gilbert, p. 625.

119 Phil Reeves, "Amid the ruins of Jenin, the grisly evidence of a war crime," *Independent*, April 16, 2002.

120 Janine di Giovanni, *The Times*, April 16, 2002, in Justin Raimondo, "The Meaning of Jenin," Antiwar.com, April 22, 2002.

121 David Rohde, "Mideast Turmoil: The Aftermath; The Dead and the Angry Amid Jenin's Rubble," *New York Times*, April 16, 2002.

122 Molly Moore, "Lives Reduced to Rubble," *Washington Post*, April 16, 2002.

123 Gilbert, p. 625.

124 Phil Reeves, "Even Journalists Have to Admit They're Wrong Sometimes," Independent, August 3, 2002.

Chapter Eight

1 "President Bush Calls for New Palestinian Leadership," WhiteHouse.gov, June 24, 2002. https://georgewbush-whitehouse.archives.gov/news/releases/2002/06/20020624-3.html

2 Ibid.

3 Ibid.

4 Ibid.

5 Ibid.

6 Ibid.

7 Ibid.

8 Ibid.

9 Ibid.

10 Ibid.

11 Ibid.

12 Ibid.

13 Ibid.

14 Ibid.

15 "Israel-Palestinian Peace Process: The Middle East Road Map (April 30, 2003)," Jewish Virtual Library. https://www.jewishvirtuallibrary.org/the-middle-east-road-map

16 Ibid.

17 Ibid.

18 Ibid.

19 Ibid.

20 Ibid.

21 Ibid.

22 Ibid.

23 Ibid.

24 Ibid.

25 Raphael Medoff, "A Holocaust-Denier as Prime Minister of 'Palestine'?," The David S. Wyman Institute for Holocaust Studies, March 2003. http://new.wymaninstitute.org/2003/03/a-holocaust-denier-as-prime-minister-of-palestine/

26 Ibid.

27 Ibid.

28 Ibid.

29 "Israel-Palestinian Peace Process: The Middle East Road Map (April 30, 2003)."

30 Gilbert, p. 627.

31 "Suicide and Other Bombing Attacks in Israel Since the Declaration of Principles (Sept 1993)," Israel Ministry of Foreign Affairs. https://mfa.gov.il/mfa/foreignpolicy/terrorism/palestinian/pages/suicide%20and%20other%20bombing%20attacks%20in%20israel%20since.aspx

32 Gilbert, p. 627.

33 "Ariel Sharon Administration: Address to the Knesset on the Disengagement Plan (October 25, 2004)," Jewish Virtual Library. https://www.jewishvirtuallibrary.org/prime-minister-sharon-address-to-the-knesset-on-the-disengagement-plan-october-2004

34 Ibid.

35 Ibid.

36 "George W. Bush Administration: Radio Address Applauding Israeli Disengagement from Gaza (August 27, 2005)," Jewish Virtual Library. https://www.jewishvirtuallibrary.org/president-bush-radio-address-applauding-israeli-disengagement-from-gaza-august-2005

37 Andy Newman, "How Old Friends of Israel Gave $14 Million to Help the Palestinians," *New York Times*, August 18, 2005.

38 Ibid.

39 Nathan Vardi, "Simply Smashing," Forbes, April 7, 2006.

40 "Palestinians in Gaza Loot Greenhouse Equipment," Associated Press, September 14, 2005.

41 Mortimer B. Zuckerman, "Israel Has a Duty to Defend Its Citizens," U.S. News & World Report, August 6, 2014.

42 "Hamas sweeps to election victory," BBC, January 26, 2006.

43 Barak Ravid, "In 2006 Letter to Bush, Haniyeh Offered Compromise With Israel," *Ha'aretz*, November 14, 2008.

44 *Reliance of the Traveller*, o9.16.

45 Itamar Marcus and Nan Jacques Zilberdik, "Olmert offered Abbas more than 100% of West Bank, says PA leader," Palestinian Media Watch, April 16, 2019.

46 "Barack Obama Administration: President Obama's First Remarks on Israel & the Palestinians (January 22, 2009)," Jewish Virtual Library. https://www.jewishvirtuallibrary.org/president-obama-rsquo-s-first-remarks-on-israel-and-the-palestinians-january-2009

47 Ibid.

48 Jeff Dunetz, "Did Years Of Obama's anti-Semitic Words and Actions Incite Pittsburgh Shooting?," Jewish Press, October 31, 2018.

49 Ibid.

50 Ibid.
51 "Palestinian Ambassador to Lebanon Abbas Zaki: Two-State Solution Will Lead to the Collapse of Israel," MEMRI, May 15, 2009.
52 Ibid.
53 "Text: Obama's Speech in Cairo," *New York Times*, June 4, 2009.
54 Ibid.
55 Yann Le Guernigou, "Sarkozy tells Obama Netanyahu is a 'liar,'" Reuters, November 8, 2011.
56 Ibid.
57 "Transcript of Obama's Speech in Israel," *New York Times*, March 21, 2013.
58 Ibid.
59 Ibid.
60 "Abbas calls terrorist prisoners 'heroes' and 'brother[s],'" Palestinian Media Watch, April 19, 2013.
61 "US Congressmen demand Abbas fire former advisor, based on PMW documentation," Palestinian Media Watch, May 15, 2013.
62 "Fatah: Abbas 'responded angrily' to US demand that Abu El-Einein be fired for glorifying a murderer," Palestinian Media Watch, June 12, 2013.
63 "US request that Al-Einein be fired for glorifying murder is "cowboy logic devoid of diplomatic tact," Palestinian Media Watch, June 17, 2013.
64 "PA Chairman Abbas incites to violence in Jerusalem," Israel Ministry of Foreign Affairs, September 21, 2015.
65 For details of how the Iran nuclear deal enabled, rather than prevented, Iran from developing nuclear weapons, see Robert Spencer, *The Complete Infidel's Guide to Iran*, Regnery, 2016.
66 Ali Khamenei, Twitter, July 23, 2014. https://twitter.com/khamenei_ir/status/531057306142650369?ref_src=twsrc%5Etfw%7Ctwcamp%5Etweetembed%7Ctwterm%5E531057306142650369&ref_url=https%3A%2F%2Fwww.timesofisrael.com%2Firanian-supreme-leader-calls-for-israels-annihilation%2F
67 "Boehner: I Didn't Want 'Interference' From Obama In Netanyahu Speech," Talking Points Memo, February 15, 2015.
68 "Full text of US envoy Samantha Power's speech after abstention on anti-settlement vote," *Times of Israel*, December 24, 2016.
69 Ibid.
70 Ibid.
71 "Statement by President Trump on Jerusalem," WhiteHouse.gov, December 6, 2017.
72 Ibid.
73 Ibid.
74 Ibid.
75 Ibid.
76 Ibid.

77 Donald Trump, Twitter, January 2, 2018. https://twitter.com/realDonald Trump/status/948322496591384576?ref_src=twsrc%5Etfw%7 Ctwcamp%5Etweetembed%7Ctwterm%5E948322496591384576&ref _url=https%3A%2F%2Fwww.nytimes.com%2F2018%2F01%2F16%- 2Fus%2Fpolitics%2Fus-palestinian-aid-refugee-un.html&module=inline

78 Gardiner Harris and Rick Gladstone, "U.S. Withholds $65 Million From U.N. Relief Agency for Palestinians," *New York Times*, January 16, 2018.

79 "US State Department withholds additional $45 million from UNRWA," *Times of Israel*, January 19, 2018; Clare Foran and Elise Labott, "US ends all funding to UN agency for Palestinian refugees," CNN, September 1, 2018.

80 Jordan Schachtel, "THIRD Rocket Arsenal Found At UN School In Gaza," *Breitbart*, July 29, 2014.

81 "UN report outlines how Hamas used kids as human shields," *New York Post*, May 2, 2015.

82 Adam Kredo, "IDF Calls Out UN for Lying About Gaza Civilian Casualties," *Washington Free Beacon*, July 24, 2014.

83 Chris Gunness, Twitter, July 24, 2014. https://twitter.com/ChrisGunness/ status/492299360164519936

84 Kredo, "IDF Calls Out UN."

85 Ibid.

86 Lazar Berman, "Palestinian kids taught to hate Israel in UN-funded camps, clip shows," *Times of Israel*, August 14, 2013.

87 "PROFILE / Slain Hamas Minister Was Key Figure in '07 Gaza Coup." Associated Press, January 15, 2009; Anav Silverman, "Do UNRWA schools encourage terror against Israel?," *Jerusalem Post*, August 22, 2011.

88 Berman, "Palestinian kids."

89 Ibid.

90 Ibid.

91 Ibid.

92 Ibid.

93 Ariel Ben Solomon, "US Congressmen to investigate UNRWA schools for inciting terrorism," *Jerusalem Post*, June 20, 2016.

94 Ibid.

95 Ibid.

96 Josh Hasten, "Group raises alarm over UNRWA's anti-Israel incitement within its Jerusalem schools," *Jewish News Syndicate*, January 30, 2019.

97 "UNRWA fakes Gaza girl campaign with image of bombed-out Damascus," *UN Watch*, June 2, 2017.

98 Ibid.

99 Edward Wong, "Trump Administration's Move to Cut Aid to Palestinian Refugees Is Denounced," *New York Times*, August 31, 2018.

100 Karen DeYoung and Loveday Morris, "Trump administration orders closure of PLO office in Washington," *Washington Post*, September 10, 2018.

101 "PLO 'suspends' recognition of Israel," *Israel National News*, October 29, 2018.

102 Patrick Wintour, "Hamas presents new charter accepting a Palestine based on 1967 borders," *Guardian*, May 1, 2017.

103 Jason D. Greenblatt, Twitter, February 6, 2019. https://twitter.com/jdgreenblatt45/status/1093225361553457153?ref_src=twsrc%5Etfw%7Ctwcamp%5Etweetembed%7Ctwterm%5E1093225361553457153&ref_url=https%3A%2F%2Fwww.i24news.tv%2Fen%2Fnews%2Finternational%2F194790-190207-trump-envoy-palestinians-take-to-twitter-to-talk-at-each-other.

104 Jason D. Greenblatt, Twitter, February 1, 2019. https://twitter.com/jdgreenblatt45/status/1091380443319070721.

105 "Poll shows Hamas leader would win Palestinian elections," *Associated Press*, December 18, 2018.

106 Deborah Danan, "Palestinian Authority Paid Terrorists and Their Families Nearly $350 Million in 2017," *Breitbart*, January 10, 2018.

107 Deborah Danan, "Abbas Vows to Use 'Last Penny' to Pay Palestinian Terrorists' Salaries," *Breitbart*, July 25, 2018.

108 "US aid to Palestinian security services to end Friday, at Abbas's request," *Agence France Presse*, January 30, 2019.

109 Ben Cohen, "US Ambassador Haley Rips Arab, Islamic States for Posturing at UN on Palestinian Question," *Algemeiner*, July 24, 2018.

110 Hugh Fitzgerald, "Mahmoud Abbas Angrily Rejects $50 Billion Dollar Aid Package," *Jihad Watch*, June 25, 2019.

111 "Marshall Plan, 1948." Office of the Historian, U.S. Department of State. https://history.state.gov/milestones/1945-1952/marshall-plan

112 "Palestinian Islamic Jihad: We can launch more than 1,000 rockets at Israel a day for months," i24NEWS, May 31, 2019.

113 "Palestinian president Abbas says certain Bahrain conference will fail," AFP, June 23, 2019.

114 Ibid.

Chapter Nine

1 Virginia Kruta, "UN Year In Review: 21 Condemnations For Israel, None For Hamas Or China," *Daily Caller*, December 27, 2018.

2 "Full text of US envoy Samantha Power's speech."

3 Bukhari, vol. 4, book 56, no. 3030.

4 Jami at-Tirmidhi, vol. 27, book 45, no. 1939. Sunnah.com. http://sunnah.com/tirmidhi/27/45.

5 Katz, p. 135.

6   Itamar Marcus and Nan Jacques Zilberdik, "'Settlers' kill Palestinians for pleasure—hate speech in official PA daily," *Palestinian Media Watch*, November 6, 2018.

7   Ibid.

8   Ibid.

9   Ibid.

10 "Holocaust libels and misappropriation," *Palestinian Media Watch*, n.d., http://palwatch.org/main.aspx?fi=808

11 Nan Jacques Zilberdik, "Fatah: Israel worse than Nazis, wants to 'crush' the Arab world, 'steal its resources,'" *Palestinian Media Watch*, May 27, 2018.

12 Dana Adams Schmidt, "Arabs Say Kastel Has Been Retaken; Jews Deny Claim," *New York Times*, April 12, 1948.

13 Eliezer Tauber, "Deir Yassin: There was no massacre," *Times of Israel*, May 28, 1948.

14 "Israel and the Arabs: the 50 Year Conflict," BBC TV documentary, 1998. https://www.youtube.com/watch?time_continue=16&v=72Ata-hY9WQ

15 Ibid.

16 Ibid.

17 Ibid.

18 Tauber, "Deir Yassin."

19 "Israel and the Arabs: the 50 Year Conflict."

20 Tauber, "Deir Yassin."

21 "Israel War of Independence: The Capture of Deir Yassin (April 9, 1948)," Jewish Virtual Library. https://www.jewishvirtuallibrary.org/the-capture-of-deir-yassin

22 Tauber, "Deir Yassin."

23 Ibid.

24 "Israel War of Independence: The Capture of Deir Yassin (April 9, 1948)"; Morris, p. 127.

25 Tauber, "Deir Yassin."

26 Itamar Marcus and Nan Jacques Zilberdik, "PA lies, presents Holocaust victims as Arabs," Palestinian Media Watch, November 5, 2018.

27 Ibid.

28 Robert Spencer, "'Palestinian' 'journalist' takes random baby photo from Instagram, claims baby was killed by Israel," Jihad Watch, August 9, 2018.

29 Ibid.

30 Nidal al-Mughrabi, "Israeli army kills Palestinian nurse in Gaza border protest—medics," Reuters, June 1, 2018.

31 Ibid.

32 Ibid.

33 Stuart Ramsey, "Gaza nurse killing: Medical official urges world 'not to keep silent,'" *Sky News*, June 4, 2018.

34 Yami Roth and Eric Sumner, "Was the Palestinian medic shot by the IDF serving as a human shield?," *Jerusalem Post*, June 7, 2018.

35 Yaniv Kubovich, "Gaza Medic Killed on Border Wasn't Intentionally Shot by Israeli Soldiers, Military Finds," Haaretz, June 5, 2018.

36 Roth and Sumner, "Was the Palestinian medic shot by the IDF serving as a human shield?"

37 "Gaza City mourns 8-month-old Layla Al Ghandour," EuroNews, May 16, 2018.

38 Ibid.

39 Ibid.

40 "Hamas paid the family of baby $2,200 to say she died in clashes with Israeli forces, Gaza infiltrator's testimony reveals," Jewish Telegraph Agency, June 21, 2018.

41 "Hamas Paying Gazans to Get Shot by IDF," Jewish Press, April 5, 2018.

42 Itamar Marcus, "Hamas is sending civilians in Gaza to die for media coverage, says Abbas' advisor," Palestinian Media Watch, April 8, 2018.

43 Deborah Danan, "WATCH: Videos Show Gaza Rioters Faking Injuries, Using Children as Human Shields," *Breitbart*, May 6, 2018.

44 "Here are three of the 'innocent civilians' killed yesterday, members of the Al Quds Brigades. One was 16 years old," Elder of Ziyon, May 15, 2018.

45 Robert Spencer, "Gaza: Ten of the 'innocent civilians' killed were members of Hamas' internal security apparatus," Jihad Watch, May 15, 2018.

46 Judah Ari Gross, "Hamas official: 50 of the 62 Gazans killed in border violence were our members," *Times of Israel*, May 16, 2018.

47 Michelle Nichols, "United Nations condemns excessive Israeli force against Palestinians," Reuters, June 13, 2018.

48 "UN report outlines how Hamas used kids as human shields," *New York Post*, May 2, 2015.

49 Aileen Graef, "Ban Ki-moon: 'Nothing is more shameful than attacking sleeping children,'" UPI, July 30, 2014.

50 "UN report outlines how Hamas used kids as human shields."

Chapter Ten

1 Ella Levy-Weinrib, "Meet the Hamas billionaires," *Globes*, July 24, 2014.

Acknowledgments

Once again I owe thanks to David S. Bernstein of Bombardier Books for giving me another chance to write one of the books I have wanted to write for years. I still have a long list of such books, and so you will be hearing from me again, David.

Hugh Fitzgerald, a man who has been called a genius by far more learned and intelligent people than I, has been a huge help, giving me numerous suggestions of material to include and looking over each chapter as I finished it, helping me sharpen it all up and eliminate numerous infelicities.

Hugh and Christine Douglass-Williams, with technical aid from the elusive Marc, again provided extraordinary assistance, keeping the Jihad Watch news website going while I was poring over the repartee of Jimmy Carter and Anwar Sadat at Camp David and hunting down the details of various vaunted agreements of the "peace process." I am particularly grateful to Christine for her indefatigable work in keeping the site going during my recent illness.

My work would be immensely more difficult without the ongoing friendship and support of David Horowitz and Mike Finch of the David Horowitz Freedom Center, and some others whom it would be imprudent of me to name here; I hope they know my gratitude is undiminished by their anonymity.

And once again, I must give a tip of the hat to the man who made all this happen, the great Jeffrey Rubin.

Index

About the Author

Robert Spencer has led seminars on Islam and jihad for the FBI, the United States Central Command, United States Army Command and General Staff College, the U.S. Army's Asymmetric Warfare Group, the Joint Terrorism Task Force (JTTF), the Justice Department's Anti-Terrorism Advisory Council, and the U.S. intelligence community.